STUDIES IN HISTORY, ECONOMICS AND
PUBLIC LAW

Edited by the

FACULTY OF POLITICAL SCIENCE
OF COLUMBIA UNIVERSITY

Number 545

# THE MOVEMENT TO AMERICANIZE
# THE IMMIGRANT

BY

EDWARD GEORGE HARTMANN

# THE MOVEMENT
# TO AMERICANIZE THE
# IMMIGRANT

BY

EDWARD GEORGE HARTMANN

AMS PRESS, INC.
NEW YORK
1967

To my parents,

LOUIS HARTMANN
and
CATHERINE JONES-DAVIS HARTMANN,
this work
is affectionately dedicated.

# PREFACE

DURING the two-year period, 1915-1916, which preceded the entrance of America into the first World War, the nation was subjected to one of those social movements or crusades, which have periodically sprung up and colored the social history of the United States. The new movement, very aptly characterized as the *Americanization Crusade,* gained momentum as German-American relations went from bad to worse and beyond, remained very active during the War years and the immediate post-war era, and then died a gradual death as the nation found itself again in the blessings of 'normalcy'.

An educative movement, the Americanization effort stressed the desirability of the rapid assimilation of the millions of immigrants who had come to America during the pre-war decades, through the attendance of the newcomers at special classes, lectures, and mass meetings, where they might be instructed in the language, the ideals, and outlook on life which had come to be accepted as the traditional American point of view. In this fashion, its advocates felt, the proper steps would have been taken toward unifying the nation in the face of external perils, while at the same time assuring the continued existence of the traditional American way of life.

As an effort to solve the many problems which had resulted from the great influx of European immigrants into America during the years 1880-1910, the movement to Americanize the immigrant takes its place along side those other manifestations of American distrust and discontent with their new neighbors,—the nativism of the 1830's, the Know-Nothingism of the 1850's, the APA-ism of the 1890's, the Ku Klux Klanism of the 1920's, and the immigrant restrictionism of the first quarter of the twentieth century. Unlike these other movements, however, the new movement drew its leadership from the intelligentsia, the educators and social workers, the industrialists, and from business and civic groups generally.

7

Unlike these others, too, it did not stress a negative program of restriction or repression as the means of solving the immigrant question. Instead, it outlined a positive program of education and guidance as a means of meeting the problem involved through the immigrant impact upon America. It manifested also, a faith in the ultimate assimilative capabilities of the immigrant and of his eventual transformation into a patriotic, loyal, and intelligent supporter of the great body of principles and practices which the leaders of the movement chose to consider 'America's priceless heritage'. The movement to Americanize the immigrant offered a program which would solve the problem of the immigrant with the least disturbance to the economic and political life of the nation; a program which would not result in the loss of an exceedingly valuable labor supply to America.

An effort has been made in this volume to trace the rise and development of this interesting and highly significant movement, and to place it in its proper niche in the social history of the United States. The author has the sincere hope that the information which he has laboriously collected and which is contained in this monograph will prove to be of such sufficient worth and interest to the reader that a clearer conception of the social aspects of a very important era in American history will have been obtained.

To Professor J. Orin Oliphant and Dr. Arnaud C. Marts of Bucknell University, and Professor Daniel J. Gage of the James Millikin University, for their constant support and encouragement of the author in his pursuit of graduate research; to Professor Merle Curti of the University of Wisconsin for suggesting the topic of this study and guiding the author through the early stages of the research process; to Professor John A. Krout of Columbia University, who read and criticized the manuscript and offered many valuable suggestions; and to Dean Harry J. Carman of Columbia College, whose capable

guidance, stimulating support, and constant attention were so
necessary in order to bring this study to a successful conclusion; to all these, to my loyal family, and to the other friends
who aided or contributed to the finished production of this
monograph, the author wishes to express his sincere gratitude
and appreciation.

E. G. H.

COLUMBIA UNIVERSITY
NEW YORK, NEW YORK
3 MAY 1948

# CONTENTS

# CHAPTER I

# BACKGROUND OF THE AMERICANI-
# ZATION MOVEMENT

THE movement to Americanize the immigrant which gripped the nation during the second decade of the twentieth century was one manifestation of the reaction of the native American elements of the population of the United States to the great impact made upon American life by the coming of the so-called 'new immigration' of the period 1880-1914. As such, it was the outgrowth of the play and counter-play of the social, emotional, and economic forces of the American nation during this very significant era of the country's growth. To understand the gradual evolution and decline of the movement, the forces at work in support of its program, and its place in the history of the United States necessitates a brief consideration of the position of the immigrant in America during the years preceding the inauguration of the Americanization crusade.

American historians, sociologists, and writers generally, speak of the history of American immigration as having occurred in two waves. The first and earlier, usually called the 'old immigration' because of the time element involved, consisted of immigrants from the British Isles, Germany, Holland, and other sections of north-western Europe, and formed the predominant element entering the country during the colonial period and the first three-quarters of the 19th century. The second or 'new immigration' on the other hand, came from eastern and southern Europe and the Levant, and formed the dominant element entering the country during the last quarter of the 19th and the first quarter of the 20th centuries.

The 'old immigration' had come from those regions of Europe which had a rather uniform background of political experience, a common fund of social mores and practices, and a somewhat similar economic experience. High standards of living, a low rate of illiteracy, a fairly active share in political self-government, and, with the exception of the German and Irish Roman Catholics, a uniform background of Protestant Christianity, characterized these people and were favorable factors which tended to make them not too dissimilar from the American neighbors among whom they settled. Although viewed generally with distrust and suspicion by many Americans upon their arrival, they adopted American ideals and habits easily and took their places as American settlers without too great a visible interference with the traditional American way of life.

Even so, the 'old immigrant' groups were very often made the butt of intolerant and openly vicious acts from the more rowdyish American elements of the population. An examination of the accounts of the riots and beatings which greeted many of the Irish immigrants upon their arrival at American ports, and the counter-action on the part of the newcomers when they were able to rally in significant numbers, will reveal a good deal of evidence to illustrate the feelings of many Americans in regard to the newcomers. The fears expressed by Benjamin Franklin concerning the possible Germanization of Pennsylvania during the period of the Palatine-German influx in the 18th century, and the rise of nativist activity during the 1830's and of the Know-Nothing movement during the 1850's, were further evidences that certain American circles found the newcomers objectionable and feared their influence would be detrimental to the best interests of the country. Difference of religion alone was evidently enough of an element of distrust to cause a considerable portion of the American populace to begin to plan ways through which this threat' to the nation's safety could be eliminated.

The 'new immigration', in contrast, came from those regions of Europe—the Russian Empire, Austria-Hungary, Italy, and the Balkans—which were comparatively backward from a political, social, and economic point of view when compared with the regions of Europe which had sent America its earlier type of immigrant. Standards of living among these people were decidedly lower, illiteracy rates ran high, experience with self-government was practically nil, and a subject ' race ' status seemed to be the general rule. Very few had the common background of Protestant Christianity which had distinguished the great majority of their predecessors and which was so characteristic of the majority of native Americans at that time. On the contrary, most of the newcomers were either members of the great Roman Catholic communion with its varied eastern and oriental-rite subdivisions, or were members of the various branches of Eastern Orthodox Christianity. In addition, vast numbers of Jews, representing all phases of orthodoxy, came from Poland, Lithuania, Hungary, and Russia to add a 'Semitic ' flavor to this ' new immigration '.

The ' new immigrant ' groups began to migrate to America in significant numbers as early as 1875 when approximately 10% of the total number of immigrants came from eastern and southern Europe. Each year thereafter saw the percentage of these newcomers increase in strength until by 1896 fully 57% and by 1902 76.2% of all immigrants were migrating from these areas. From approximately 24,584 in 1874, the number of such immigrants rose to 38,071 in 1880, to 55,584 in 1881, 84,973 in 1882, 129,349 in 1887, 141,281 in 1888, 270,084 in 1892, 301,785 in 1899, 486,554 in 1902, 617,931 in 1903, 717,391 in 1905—979,661 in 1907. In an ever increasing torrent the peasant masses of Austria-Hungary, Italy, Russia, and the Balkans poured into America to find employment in the mines, mills, and other types of industrial enterprise of the growing republic. From 1873 to 1910, it has been estimated that approximately 9,306,370 immigrants from southern and eastern Europe migrated to the United States.[1]

1 For complete statistical data on the "new immigration" and other material of interest, cf. U. S. Immigration Commission, *Abstracts of Reports of the Immigration Commission*, I and II, Washington, 1911 ; for specific reference cf. I, pp. 61-63.

Forming as they did the great source of unskilled labor for America's growing industries, these people tended naturally to settle in the great industrial and urban centers of the northeastern seaboard region and in the middle west where opportunities for finding employment were most favorable. Here, in such centers as the New York—New Jersey metropolitan area, Boston, Pittsburgh, Buffalo, Cleveland, Chicago, the Pennsylvania anthracite and bituminous coal fields, and a score of other communities, they gathered together in little neighborhood groups which in most cases quickly spread out into the surrounding areas to form little ethnic colonies in the midst of their urban surroundings. It was only natural that colonies of this sort should form. To the foreigner, ignorant of the English language, bewildered by his new surroundings, and homesick for his native environment, association with his own kind offered a sense of security in the midst of confusion, a kind of haven from the new, vigorous, competitive environment which he found all about him. Here in these growing colonies, he heard the friendly sound of mother tongue, saw many of the old familiar customs, and obtained the advice and friendship of those who had arrived before him.

Unfortunately, the already crowded conditions existing in the great urban areas forced the newcomers to occupy the poorest and least desirable residential sections where housing conditions were deplorable, sanitation almost unheard of, firetraps the rule, and crime often the inevitable associate. Exploitation of the immigrant which began immediately upon his arrival at American ports continued to follow him here. Rents rose to such heights that it was usually impossible for the immigrant family to meet its expenses without recourse to the expedient of ' taking in boarders '.

Continued overcrowding of already overcrowded areas resulted in many people frequently occupying common sleeping rooms. Deplorable unsanitary conditions were prevalent. Situations breeding immorality were far from unusual with many bachelor and unattached male immigrants sharing the same rooms with growing children. A good deal of evidence was unearthed to show that situations were common where the same beds were occupied by immigrants in eight-hour shifts throughout the entire day. These and other unbelievable conditions were discovered and reported by social workers and others during the period 1895-1910.[2]

Today, most sociologists seem agreed that many of these people have become fully assimilated to American ways, and have assumed a good many of the traditional American behavior patterns. Moreover, there is every indication that we can expect the remainder to conform over a reasonable period of time. Yet to most native Americans, these people, with their lower standards of living, their strange manners and customs, their tendency toward congregating in ' little Italys ' and ' ghettos ' in our larger cities, and their affiliation with the Roman Catholic, the Orthodox Christian, and the Hebrew faiths, seemed definitely inferior, and for the most part largely incapable of assimilating themselves to a proper appreciation of the traditional American ideals and the American way of life.

Since antagonism toward the immigrant had expressed itself upon the arrival of such culturally similar ethnic groups as those of the so-called ' old immigration ', it would have been exceedingly strange if the arrival of this new, foreign-type of immigration did not result in the growth of a movement of opposition on the part of the native American elements. Such a movement began to shape itself in the decade of the 1890's, and gained its first successes in the decade of the 1910's.

Labor, in particular, reacted in a very hostile manner to the immigration of the newcomers, because of their comparatively

2 For description of typical living conditions in immigrant colonies, cf. *Report of the Commission of Immigration of the State of New York*, Albany, 1909; *Report of the Commission on the Problem of Immigration in Massachusetts*, Boston, 1914; and the *Report of the Commission of Immigration of the State of New Jersey*, Trenton, 1914.

lower standards of living, their docility in the face of the most trying labor situations, and their use by the industrialists to break strikes and destroy collective bargaining. American labor leaders naturally viewed the immigrants as a definite menace to the struggle to raise wages and to reduce hours at that time in its infancy.

Although quiescent at first, various labor groups soon began to agitate for some sort of restrictive measures to protect themselves from cheap immigrant competition. As early as 1894, sentiment of this sort had expressed itself at a meeting of the Farmers' National Congress of America at Parkersburg, W. Va. Although representing primarily agrarian interests, delegates from 36 states put themselves on record as feeling that the immigrant tide had trespassed upon the interests of American labor. A call for adequate legislation to meet the growing evil was sent to Congress in the form of a memorial.[3] Thereafter, organized labor began to play an ever increasingly important role in the movement for immigration restriction.

Labor's objections to the newcomers were chiefly of an economic nature, but to many other Americans the assimilative possibilities of the 'new immigration' began to assume importance. Alarmed by the great numbers which came constantly to America's shores during this period, a score of articles began to appear in the periodical press of the nation, that stressed the menace to America's unity which these hordes of immigrants represented. The authors pointed to the unsanitary conditions existing in the immigrant areas, to the tendency of the 'new immigrants' to congregate in 'unassimilative' blocs in the midst of the great urban centers of the nation, to their great tendency to vagrancy and crime, to their undemocratic background and lack of understanding of American institutions, and to a host of other evils, real and

3 George M. Stevenson, *A History of American Immigration*, Boston, 1926, p. 148.

imaginative, to support their belief that the 'new immigrant' was unworthy of residence in America if not an actual menace to the country.[4]

Many of these writers were undoubtedly influenced by the growing consciousness of 'racialism' which began to make itself felt in certain of America's intellectual circles. The findings of Darwin and Spencer began to be read into the social sciences as well, and the belief of intellectuals and teachers like Moses Coit Tyler, Andrew D. White, John W. Burgess, Albert Bushnell Hart, John Fiske, and many others in the 'Teutonic' origin of American institutions, and the rather unique supremacy of the 'Teutonic' peoples in the realm of government, did much to strengthen this growing racial consciousness. An increasing belief that American institutions were peculiar 'racial' products, made these intellectuals and many of their followers ever more aware of the supposed 'racial' differences between the 'old immigration' and the 'new'. From their observations it became easy to conclude that since American institutions were the unique creation of 'Teutonic' peoples and were meant for their use, it would be considerably doubtful if these newcomers could carry on the traditional conception of freedom, individual liberty, local self-government and federalism in government.[5]

As the result of this growing spirit of hostility toward the 'new' type of immigrant, it was only a matter of time before organizations came into existence which had definite programs of an anti-immigrant nature. The first of these, the American Protective Association, represented a revival of the nativist spirit of the mid-19th century. A strongly anti-Roman Catholic movement, the APA, as the organization was dubbed by Americans, was formed as early as 1887, and did much during the short span if its existence to embitter religious feeling through-

4 For bibliography of such writings, see Appendix A.

5 Edward Norman Saveth, "Race and Nationalism in American Historiography: The Late Nineteenth Century", *Political Science Quarterly*, LIV (Sept. 1939), pp. 421-441; Julius W. Pratt, *Expansionists of 1898, the Acquisition of Hawaii and the Spanish Islands*, Baltimore, 1936, Chapter I.

out the nation. The Association agitated constantly for a tighter control of immigration and for stiffer requirements for admission to citizenship. An examination of the creed of the APA, adopted by the supreme council at Des Moines, Ia., reveals the usual nativist emphasis. Planks were inserted which advocated the prohibition of further importation of 'pauper' labor, the restriction of immigration to persons capable of proving their intention of becoming self-supporting citizens, the strengthening of the naturalization laws and suffrage requirements to include the ability to speak the language of America and a continuous residence of seven years after filing declarations of intention, the exclusion of teachers in public schools who were subjects of an un-American ecclesiastical institution, and finally the prohibition of state support of parochial schools.[6] Although influential in certain districts as late as 1896, the APA failed to gain any considerable number of permanent adherents and soon disappeared as an active movement.

A second organization appeared in 1894 which had a much more successful career. It soon became the spearhead of the growing movement to restrict immigration. The Immigration Restriction League, which the new organization called itself, was composed of New Englanders of old American stock at first and represented the views of the 'Teutonic Supremacy' school of thought. John Fiske, the historian, was one of its first presidents. Prescott F. Hall, its executive during the greater period of the League's existence, wrote books and pamphlets in opposition to the further penetration of the 'new immigration' and stressed therein the usual arguments of the racialists.[7]

A voice of old-American New England at its formation, the League gained influence rapidly in other quarters until it could count upon supporters from practically every section of the

6 *Chicago Tribune*, May 6, 1894; *cf.* Humphrey J. Desmond, *The APA Movement*, Washington, 1912, pp. 38-44.

country. From its organization in 1895 until the final passage
of the literacy test in 1917, the Immigration Restriction League
carried on an active campaign, which sought to educate the
American public to the menace of unchecked immigration by
means of pamphlets, handbills, and form letters. As a lobbying
agency, the League agitated for immigration restriction at the
nation's capitol for two decades, and was largely instrumental
in keeping alive the issue of immigration restriction during
the entire pre-World War I period.[7]

As a result of the joint agitation of the Immigration Restriction League, organized labor, intellectuals, and others of
prominence having a restrictionist outlook, enough pressure
was exerted to bring the question of immigration restriction
before the Congress of the United States upon many occasions
during the years 1890-1917. From 1894 onwards, the oppon-
ents of unrestricted immigration began to concentrate more
and more upon the literacy test as the means best suitable for
checking further immigration. The whole question of immigration restriction began to assume a 'racial' cast which it
never lost thereafter. Bills adding illiterates to the excluded
classes of immigrants (and since illiteracy ran exceedingly
high among most of the newer immigrant groups, the passage
of such legislation would have had the effect of decreasing
immigration from southern and eastern Europe considerably,
and would have met the aims of the racial theorists) passed
both houses of Congress in 1896 only to receive the veto of
President Cleveland because of his objection to any interference
with the nation's traditional policy of free and generous admission of immigrants. Seven such bills passed at least one of
the houses of Congress during the ten year period 1893-1903,
—definite evidence of the ardour and persistence of the restrictionists in opposition to any further penetration of unrestricted
immigration from southern and eastern Europe.[8]

7 Immigration Restriction League, *Papers*, and other publications.

8 Stevenson, *A History of Immigration, op. cit.*, pp. 150-151.

The attacks made upon the 'new immigrant' by the re-strictionists brought forth a series of articles in his defense from social workers, educators, and intellectuals, who felt the arguments used against the immigrant were based upon insufficient data and superficiality of approach. Pointing to the fact that America had always absorbed her immigrants in the past without apparent harm to her ideals or institutions, and had profited in no small way as the result of their labors, these writers declared it unfair to say that the newcomers were lacking in the assimilative qualities which the 'old immigrant groups' had possessed. They acknowledged that living conditions in most immigrant areas were deplorable, but insisted that these conditions were not the fault of the immigrant because such slum conditions had existed long before the newcomers arrived. The problem was one which concerned a too rapid urbanization rather than one of ethnic make-up. They argued: to blame the 'new immigrant' for the deplorable environment into which he had been forced through circumstances beyond his control was merely blinding oneself to the true facts.

In further refutation of the claims made by the restrictionists, they cited the revelations uncovered by various educators which showed beyond doubt that the children of the newer immigrant groups were rapidly becoming assimilated to the American behavior patterns through the influence of the public schools. Obviously, they admitted, the great bulk of those who had migrated would continue to conform to many of the traditions and ways of life of the old country, but this did not necessarily prove that their capacity for understanding the ideals for which America stood and for appreciating the American way of life was poor. The more ardent defenders thought they could detect enough evidence already of a change of habits of many of the first generation 'new immigration' stocks to warrant making the assumption that complete assimilation would take place over a mere period of years. If anything was to be deplored and feared, they declared, it was the too rapid assimilation by the children of the foreign-born of the undesirable features of American life about them, the psychological maladjustments which often resulted from the feeling of inferiority aroused through their contacts with native-born children, the engendering of contempt for their parents because of the latter's foreign ways with the consequent loss of parental control over the family, and the loss of many of the better features and contributions of the various ethnic cultures without any satisfactory cultural recompense.

The great existing danger in the immigrant situation, they pointed out, lay not in the fact that these people could not become assimilated to American ideals and to the American way of life, but in the fact that very little effort was being made to help the process of assimilation by bettering relations between the newcomers and their American neighbors, by helping to preserve the hold of the immigrant parents over their children, or by seeking to amalgamate the better features of the various immigrant cultures with the native American one as a lasting contribution from abroad. Writers of this school of thought began to stress more and more, the need for social action to educate the immigrant in American ways as one means of solving the problem.[9]

Social action of this sort had expressed itself already in many of the programs of the social settlement houses located in the larger industrial areas, where workers and nurses circulated among the members of the immigrant populations teaching them the fundamentals of personal hygiene and sanitation, and introducing them to the better aspects of American life. Leaders of the settlement house movement such as Jane Addams, Stanton Coit, Charles B. Stover, and Jacob A. Riis, were ever alert to the great assimilative role which their peculiar institution could play for the immigrant. As interest in settlements grew, and more and more Americans threw their support to institutions of this sort, a virtual chain of little centers of im-

9 For bibliography of such writings, see Appendix B.

migrant welfare work became active in practically every urban area of significance in the nation.

Debate over the status and future of the immigrant led an increasingly large number of individuals to feel that some sort of program for educating the immigrant, particularly in the fundamentals of the English language and civics, would be the best means of solving the many evils supposedly arising from his entrance upon the American scene. Many of these people felt that if a concerted effort were made to teach the language of America to the immigrant, the first step toward his full assimilation would have been taken. They believed confidently that the immigrant's command over the English language would eventually result in his having a better understanding of the American way of life and in his participating fully therein —imbued with the same ideals and the same aspirations as those of his native-born neighbors.[10]

Certain of the larger American cities had embarked incident-ally toward the end of the century upon programs of immi-grant education work in connection with their night school activities. In practically every case, these classes were organized upon the request of the immigrants themselves. New York City reported very satisfactory results in the way of special instruc-tion for its adult immigrants as early as 1901.[11] Chicago started special classes for foreigners in 1903.[12] Detroit noted great interest in the night schools on the part of many immi-grants in 1904, and set up special classes for Jews, Italians, and Greeks in 1906.[13] Rochester, Cleveland, Philadelphia, Buf-falo, Cincinnati, and Boston, were also among the cities which took the lead in immigrant education work during the first decade of the 20th century. It remained, however, for certain

10 For bibliography of such writings, see Appendix B.

11 New York, N. Y., *Third Annual Report of the City Superintendent of Schools for the Year Ending, July 31, 1901*, p. 51.

12 Chicago, Ill., *Forty-Ninth Annual Report of the Board of Education for the Year Ending, June 30, 1903*, pp. 65-66.

13 Detroit, Mich., *Sixty-Second Annual Report of the Board of Education of the City of Detroit for the Year Ending, June 30, 1906*, p. 94.

private groups to take the initiative in an active campaign to educate the immigrant to a better appreciation of his American environment and of the good 'old fashioned' American ideals.[14]

Particularly active in this respect was the Educational Alliance of New York City, established on the lower East Side in the 1890's to 'Americanize' the Jewish immigrants from central and eastern Europe. The Alliance came into existence as the result of a realization on the part of certain Jewish societies that a center for assimilative activities was a necessity in the 'ghetto' districts of New York City. Three organizations, the Hebrew Free School Association, the Aguilar Free Library, and the Y.M.H.A., succeeded in organizing a committee of public-spirited citizens to raise the necessary funds to build and equip a suitable building for that purpose. At a 'fair' given in 1889, upwards of $125,000 was secured, and a plan agreed upon whereby the three interested societies embarked upon the construction project. The resulting corporation took for its name the Educational Alliance, and devoted itself to the management of the new building.[15]

From the very beginning, arrangements were made for free lectures by eminent citizens through the cooperation of the New York City Board of Education and the United Settlement Society. Classes in biology, American history, English literature, dress-making, and kindergarten work were inaugu-

14 Boston, Mass., *Twenty-Eighth Annual Report of the Superintendent of Public Schools*, July 1908, p. 65; Buffalo, N. Y., *Annual Report of the Superintendent of Education of the City of Buffalo, 1904-1905*, p. 37; *ibid., 1905-06*, p. 24; Cincinnati, Ohio, *Seventy-Ninth Annual Report of the Public Schools of Cincinnati for the School Year Ending August 31, 1908*, p. 71; Cleveland, Ohio, *Sixty-Seventh Annual Report of the Board of Education for the School Year Ending August 31, 1903*, p. 84; *ibid., Sixty-Ninth Annual Report, 1905*, p. 63; Philadelphia, Pa., *Eighty-Ninth Annual Report of the Board of Public Education for the Year Ending, December 31, 1907*, p. 47; Rochester, N. Y., *Fifty-Second Annual Report of the Board of Education of the City of Rochester, New York, for the Years 1900-1901-1902*, p. 36; *ibid., Years 1903-1904*, p. 31; *ibid., Years 1905-1906-1907*, p. 30.

15 *First Annual Report of the Educational Alliance*, New York, 1893, pp. 9-22.

rated, and special work with boys and girls to prepare them for attendance at the public schools was undertaken. In addition, the Alliance carried on the usual activities associated with social settlement work. Evening classes in English for immigrant men and women were offered, and daily classes for teachers on how to teach English to the immigrants. An examination of the annual reports of the Educational Alliance during the next ten years reveals that the work started along the lines indicated above was continued among the Jewish immigrant populace of the lower East Side on a large and expanding scale, with special emphasis on classes for immigrant children, the teaching of English to adult immigrants, and work of a school and Americanization nature.[16]

Of peculiar significance was the financial aid given to the Educational Alliance by the Baron de Hirsch Fund for the purpose of carrying on the work of educating the immigrants. Founded in 1891 by Baron Maurice de Hirsch, who gave $2,400,000 in trust to assist Jewish immigrants and to establish them as useful members of the community in which they settled, the Fund maintained its own classes for the education of Jewish immigrants in New York City at first, but later in 1899 turned to the Educational Alliance to carry on the work instead. Henceforth, the Fund financed the educational program of the Alliance. In addition, the Baron de Hirsch Fund aided the Hebrew Educational Society of Brooklyn, the Philadelphia Hebrew Educational Society, the Columbian Council of Pittsburgh, and the Jewish Educational Society of St. Louis, in carrying on work of a similar nature with the Jewish immigrant.[17]

16 *Ibid.*, pp. 9-22; *cf.* Educational Alliance, *Souvenir Book of the Fair in Aid of the Educational Alliance and the Hebrew Technical Institute*, New York, c. 1895, *passim.*

17 Maurice H. Harris, " The National Conference of Jewish Charities ", *Charities and the Commons*, XVI (May 19, 1906), pp. 255-284. For excellent account of the work of the Educational Alliance, *cf.* Paul Abelson, " The Education of the Immigrant ", *Journal of Social Science*, XLIV (Sept. 1906), pp. 163-172.

Another organization, the Society for Italian Immigrants, attacked the same problem for the benefit of the Italian immigrant during the same period. The Society was organized in 1900 by leading Italian-Americans and Americans of native origin for the purpose of helping and protecting the newcomers from Italy by guiding and advising them both upon their arrival and later at their final destinations. Because many of the incoming Italians found employment on the laboring gangs and in the construction camps throughout the United States, the Society devoted most of its educational work to the Italians found in these isolated communities.[18]

In an effort to better the lot of the poor wretches forced to live in construction camps, the Society engaged the services of Miss Sarah W. Moore, an experienced teacher and social worker. Miss Moore started an experiment in the way of labor-camp schools which proved to be of such value that both New York and Pennsylvania passed legislation in support of such ventures on the strength of the success of her first school of this sort.

With the assistance of an executive of the corporation engaged in the construction of a new infiltration plant at Aspinwall, Pa., Miss Moore opened an experimental night school for day laborers on September 5, 1905. Using a shanty given to her for that purpose by the contractors, she soon had forty men enrolled. The experiment was a success from the very start. Finding no suitable textbook for her new pupils, Miss Moore wrote her own. By 1906, the school had an enrollment of 80 students divided into three classes according to their knowledge of the English language.[19]

The success of the experiment at Aspinwall encouraged the Society of Italian Immigrants to open a similar school at Ambridge, Pa., upon the completion of the Aspinwall project in

18 Society for Italian Immigrants, *Annual Reports,* 1904-1920.

19 Jane E. Robbins, " Immigrants in Labor Camps and in Isolated Communities ", United States Bureau of Education, *Bulletin,* 1913, LXI, pp. 15-18.

1909. This school carried on the program inaugurated in the Society's initial effort, and remained in the hands of the organization until 1912 when a local committee took over control and henceforth ran it as a community venture. Other schools were opened by the Society at Wappinger's Falls, Stoneco Dam, and Ashokan Dam in New York. A fourth school was started at Valhalla, N. Y., but was later taken over and conducted by the North American Civic Leangue for Immigrants in 1912.[20]

The Young Men's Christian Association also began to focus some of its welfare work among the immigrants arriving yearly through the various ports of the nation. Special work for non-English-speaking people began in 1907, when the New York Association established the first of its evening schools. Emphasis was placed upon teaching the alien the language of America, the requirements of naturalization, the nature of American government, and something of the background of the new country into which he had come. By 1908, the movement to educate the immigrant through evening classes had spread to the YMCA's of other cities, and between five thousand and six thousand immigrant men were meeting in groups of from ten to one hundred in 130 cities and towns of America. Some took their lessons at noon-time in the shops and factories, some at mid-night lunch hour, others during the day-time when special arrangements could be made. The great majority of classes met, however, in the evening after the day's work had been completed.

---

20 Sarah Wool Moore, " Teaching of Foreigners ", *Survey*, XXIV (June 4, 1910), pp. 386-392. For other articles on Miss Moore's work, *cf.* Moore, "Labor Camp Schools ", National Conference of Charities and Correction, *Proceedings*, 1909, pp. 236-238; Moore, " New Recollections—Notes on Camp School No. 1, Aspinwall, Pa.", *Charities and the Commons*, XVII, pp. 894-902; Umberto Coletti, " The Italian Immigrant ", National Conference of Charities and Correction, *Proceedings*, 1912, pp. 249-254; Coletti, "Assimilating the Adult Immigrant ", *Outlook*, LXXXVIII (Feb. 1, 1908), pp. 244-245; Coletti, " Schools for Immigrant Laborers " *Outlook*, XCII (Aug. 7, 1909), pp. 823-824.

While most classes met in Association buildings, many were held in rented rooms or halls in immigrant sections, and occasionally in lodge rooms, church basements, or in boarding houses. The teachers were generally young men who knew very little if anything about the languages of the newcomers, but succeeded in obtaining considerable success in spite of this handicap. An elaborate system of teaching English to the newcomers was worked out by Dr. Peter Roberts, secretary of the industrial department of the New York Association. Later, he assumed complete charge of all activities of the Y.M.C.A. along this line. Roberts' system received great praise from many educators because of its fundamental approach to the problem.[21]

By 1912, it was estimated that more than fifty-five thousand immigrants had been helped by the Y.M.C.A. to learn English and that approximately three hundred branches of the Association scattered throughout the United States were offering training in English. In addition to such classes, illustrated lectures were given for the benefit of the newcomers. These dealt with all phases of American life and included such subjects as personal hygiene, sanitation, geography, industrial safety, and government.[22]

21 Peter Roberts, "The Y. M. C. A. Teaching Foreign-Speaking Men", *Immigrants in America Review*, I (June 1915), pp. 18-23. Roberts stressed the necessity for compulsory education for immigrants as a means of avoiding election frauds, industrial accidents, and providing for better sanitation conditions. He also praised the efforts of the men who cooperated with the Association in conducting the classes. Roberts offered the Y's immigrant education program as suggestive of what could be done by other groups. The Y viewed its work as tremendously successful and at least one answer to the "immigrant problem". *Cf.* Roberts, "Night Schools", National Conference of Charities and Correction, *Proceedings*, 1909, pp. 232-236.

22 Roberts, "The Y. M. C. A. among the Immigrants", *Survey*, XXIX (Feb. 15, 1913), pp. 697-700. The Y also established an elaborate system of port and railroad service for the immigrant. Arrangements were made whereby the Y's representatives abroad distributed cards to the departing immigrants telling them to be on the lookout for the Association's representatives upon their arrival in America. The latter, upon meeting the newcomers at the ports, offered to help them learn English. The immigrant was

Still another pioneer institution to enter the field of immigrant education in a serious way was that started by Dr. R. DeWitt Mallary in New England—as a center of learning to meet the needs of educated leaders among the various immigrant nationalities. Backed financially by the various Protestant bodies, Dr. Mallary transformed the Congregational French Protestant College of Springfield, Mass., into a nonsectarian collegiate center for the education of immigrant leaders, teachers, members of the professions, and men in the industrial and commercial fields. Mallary planned to have these people go forth trained in a knowledge of America and of American ideals, and capable of guiding, advising, and leading fellow members of their nationality. He hoped in this way to break the rule of the padrone, the political boss, and the demagogue.

Dr. Mallary aimed to place the American International College, as the new institution was called, on the same liberal basis that distinguished such schools as Amherst and Williams. At the same time, marked emphasis upon religous ideals was retained, and useful training for the students afforded through an industrial department as a means of paying their way through school. The college had an enrollment of fifteen at the start. In addition to the usual collegiate subjects, it set up a School of Citizenship conducted by Professor Louis F. Giroux, where English was taught by a system of phonetics aimed to give the student a command of a vocabulary of 3,000 words after thirty-six weeks of study. Other subjects included American history and ideals (in the form of talks by instruc-

---

asked to help organize classes at the boarding house or at some other convenient place where the YMCA could send teachers to carry on the classes. The Y also distributed cards in thirty languages through its agents informing the immigrants of the services of the Association, and other useful literature containing information about America and warning them about the activities of quacks and other types of parasites which preyed upon the unsuspecting immigrant. *Cf.* Edward A. Halsey, "Our Brothers, the Immigrants", *World Today*, XIX (Dec. 1910), pp. 1375-1381; also, Roberts, "The Y. M. C. A. among the Immigrants", *op. cit.*, pp. 697-700.

tors based on the lives of eminent Americans), American government, patriotism, sanitation, and personal hygiene. An effort was made to infuse a spirit of Americanism through the reading of the Declaration of Independence, Washington's Farewell Address, Benjamin Franklin's *Autobiography*, the Gettysburg Address, and other patriotic literature.

Although the College received financial aid from the various Protestant bodies, Roman Catholics, Jews, and others were welcomed as students. The enrollment of 1910 numbered 100 students. From its transformation into a college for the exclusive education of immigrant leaders in 1908, the American International College yearly sent forth educated immigrants, who returned to their respective communities imbued with the teachings of the College and trained to help their fellow countrymen adjust themselves to their new environment.[23]

With all the hubbub over the immigrant question during this period, it was only natural that certain of the old established patriotic organizations should enter the lists and engage in the work of winning the immigrant over to a better appreciation and a better understanding of America. Two of these, the National Society of the Colonial Dames of America and the National Society of the Sons of the American Revolution, took an active part in the education of the immigrant through the publication of tracts and other informative literature for the benefit of the immigrant and through the sponsorship of lectures and classes of a patriotic nature.

The National Society of Colonial Dames of America was the first of the large patriotic American societies to realize the opportunity for rendering patriotic and educational work among the immigrants. During the opening years of the new century, it began, in the words of one of its spokesmen, " this wonderful and valuable work and kindled a torch which, we

23 Charles G. Fairman, " College-Trained Immigrants, a Study of Americans in the Making ", *New England Magazine*, new series, XLII (July, 1910), pp. 577-584; also, *Annual Reports of the American International College*, 1908-1925.

trust, shall never go out. . . ." [24] The Illinois chapter started the work in 1904 by appropriating $1,500 for a five-year scholarship at the University of Chicago, based upon competitive examinations, and with the proviso that the successful candidate agree to engage in patriotic educational work in the foreign settlements of the state at the request and under the direction of the Illinois Society. The experiment worked out very satisfactorily from the Society's standpoint. Not only did the beneficiaries perform the services required of them successfully, but other and unexpected forces were set in motion.

The Society's new venture aroused the interest of the press of the state, which ably and persistently seconded the efforts of the Colonial Dames in respect to the immigrant. One of the daily newspapers established a series of free lectures for foreigners at its own expense in 1906. Pastors of the foreign communities became interested and lent their aid to the work, while talks by leaders of the immigrant groups in their own languages upon the advantages of citizenship and the requirements necessary for this status were given under the sponsorship of the Society. In some cases, the Illinois group sponsored and furnished the textbooks for carrying on citizenship classes, while a special civic primer for the use of the immigrant was prepared by one of its scholarship holders. The latter set forth in simple language the fundamentals of American political institutions and was printed in Czech and English and distributed broadcast among the immigrant classes.[25]

The work of the National Society of Colonial Dames spread. In 1909, the Illinois chapter established a second scholarship at Northwestern University, while the Missouri chapter set up a similar one at Washington University in St. Louis. The

24 National Society of the Colonial Dames of America, *The National Society of the Colonial Dames of America, Its Beginnings, Its Purpose and a Record of Its Work, 1891-1913*, 1913, p. 61.

25 *Ibid.*, pp. 59-66.

Michigan chapter provided lectures for Italians in their own language in Detroit. During the same years, the Minnesota chapter inaugurated a series of stereopticon lectures delivered to the immigrants by a Polish rabbi. The Massachusetts chapter continued to carry on the classes in history and civics for the Rumanian and Italian immigrants of Boston, which it had started in 1904. By 1913, the National Society of Colonial Dames of America was engaged in some sort of educational and patriotic work among the immigrant groups of Colorado, Ohio, Wisconsin, New York, Iowa, and Tennessee, in addition to the states mentioned above.[26]

While the Colonial Dames approached the problem of the immigrant's education and indoctrination in American ideals and practices chiefly through individual effort on the part of the various state subdivisions, the National Society of the Sons of the American Revolution centered its activities along this line in the national body itself. As early as 1893, the Sons had discussed the problem of the immigrant and the need for his education at their annual congress. It was not, however, until after the assassination of President McKinley that the Society commenced its active work in this field. At that time the organization published and distributed a small leaflet entitled, *A Welcome to Immigrants and Some Good Advice,* which outlined briefly the natural advantages which the country offered and urged the immigrants to abide by the laws of the land and to become American citizens as quickly as possible. Because of lack of funds, the leaflet was published in English only and never had a very large circulation.[27]

No further steps were taken until 1907, when the question of the assimilation of the immigrant was discussed at the national congress held at Denver that year. As a result, a special Committee on Information for Aliens was created. At

26 *Ibid.*, pp. 59-66.

27 John H. Moore, "The Sons of the American Revolution and Better Citizenship", *Immigrants in American Review*, I (Sept. 1915), pp. 40-41.

the next meeting of the Society's executive committee, a plan was outlined to care for the new program, and over one-half of the Society's income was appropriated to carry on the work.[28]

In May 1908, the Committee on Information for Aliens announced the printing of one million copies of a new leaflet, entitled, *The United States: Information for Immigrants,* in thirteen different languages. It announced also that plans had been completed for its distribution. The pamphlet was an enlarged edition of the Society's earlier publication and contained the same sort of information only in greater detail. By October of the same year, the leaflet had received such a popular reception that many of the large cities adopted it for use in their night school classes. Plans were set in motion immediately for the publication of a second leaflet dealing with the naturalization process. This second leaflet, entitled, *Naturalization of Aliens, How to Become Citizens, What is Required, Rights and Duties,* was printed in English, and submitted to the United States Department of Commerce and Labor for its approval and eventual adoption. The Society deemed it best that this leaflet be published in English only in view of the fact that the naturalization process itself required a knowledge of English.[29]

In December 1908, the Committee reported that over 40,000 copies of Leaflet Number One had been distributed, and that a great deal of interest had been aroused in the leaflet on naturalization. In March 1909, the Society received assurances from the Department of Commerce and Labor that its second pamphlet had been approved and that plans were being con-

[28] National Society of the Sons of the American Revolution, " Statement of Committee on Information for Aliens ", U. S. Immigration Commission, *Reports of the Immigration Commission, Statements and Recommendations Submitted by Societies and Organizations Interested in the Subject of Immigration,* XLI, p. 7.

[29] National Society of the Sons of the American Revolution, *Official Bulletin,* III, No. 2 (Oct. 1908), pp. 5-6.

sidered for its translation into several languages. To its disappointment, the installation of a new administration resulted in the dropping of the project. Despite this blow, the Society continued to publish both pamphlets, and estimated that approximately 134,000 copies of both had been distributed by December 1908, a figure that rose rapidly to 433,529 by May 1909. An examination of the *Reports* of the Society indicates a constant and ever increasing demand for both publications as the new century wore on.[30]

Eventually, an edition of one million copies of the leaflets was published in English, Yiddish, Polish, Italian, Magyar, Greek, Swedish, Danish, Norwegian, German, Slovak, Lithuanian, Czech, Slovene, and Croatian, distributed gratis. The organization found that it was a comparatively easy matter to interest manufacturers, mining companies, employers of immigrant labor, settlement workers, and many private individuals in the distribution of the leaflets. Thousands were distributed in pay envelopes and in the night schools of the large cities to be carried home and read by the members of the family. Patriotic societies aided in the general distribution, while newspapers like the *New York Herald* and many of the foreign-language newspapers published the entire texts of the pamplets in their editions.[31]

Judging from the reports received from the many state societies and sub-chapters, the Committee for Information for Aliens did not hestitate to state that the work it had been carrying on along this line had been beneficial. The Committee felt that the leaflets had been gratefully received in most cases and that great work had been done to teach the newcomers an appreciation for the principles and ideals for which America stood.[32] " The millions of aliens in the United States are being

---

30 *Ibid.*, III, No. 3 (Dec. 1908), pp. 4-7; also, III, No. 4 (Mar. 1909), pp. 5-10, and subsequent issues.

31 *Ibid.*, VI, No. 2 (Oct. 1911), pp. 1-2.

32 National Society of the Sons of the American Revolution, " Statement of Committee on Information for Aliens ", *op. cit.*, p. 7.

taught what the nation stands for, what it means for them to become a part of the body politic, participating in the duties and responsibilities of active citizens in an intelligent manner. The immigrants of today may be the good Americans of to-morrow, if they are made to know their privileges and their duties in their adopted country. The children of our alien population may become leaders in the advancement of American ideals." [33]

Indicative, too, of the growing interest in the education of the immigrant was the passage of the first state legislation, by New Jersey, in 1907 in support of evening classes in English and civics for the foreign-born. As the result of this action, boards of education of any school district in the state were authorized to establish and to maintain evening schools and classes for the instruction of the foreign-born residents of their respective districts in the English language and in the form of government and laws of the State of New Jersey and the United States. To insure uniformity of administration and of instruction, provision was made by the State Board of Education to prescribe rules for the proper control and management of the schools, for their inspection, for granting certificates to teachers to teach in such schools, and for carrying into effect the provisions of the act. Establishment of such evening schools was to be encouraged. By the law, state aid to local schools was authorized in equal proportion to the amount raised in support of the schools by the local boards. This was the first instance where the necessity for special facilities for foreign-born residents of a state was recognized by statute.[34]

Thus the opening years of the new century witnessed an active and growing interest in the immigrant and the problems related to his entrance upon the American scene. A strong

33 Sons of the American Revolution, *Official Bulletin*, VI, No. 2 (Oct. 1911), pp. 1-2.

34 H. H. Wheaton, "Recent Progress in the Education of the Immigrant" *Report of the Commissioner of Education for the Year Ended June 30, 1914*, I, pp. 427-428.

movement had been set afoot, based upon a combination of economic and racial motives, which agitated for the passage of restrictive legislation to halt or slow the further infiltration of these 'undesirables'. A growing feeling of distrust had led certain of the patriotic societies to inaugurate programs which attempted to acquaint the newcomers with the ways of life and ideals of their new home. An awakening consciousness of the need for humanitarian measures to alleviate some of the deplorable conditions in the immigrant slums and the help-lessly dependent position of the immigrant from the first day of his arrival had led to the establishment of social settlement ventures and Y.M.C.A. bureaus in an attempt to meet this need.

A growing awareness of the need for action on behalf of their fellow immigrants had led certain of the more progressive immigrant circles to organize immigrant welfare societies and educational groups to aid in easing the lot of their fellow countrymen. The stage was set for the formation of a tra-ditionally American pressure group to agitate for a domestic program on behalf of the immigrant; for a domestic program which would stress the need for action leading to the eventual assimilation of the immigrant. Such a program, these people felt, would be the best answer to the queries concerning the means of solving the 'immigrant problem'. This pressure group was not long in forming. As a result of its efforts, the movement was inaugurated which accumulated eventually in the Americanization crusade of the years immediately pre-ceding, accompanying, and succeeding World War I.

# CHAPTER II

# THE NORTH AMERICAN CIVIC LEAGUE FOR IMMIGRANTS AND AFFILIATED ORGANIZATIONS

IN February 1907, the International Committee of the Y.M.C.A. sponsored a conference in New York City of representatives from the chief ports of entry—philanthropists, social workers, writers, leaders in the industrial field, and others of prominence in the public life of America—for the specific purpose of forming an organization to accomplish the civic betterment of the immigrant. After deliberation and discussion, the members in attendance agreed to band themselves together under the name of the North American Civic League for Immigrants, and to embark immediately upon a program to meet the many problems inherent in the immigrant situation through protecting, aiding, educating and inspiring the newcomer with a better appreciation of the new life about him. Thus was born the first of the active Americanization groups.[1]

Composed by and large of representatives of the more conservative economic interests, the new League was soon to exert a powerful and influential pressure to achieve its goal. " To change the unskilled inefficient immigrant into the skilled worker and efficient citizen, to strike at the cause of poverty, to improve the environment and the spirit of America, the knowledge of America, and the love of America and one's fellow-men into the millions gathered and gathering here from the ends of the earth. . . ."—this was the stated humanitarian and idealistic aim of the new organization.[1]

1 D. Chauncey Brewer, "A Patriotic Movement for the Assimilation of Immigrants", *Editorial Review*, III (Aug. 1910), pp. 786-800. See also, North American Civic League for Immigrants, *Annual Report*, 1910-1911, p. 9. Officers and members of the League were: D. Chauncey Brewer, lawyer and civic leader, and active in the Boston Chamber of Commerce, president; Bernard J. Rothwell, industrialist and president of the Boston Chamber of Commerce, vice-president; Francis B. Sears, treasurer. Board of Managers:

The organization of the League reflected that fear for the continued safety of American institutions so current among native American groups during the first decade of the 20th century. Writing in the *Editorial Review* of August 1910, the new League's president, D. Chauncey Brewer, summarized succinctly the underlying fears and reasons motivating the League's membership to embark upon its new program. After noting the great influx of new immigrants since 1880, the seriousness of the problem which had emerged as a result, the apathy of the native stock to the new menace because of its intense interest in " commercialism " and self-gain, Brewer intimated that something portentous might happen unless positive and sufficient action were taken to meet the exigency. It was a cognizance of this possibility that explained the formation of the League. He then went on to explain:

> For some time those in the community, whose thoughts are not limited by the requirements of the day's toil or pleasure, have been noting with uneasiness the changing character of our population. Especially is this true of the men at the head

Nathan L. Amster, Jacob P. Bates, Lucius Tuttle, president of the Boston & Maine Railroad, Samuel B. Capen, officer and director of Torrey, Brighton, & Capen Co., Edward H. Haskel, president of the Haskell-Dawes Machine Co., and the American Rotary Power Co., Richard C. Humphreys, Arthur S. Johnson, president of the Boston Y. M. C. A., the Rt. Rev. William Lawrence, William E. Murdock, Bernard J. Rothwell, the Most Rev. William H. O'Connell, William T. Rich, and the officers of the League, all of Boston. Non-Boston members included: Frank A. Vanderlip, president of the National City Bank of New York City; Thomas M. Mulry, Jacob A. Riis, Felix Warburg, prominent banker and philanthropist, and Robert Watchorn of New York City; James Cardinal Gibbons, Charles England, president of the Baltimore Chamber of Commerce, and Jacob H. Hollander, economist and financial advisor, of Baltimore; Clinton R. Woodruff, lawyer and member of the Pennsylvania legislature, and William R. Tucker, secretary of the Philadelphia National Board of Trade, of Philadelphia. Later members included E. J. Buffington, president of the Illinois Steel Company, L. Wilbur Messer, general secretary of the Chicago Y. M. C. A., George E. Roberts, and John F. Smulski, immigrant banker, president of the Northwestern Trust and Savings Bank, and vice-president of the Chicago Chamber of Commerce, of Chicago; Charles H. Pugh, financier, and John Wanamaker, prominent merchant, of Philadelphia.

of industrial activities and the teaching forces of the nation. The nature of their activities keeps them informed. They know by experience that the number of the people in our mills who do not speak English is constantly increasing and that children brought into public schools are often ignorant of the tongue in which they are to be taught.

Bearing these facts in mind, they have communicated their uneasiness to others. Thus a large number of citizens has been ready to initiate action and respond to any reasonable call.

If, therefore, the peril menaces, that Americans by birth or naturalization will be crowded out of their possessions by newcomers, it is true that they are waking to the situation. Should they falter at some self-sacrifice to adjust themselves to the need of the hour, it will be because they have lost their virility and power of adaptation. In this case it may be expected that historians will claim that our composite people were weakened rather than made strong by amalgamation.

Meanwhile, men who have become conversant with the status through the above named channels or by the accident of position, are urging their fellow-citizens to meet a growing menace man fashion. This can be done only by each individual being loyal to our institutions and agreeing to stand in his or her place and assume a responsibility commensurate with the influence, ability and wealth possessed by each.

Unless this be done or unforeseen causes discourage immigration, it is believed by many that what our fathers won for themselves and humanity will be forfeited. Not only shall we have proved ourselves unworthy of a sacred trust, but we shall have knowingly disregarded the interests of our children.

Those who have made the cause of the League their own, have abundant faith in the American people and in the future of constitutional government as it exists in North America. They also believe that the majority of the immigrants entering the continent or who may become resident here, are well meaning, and may become useful citizens if they receive the attention to which they are not only entitled as a matter of humanity, but which prudence necessitates because of their relation to our economic and political affairs.[2]

Yet, Brewer continued, this could only be possible if efforts were taken at once along the lines suggested by the League, namely, through agitation that would inform the public as to the conditions which existed and were developing through immigration; through protecting incoming immigrants and resident aliens as well as bringing them into close sympathy with that part of the community which was devoted to law and order; and through such education of immigrants and resident aliens as would make them familiar with the English language and fit them to become citizens if they so desired. It was such a program that the League presented to the American public for its consideration and support, and by so doing can be said to have inaugurated the movement to Americanize the immigrant.[3]

Stressing the need for a non-sectarian organization as one of the reasons for its founding, the League's members pointed out that a comprehensive movement for the Americanization of the immigrant must of necessity be independent of any organization which could evoke the criticism of any religious body. They felt the need for an organization devoted exclusively to impartial immigrant aid work rather than to work of a missionary or proselytizing variety. They wanted their organization to be acceptable to Protestants, Catholics, and Jews alike.[4]

The first work of the League was to investigate conditions among the immigrants. Findings similar to those revealed by the national and various state immigration commissions (of

2 Brewer, *op. cit.* This article was later published by the North American Civic League for Immigrants in pamphlet form under the same title, *A Patriotic Movement for the Assimilation of Immigrants*, 1910. For specific quotations, see pp. 4-10 of pamphlet.

3 Brewer, *op. cit.*, pp. 9-10.

4 North American Civic League for Immigrants, *Report, 1910-1911*, *op. cit.*, p. 9.

which more will be said below) were obtained. But in addition, the League found, that, smarting from real or fancied wrongs, and not being able to distinguish good Americans from rascals, the immigrants were frequently brought under the influence of "mischievous radicals", whose harangues enlisted the immigrants in the forces making for disorder. The League found also, that ignorance of the American language, a "negative philosophy", and an inherited distrust of government, combined to make the immigrants readier after such experiences to ally themselves with "destructive forces" rather than with those making for order. Forearmed with this information, the League then set about putting its program into effect.[5]

Analysis of the existing immigrant situation led the League to select Boston, the second port of entry, as the experimental center of the new movement, in as much as this city contained most of the immigrant problems that existed in New York City yet in a much less confused way and without the adverse political and commercial influences that played such an important part at that time in the great metropolis. The New England post was therefore chosen as the laboratory to try out methods for dealing with the problem of the immigrant as the League saw it.[6] It then proceeded to put into effect its three-fold program of agitation, protection, and education of the newcomers in the English language and good citizenship as indicated above.[7]

To assure the success of its program, the Board of Managers of the League commissioned committees of leading residents in the larger cities and representative ones in the smaller towns to adapt the scheme of campaign to local needs.

5 Brewer, *op. cit.*, p. 6.

6 "Statement of the North American Civic League for Immigrants", *Reports of the Immigration Commission, Statements and Recommendations, op. cit.*, Chapter I, XLI, p. 97.

7 North American Civic League, *Annual Report, 1909-1910*, pp. 3-4.

Special efforts were made with considerable success to arouse the interest of business circles in the League's program on behalf of the immigrant. Meetings were held to discuss the immigrant problem and its industrial ramifications. Appeals were made by agents of the League to the patriotism of business groups in many of the industrial areas of the nation, and sufficient response was aroused by the end of its first year of existence to enable the League to organize committees in 36 cities in nine different states to assist it in its program of assimilation.[8] As a result of these successful efforts, the League's Board of Managers were spurred on to continue the 'good work', convinced more than ever, that they had the backing and support of a considerable portion of the more progressive business elements in these various centers.[9]

The League set to work immediately to organize a staff of workers to meet the immigrant ships coming into New York, Boston, and Philadelphia, in order to advise and direct the newcomers, and to endeavor to protect them from those seeking to exploit them. Agents of the League were ordered to cooperate with representatives of other societies at work in the ports and to correlate the activities of these societies in so far as possible to avoid duplication of effort. In Boston, a

8 " Statement of the North American Civic League ", *op. cit.*, pp. 97-98. Centers mentioned were: Baltimore, Md., Beverly, Boston, Everett, Fall River, Fitchburg, Great Barrington, Haverhill, Lawrence, Lowell, Lynn, New Bedford, Newton, North Adams, Pittsfield, Salem, Springfield, Waltham, Williamstown, and Worcester, Mass., Harrisburg, Hazleton, Philadelphia, Pottsville, Reading, Shenandoah, and St. Clair, Pa., Hartford, New Britain, and New Haven, Conn., Los Angeles, Cal., Patterson, N. J., Providence, R. I., Chicago, Ill., and New York City.

9 Indicative of the optimism of the League in this respect was the statement which appeared in its *Report* for 1909-1910, p. 3: " That the issue it has organized to meet is of extraordinary significance is proved by the character of the men who have responded to its call. It is cause for great encouragement that American business men are still quick to note a national exigency. Evidently commercialism has not clouded all our sensibilities. Men still love their country, and will respond adequately when the appeal is made to their patriotism."

similar service was performed at railroad stations and terminals, where arrangements were worked out whereby the League received advance notification each day from the immigration authorities in New York City as to the number and nationality of those immigrants en route to Boston. At the latter's South Terminal building, agents of the League met the newcomers and directed them to their proper destinations. Literature of a helpful nature was handed out to the immigrants at the same time. Thousands of pamphlets were distributed in Yiddish, Italian, and English. A similar service was performed by agents of the League in New York City.[10]

The new organization found upon investigation that, except for routine federal activities, there was little systematic work being done at the docks where the immigrants were being landed, especially so at the North Atlantic ports. Representatives of certain societies aided officials in the detention rooms and did some work outside, but most of them deplored the fact that they were without influential support. Much of the work fell into the category of fruitless and mistaken effort. Colporteurs of religious societies distributed religious tracts to people who needed immediate protection and information. The League cited cases where Italians were given Scandinavian literature and *vice versa*. Little, too, was being done to discourage the legion of scamps who met the immigrants as soon as they passed beyond the confines of the federal immigration authorities. Everywhere the League reported a lack of cooperation.[11]

To remedy the situation, the newly organized group offered its services freely as a civic agency with no religious or political bias. To the satisfaction of its members, noticeable results were reported. Its secretaries and representatives gained the confidence of the Commissioner of Immigration in all the northeastern ports of the United States, and endeavored to learn how best they could supplement the work of the government

10 " Statement of the League ", *op. cit.*, p. 98.

in its endeavors to guard new residents. Aggressive work was pushed in the urban areas where immigrants were most likely to congregate. A great deal of data was collected for reference purposes concerning immigrant aid societies, boarding houses available for immigrants, the character and availability of interpreters, and a host of other possible services. The League's agents remained ever on the alert for evidences of fraud or other illegal actions committed against the immigrant, and attempted to stamp out such abuses in every possible way.[11]

Many immigrants were invited to visit the offices of the League in order to obtain information and advice. In Boston, a special Italian branch of the main office was established with an Italian secretary to work with people of that nationality. Most satisfactory work was reported as having been accomplished in this way. The Board of Managers proudly stated that many immigrants in search of work, and those desirous of receiving advice regarding the naturalization process, were quick to come to the offices of the League to be aided and so directed.[12]

Believing wholeheartedly in a campaign of education for the immigrant, the League shaped its educational program so that the utmost cooperation with the public school authorities in advertising and sponsoring night school programs and lectures for the adult could be achieved. It did not attempt to teach the immigrants directly for it did not feel that it should embark upon actual class work itself. Instead, it tried to induce the public schools to increase their educational facilities in order to reach a larger number of immigrants. Public school authorities were asked to open more classes for foreigners and to keep such classes as were already in existence open for a longer period during the year.[13]

[11] North American Civic League for Immigrants, *Annual Report, 1909-1910*, pp. 6-7.

[12] "Statement of the League", *op. cit.*, p. 98.

[13] In a plea for more and better opportunities for the education of the immigrant, the League's president, Brewer, stated: "That enlightened

In an effort to attract the residents of the foreign colonies to the schools in their neighborhood, the North American Civic League provided a series of illustrated lectures on civics for evening schools. At the same time, it hoped to give regular pupils in attendance at the evening schools simple instruction in matters which had to do with their practical welfare or with those things with which they should be familiar before receiving citizenship. During the period 1909-10, more than forty such lectures were given in Boston and elsewhere throughout New England in English, Yiddish, Finnish, German, Greek, Hungarian, Italian, Lithuanian, and Polish. Throughout the following year, over one hundred and fifty lectures were delivered in thirteen New England cities in co-operation with the public school authorities.[14]

---

governments only endure by making adequate provision for the education of those who exercise the franchise will be admitted by all informed Americans. It might be well if the negative of this position were championed. Then more thought would be given the reasons underlying the assertion. As it is, many on this side of the North Atlantic must believe in schools without appreciating their full significance. If such people understood that cherished political institutions could only be perpetuated by educating the public, they would provide schools not only for children but for the unnumbered adult immigrants who are crowding into their communities. It is absurdity to claim that such can intelligently perform a voter's duty until they understand something of the language and obligations of citizenship. Therefore nothing is more essential to the welfare of any city or town than the maintenance of night schools in which these people may be instructed. The argument that immigrants are too old to be instructed is without foundation, as eighty-three per cent of those entering the United States in the year ending June 30, 1909, were between fourteen and forty-four years of age. The contention that they are handled to better economic advantage if kept ignorant is unworthy, besides being stoutly contested by the largest employers of labor. Politically this latter is a dangerous principle. The North American Civic League for Immigrants has no more important function to perform than to push the teaching of English and Primary Civics to the immigrants ". *Cf. Annual Report, 1909-1910*, pp. 20-21.

14 " Statement of the League ", *op. cit.*, p. 98. The cities were : Boston, Beverley, Fitchburg, Lowell, Lynn, Springfield, and Quincy, Mass., New Britain, New Haven, Meriden, Conn., Westerly, R. I., and Elizabeth, N. J.

Most of the lectures were based upon material contained in the League's *Messages for Newcomers to the United States,* a series of eight lectures issued in pamphlet form in English and in nine foreign languages—Italian, Yiddish, Hungarian, Arabic, Finnish, Greek, Lithuanian, Polish, and Russian. The *Messages* dealt with such topics as *The United States, Its People and Its Laws, The Need of Learning English and the Advantages of an Education, The Story of the American People, Abraham Lincoln, How to Become a Citizen of the United States, The New Homeland and Opportunity Offered in Various Sections, George Washington,* and *A Primer for the Alien Desirous of Becoming a Citizen.*[15]

The *Messages* achieved an almost instant popularity with both immigrant and educational groups according to the League. Sold at virtual cost, public libraries, schools, social agencies, and many individuals found them invaluable in their work with the immigrant. The New York Public Library purchased 2,000 copies, while public libraries in at least thirty-one other cities distributed 4,500 more. An estimated thirty-two cities used the *Messages* in connection with their night school work. Philadelphia alone purchased 6,500 copies.[16]

The League also believed that wholesome recreation was essential to sound teaching, and frequently included music and other entertainment in addition to the lectures. Students of Harvard, Columbia, and the University of Pennsylvania, as well as many ' public-spirited ' men and women furnished the entertainment. In order to make the lectures a greater success, systematic advertising was carried on in the foreign-language press. Announcements were inserted telling of the coming talks and inviting the immigrants to attend the meetings. Fliers and tickets proved a successful means of arousing interest. By

15 North American Civic League *Annual Report, 1909-1910,* p. 27; *cf.* North American Civic League, *Messages for Newcomers to the United States,* Boston (no date) ; issued individually under the above mentioned titles and in a complete volume of eight.

16 North American Civic League, *Annual Report, 1910-1911,* pp. 11-12.

the end of the League's second year of existence, the lecture program had become one of its most successful activities.[17]

The League's Board of Managers emphasized cooperation with all other groups aiding the immigrant as a major part of its program. It sent inquiries to and counseled with many organizations of this character in the Boston area, including the Good Government Association, the Young Traveler's Aid Society, the Associated Charities, the Italian Immigrant Aid Society, the St. Vincent de Paul Society, the Y.M.C.A., and many others. It soon assumed the leadership of all these various organizations dealing with the immigrant in the Boston area by presenting a joint petition to the federal immigration authorities asking them to appoint it the representative of all the groups at the new immigration station about to be erected in that city. The organization asked also that it be assigned space in the building to carry on its work. Both requests were granted. The League's Board felt that it was gradually assuming a very important function as a coordinating organization and hoped eventually to become a clearing house for the various immigrant-aid groups of the vicinity.[18]

Sympathetic connections were formed between members of the League's Board of Managers and prominent foreign-born individuals of the various nationalities. The zeal with which many of these took up the work of the League impressed the members of the organization greatly and made them feel that their efforts were fully justified. President Brewer, in particular, felt that the cooperation of people of this sort refuted the contention of pessimists who were satisfied that the United States could not solve the mighty problems which immigration had developed. The love and appreciation for American ideals shown by these people, Brewer concluded, went far to encourage the League to carry on its program.[19]

17 *Ibid.*, p. 17.

18 " Statement of the League ", *op. cit.*, pp 96-97.

19 North American Civic League, *Annual Report, 1908-1909*, pp. 5-6.

By the end of its first year of existence, the League reported a gratifying patriotic reaction had been made to its appeals to the public for concerted action to Americanize the immigrant. Cordial response greeted its efforts in New York City, Boston, and Philadelphia, from the newspaper press of those centers, while such periodicals as the *Outlook* and *Survey* praised the League's program in strong editorials. The school authorities of Boston acceded to the League's request that immediate measures be taken to render the public-school system more adequate to the education of the immigrant by holding a conference of ungraded classes on November 11, 1910, and a second conference on immigrant education on March 24, 1911. A much clearer comprehension of the problem, it was claimed, was achieved as a result.[20] Requested to present its case to men's gatherings, patriotic and economic societies, and women's clubs, the League did so, and reported the response waxed so enthusiastic that the Board determined to form auxiliaries among those who desired to share in the growing movement. Arrangements were made whereby women's clubs could cooperate in publicizing the campaign. By means of circulars, the League further publicized its goal. Pastors of immigrant communities were requested to aid in interesting the immigrants in attending classes through the distribution of these circulars among their parishioners, while pastors of American congregations were urged to cooperate in every possible way.[21]

As outlined above, the League had taken the first steps toward interesting the nation in a concerted movement on behalf of the education of the immigrant. Within the next decade, the North American Civic League for Immigrants, as the pioneering agency in support of the Americanization of the immigrant, was to witness the consolidation of the movement

---

20 *Ibid., Annual Report, 1910-1911*, p. 21.

21 *Ibid., Annual Report, 1908-1909*, pp. 4-5.

it had set afoot and the growth of the campaign to educate the immigrant until it assumed a nation-wide significance.[22]

While the North American Civic League was at work in the east, a somewhat similar organization was founded in Chicago to serve a like purpose. The new organization grew out of the interest shown by the Women's Trade Union League of Chicago in immigrant problems in that city. The latter group organized a committee to visit immigrant girls to help them to escape the many pitfalls which constantly threatened their moral well-being while living in the great midwestern metropolis. The Trade Union League soon discovered, however, that the undertaking was quite beyond the ability of the organization to handle.[23]

As more information was secured, those interested in the immigrant became convinced of the need of a protective agency for the immigrant men and women of the Chicago area and, accordingly, organized the League for the Protection of Immigrants in the spring of 1908. It later changed its name to the

22 Describing the evidences of the League's growing popularity among all sorts of groups, President Brewer stated: "Not only have officials of the Federal and State governments, societies working for the betterment of economics and social conditions, the headmasters of evening schools, and local authorities, endorsed the movement and extended marked courtesies, but citizens of every class have been generous in personal service and financial support". He added: "This is as it should be. The movement is a direct evolution of a growing sentiment in the United States that something practical and immediate should be done to assimilate and Americanize the immigrant. No other organization of a national character has taken up this special work as its sole object, although many societies, religious, social and civic, are rendering invaluable service to the same end. It is our purpose to stimulate and assist these and to enthuse others with the same spirit, to work through constituted authorities wherever possible, and to create helpful agencies where none exist at present. If our plans do not miscarry, it will not be long before men of foreign-birth admitted to the privileges of the franchise will have some intelligent idea of the responsibilities of an American citizen." Cf. Annual Report, 1908-1909, pp. 6-7.

23 League for the Protection of Immigrants, Annual Report of the League for the Protection of Immigrants, 1909-1910, p. 8; cf. "Statement of the Immigrants' Protective League", Statements and Recommendations Submitted by Societies, op. cit., p. 63.

Immigrants' Protective League in 1910. The new organization embarked upon a campaign in many ways complementary to that which was being carried on by the North American Civic League for Immigrants, but whereas the latter organization and its affiliates gradually assumed a role of nation-wide significance, the Chicago organization confined its activities to the Chicago region with occasional state-wide drives.[24]

The League sponsored a program of action which included welcoming the newcomers, seeing that they reached the homes to which they were destined, guarding them against wrongs at railroads stations, labor employment agencies, and work camps, assisting the immigrants to secure work, and advising and encouraging them to take advantage of the many educational opportunities that were being furnished by the night schools, the settlement houses, the Y.M.C.A., and other helpful organizations.[24] It supplemented these activities when necessary by protecting immigrant girls and women from the white slave traffic and prostitution. Personal visits to stations and homes by its agents and conferences with local, state, and na-

---

24 The League stated that its chief object was to help the bewildered immigrant unacquainted with the English language and American habits and customs. It outlined the necessity for such action as follows: "His entire future and patriotism to the country that is going to be his home may be seriously affected by his first contact with its men and women. Not merely as a matter of humanity toward the brother or sister in need, but as a matter of duty to ourselves and to our children it is important that the newcomers receive the best possible impression of those who are to be their fellow citizens." Pointing out that the immigrants were often the pliant tools in the hands of certain political workers, because they had been befriended by these in time of need and felt a debt of gratitude in return, the Society emphasized and reiterated the necessity for a more active interest in the immigrant from the native American elements. "It therefore behooves those whose interest in the development of their own country is pure and unselfish and whose humanity is broad enough to overlook the differences of race and creed and habit, themselves to extend this welcoming hand, to take measures to guard the foreigners against the perils to which they, more than the average man, are subject, and finally to open up to them opportunities for education and patriotic citizenship." Cf. *Annual Report, 1910-1911*, p. 5.

tional authorities as well as with the police and private agencies formed the basis for work of this sort.

In addition, the League had its executive secretary, Miss Grace Abbott, undertake studies of two of Chicago's ethnic groups, the Bulgarians and the Greeks, and of the existing employment agencies which catered to the immigrant. Miss Abbot undertook also a study of the role which the municipality could play in correcting existing evils in regard to the immigrant. As a result of her studies, the Illinois State Legislature amended and improved greatly the existing legislation in regard to employment agencies. Although Miss Abbot felt most of the work concerning the immigrant would have to be done by private philanthropic organizations like the League, she insisted that municipal, state, and federal authorities could render an important and necessary measure of assistance.[25]

The League negotiated with the federal authorities in 1910 to obtain the names of immigrants destined for Chicago, and for the establishment of a federal bureau in Chicago to which the immigrants could come upon their arrival, supplemented by federal inspectors on immigrant railroad trains and by matrons at railroad stations. The organization felt that such a bureau would offer an opportunity for all agencies to confer with the immigrant under the proper supervision. It enlisted the aid of the Commercial Club of Chicago in sponsoring a bill providing for the establishment of such a bureau. It was not, however, until 1912 that Congress passed the measure and the bill received the President's signature. The new act authorized the setting up of such a station in Chicago by the Secretary of Commerce and Labor, and provided the sum of $75,000 for that purpose. By the terms of the act, the Secretary

25 Immigrants' Protective League, *Annual Report, 1910-1911*, p. 6; Miss Abbott's findings and recommendations were published in the *American Journal of Sociology, Survey,* and the *Proceedings of the National Municipal League in the Cincinnati Conference for Good Government.* See Bibliography.

was authorized also to establish similar stations at other points in the interior of the country.[26]

The Immigrant's Protective League continued its work well into the post-war period very much along the lines outlined above. Cooperation between the Chicago organization and the North American Civic League for Immigrants was often very close and mutually beneficial, although the fond hope held by the New England group that the Immigrants' Protective League would become eventually a branch of its chief agency in Boston never materialized.

The third and last of the Americanizing agencies launched during the first decade of the 20th century, and the one which proved to be the most aggressive champion of the new movement eventually, was founded as the result of the findings of the New York State Immigration Commission. The year 1907 had seen the creation of the Federal Immigration Commission, one of the great triumphs achieved by the immigration restrictionists in their campaign to halt the flow of the newcomers to America. As a result of the general publicity occasioned by the vociferous adherents of a strong federal policy of restriction, those interested in the welfare of the immigrant succeeded in having a similar commission appointed to investigate conditions existing among the immigrant groups living in New York State.[27]

The Commission, consisting of nine members, was appointed by Governor Charles Evans Hughes in 1908. It made a thorough survey of the general social conditions of the aliens, their relationships with private banks, steamship ticket agencies and notaries public, the relationship of the immigrant to the civil and criminal code, naturalization, transportation, conditions in immigrant homes, sanitation, contract labor laws, unemployment, employment opportunities, conditions in labor

---

26 *Ibid., Fourth Annual Report for the Year Ending January 1st, 1913,* p. 7.

27 State of New York, *Laws of 1908,* Chapter 210.

camps, and the progress of immigrant education and assimilation.[28]

Holding its first meeting in New York City on August 11, 1908, the Commission held 42 meetings, 9 conferences, 37 hearings, and examined 193 witnesses, before handing in its report to the New York Legislature on April 5, 1909. It felt it had made a full inquiry, examination, and investigation into the condition, welfare, and industrial opportunities of aliens in the state as the law creating it had demanded. It found to its dismay what many social workers had been well aware of for quite some time, namely—that unbelievable living conditions existed in the areas of urban life occupied by the immigrants and that conditions of fraud and deception whereby the ignorant newcomers were taken advantage of. were almost universally prevalent. The Commission discovered further that very little effort was being made to correct those evils or to educate the immigrant to higher standards of living, and that practically no interest existed among the native white American population in the immigrant strangers that had flocked into New York's cities during the past two decades.[29]

On the basis of its findings, the Commission recommended that the state establish a bureau or department of industries and immigration. This was to be given duties which would tend best to secure to the state the economic advantages derived from an intelligent utilization of the immigrant in all fields, and which would at the same time protect him from exploitation, fraud, and abuse. A further duty would be to facilitate his development into intelligent and useful citizenship. Such a bureau, the Commission felt, could act as a clearing house and as a medium of communication with the several agencies

28 State of New York, *Report of the Commission of Immigration of the State of New York*, Albany, 1909, p. v. Members of the Commission were: Louis Marshall, chairman; Miss Frances A. Kellor, secretary; Marcus A. Marks, James B. Reynolds, Gino C. Speranza, Lillian D. Wald, Edward B. Whitney, Philip V. Danahy, and Charles W. Larmon.

29 *Ibid., passim.*

and activities with which the alien might come in contact or with which it might be desirable that he communicate. It drew up a bill creating such a bureau of immigration and industry, and attached it to the *Report*.[30]

Members of the Commission praised the immigrant education law passed by the legislature of New Jersey in 1907, and stated that the principle involved in such legislation, namely, the granting of appropriations for night schools for non-English-speaking residents, was a sound one.[31] They therefore recommended that the New York legislature enact similar legislation and provide a similar appropriation to begin this experiment with immigrant education. The Commission also praised the work of Miss Sarah W. Moore in connection with her labor-camp schools, and recommended that such camp schools be established as an experiment at the expense of the state at such construction camps as were then conducting work for the state. It was suggested that such camps should be placed under the direction of the Commissioner of Education of New York. An appropriation of approximately $10,000 was recommended for this purpose.[32]

Although the Commission made its report in March, 1909, the recommended legislation was not passed due to the lateness of the *Report*. Since the work of the Commission terminated with the submission of its report, there remained no state agency which could continue to advocate the measures proposed along the broad generalities covered by the investigations of the Commission. Its report had shown the need for definite state action. The members of the Commission determined therefore to form some organization to agitate for the bill and to take up the immigration questions within the state from a point of view broader than mere race or religion, or of exclusion or admission, and to direct special attention to the condi-

30 *Ibid.*, p. 140.

31 *Cf.* Chapter I, p. 36.

32 *Report of the Commission of Immigration, op. cit.*, pp. 103-107.

tions of the American workingman and the unskilled immigrant workman in their relation to each other and in their
labor adjustment. This latter the members of the Commission
felt was the most immediate and important phase of the immigrant's new life in America.[33]

While some of the members of the State Immigration Commission were considering the advisability of creating a special
citizen's committee to assist in carrying out the Commission's
recommendations, their attention was called to the work of the
North American Civic League for Immigrants, then embarked
upon its first year of immigrant aid and educational work in
the New England region. The latter organization was desirous
of extending its work to New York City in order to obtain
better cooperation between the two important ports of Boston
and New York. The members of the Commission therefore
felt it advisable to organize a New York City Committee of
the League rather than to establish a new organization. This
was soon arranged. Miss Frances A. Kellor, who had acted as
the secretary for the State Commission, became the secretary
of the new committee, which was composed of John Hayes
Hammond, mining engineer and financier, chairman, Frank
Trumbull, chairman, Chesapeake and Ohio R. R., vice-chairman, Frank A. Vanderlip, president, National City Bank of
New York, treasurer, and D. Chauncey Brewer, John B. Carse,
Miss Anne Morgan, Thomas Mulry, and Felix Warburg. The
New York Committee of the North American Civic League
for Immigrants, which it took for its name, was organized in
December 1909. It began its work of furthering the recom-
mendations of the New York State Immigration Commission
in 1910.[34]

In addition to embarking upon a campaign which urged the
state to assume some of its long neglected duties in regard to

33 *New York—New Jersey Committee of the North American Civic
League for Immigrants, December 1909–March 1911*, pp. 5-6 [title of the
League's Report for the period].

34 *Ibid.*, p. 6.

the immigrant, the New York Committee undertook also to do educational and civic work that governmental agencies could not undertake at the time, and to conduct experiments and studies upon which practical measures could be based. It sought also to correct some of the prevalent abuses which were not being remedied by existing agencies.[35]

The new Committee felt the characteristics and problems concerning the immigration question could be met best through a five-point program which it drew up. This program was to include first, *assimilation*—or the alternative of restriction; second, *education,* elementary, industrial, civic, and English—or a change in American standards and ideals; third, *distribution*—or congestion, maladjustment, and unemployment with all their attending evils; fourth, *naturalization* and direct and permanent contact with American institutions and standards—or constantly increasing colonies and camps, isolation, the establishment of ' race ' communities within cities and persistent racial prejudices; and fifth, *protection*—or exploitation industrially, financially, and socially which caused aliens to become penniless, diseased or exhausted members of the community within a few years after they had been admitted on the basis of a rather high physical standard.[36]

The Committee decided that an immediate campaign in support of the first of the above alternatives seemed to be the most logical and reasonable course of action. The members therefore determined to conduct the campaign in three ways,—by strengthening, unifying, and standardizing the work already being done; by developing new agencies and pressing for the passage of new laws where no adequate provisions existed; and by conducting field surveys, including studies of conditions and practical experiments for the benefit of both the alien and the country generally, and for the education of the public.[37]

35 *Ibid.,* p. 7.

36 *Ibid.,* p. 11.

37 *Ibid.,* pp. 11-12.

Like the mother organization in Boston, the New York Committee rendered its aid in helping aliens en route to their destinations through representatives at Ellis Island and at the various railroad terminals. It investigated and recommended employment agencies, savings banks, proper land investments, notaries public, and rendered legal aid to the newcomers. It embarked upon a survey of practically all laws passed in New York State, and prepared a report of its findings for reference purposes.[38]

Ever stressing the importance and need for a knowledge of English for aliens, and deploring the existing evils in the naturalization process and in the labor camps, the Committee set about meeting these problems by securing the records of all children of school age entering the port of New York from the ships' manifests at Ellis Island, and transmitting these to the proper school authorities throughout the state. By constant agitation, it succeeded in getting the federal authorities to agree to furnish such records of entering children to the educational authorities of the states of New York, New Jersey, Massachusetts, and Illinois.[39] The Committee also started an experimental camp school at Valhalla, N. Y., in December 1910, in cooperation with the Society for Italian Immigrants. It continued to operate the school for the next two years until the completion of the building project necessitated its closure. A special hall was opened in 1911 as a day school for the children. A program of English classes for the men in the evening, and classes in household economics for the women and girls in the afternoon was carried on very successfully by the Committee's teachers. Special moving pictures on Saturday nights and dances once a month completed the program.[40]

38 *Ibid.*, p. 26.

39 *Ibid.*, p. 26.

40 *Ibid.*, pp. 32-33; *cf. New York–New Jersey Committee of the North American Civic League for Immigrants, December 1, 1909–February 1, 1913,* p. 14. This was the second report issued by the Committee.

In 1911, the Committee made the experiment of providing recreational facilities in the series of labor camps along the new New York City water aqueduct then being built. Moving pictures and victrola records were used to furnish entertainment. A circuit of the fourteen camps on the aqueduct was made, fifty entertainments in all, with an attendance of 6,000. The experiment proved such a success that several contractors agreed to purchase equipment to inaugurate programs of their own for the entertainment of the men. At Mineville, N. Y., an iron-ore community, the cooperation of one of the iron-mining companies was secured in starting domestic education work for the benefit of the immigrant mothers. In June 1912, an experiment in educative work in railroad camps was started by the Committee at Campbell Hall, N. Y. Here a discarded freight car was used as a class room. On the basis of this experiment, definite recommendations were prepared and submitted to the railroads for future programs of immigrant education. At Albion, N. Y., the Committee supervised a camp school supported by the Burt Olney Canning Company, which functioned during the canning season, and consisted of a class for children, a kindergarten, and domestic educative work for the mothers. From its experience with these ventures, the League's New York Committee prepared a bill authorizing the State Department of Education to set up schools in labor camps and submitted it for the consideration of the New York legislature.[41]

The new Committee credited itself with much of the success of the passage of the four immigration bills drawn up by the chairman of the former New York Immigration Commission and passed by the New York legislature in 1910. It felt that their passage was due largely to the interest and support given by the Committee's members individually.[42] With the establishment of the state's new Bureau of Industries and Immigra-

41 *Ibid.*, pp. 15-16.

42 *Ibid.*, pp. 16-17.

tion in the Department of Labor and the inauguration of the new regulations controlling the activities of immigrant banking houses, the Committee contributed its services through its investigators and its accumulated data to help make the new agencies function properly.[43]

Expanding its regional scope in January 1911, the Committee included the State of New Jersey in its area of activity. It thereupon changed its name to the New York-New Jersey Committee of the North American Civic League for Immigrants. Immediate arrangements were made to start a campaign of education in support of the League's program in the new area. At Morristown, N. J., an experimental class in English for Italians was started, and as a result, the Committee succeeded in persuading the board of education of that city to vote an appropriation of $1,000 for the establishment of a permanent evening school for adults in 1912. The Committee also took an active part in sponsoring adult immigrant education in Raritan, and at Passaic, N. J., where a meeting of representative people voted in January 1913, to secure sufficient money to support a domestic education experiment under the supervision of the Committee.[44]

In February 1911, the Committee took over the work of the Bureau of Promotion and Information of Foreigners in Rochester, N. Y. It then embarked upon a study of employment agencies dealing with immigrants in that city, an analysis of the influence of benevolent fraternal and philanthropic societies on the immigrant in the Rochester area, and a study of the facilities which the public schools were offering the adult immigrant. A special reading room and library were set up for the use of immigrants at the League's headquarters, and a handbook containing a compilation of the local laws affecting

43 For activities of the new New York State Bureau of Industries and Immigration, *cf.* Chapter III below; also, New York–New Jersey Committee, *Report, December 1909–March 1911, op. cit.*, pp. 37-38.

44 New York–New Jersey Committee, *Report, December 1, 1909–February 1, 1913, op. cit.*, p. 17.

immigrants and other general information was prepared in several different languages and distributed. The Committee also arranged for special instruction in the methods of naturalization and preparation for it. Home visitors were sent out from time to time, and all possible aid was furnished in helping the immigrant to become adjusted to his new conditions in the city. Cooperation with all organizations furnishing relief to the immigrant and securing of legal aid when needed were also rendered by the Committee.[45]

A survey made by the organization revealed that Rochester had no public school in the Polish immigrant section despite its population of approximately 7,000. Accordingly, in June 1912, the Committee opened a Polish Institute in small rented quarters to furnish facilities for adult immigrants of that nationality aspiring to learn English. Special classes for immigrant women were set up, while a branch of the Rochester Public Library was established at the Institute in cooperation with the Polish National Alliance which furnished the books.[46]

A similar campaign to aid the immigrant was inaugurated by the New York-New Jersey Committee in Buffalo when investigation revealed that no organization was at work on the immigrant problems of that city. A special office was opened there March 15, 1911, to arouse interest in the immigrant. Within a comparatively short time, the Committee reported, active steps had been taken to alleviate the existing conditions. Activities along the lines introduced in Rochester earlier in the year were in full swing by the end of 1911.[47] A corps of six domestic educators formed a visiting staff of workers that labored among the immigrant homes of the community. A special vocational school was opened in the Polish-speaking section of the city in the fall of the year, while during the winter season, the Committee prepared a *Course in Citizenship*

45 *Ibid., Report, December 1910–March 1911, op. cit.*, pp. 39-40.

46 *Ibid., Report, December 1, 1909–February 1, 1913, op. cit.*, p. 14.

47 *Ibid., Report, December 1910–March 1911, op. cit.*, p. 40.

*for Foreigners,* and introduced it into the Buffalo evening schools as part of the regular curriculum. It was largely through the Committee's influence that the board of education set up a separate department of evening schools to meet the new immigrant situation. By 1913, the League had succeeded in gaining municipal support for its domestic education program, and during that year, the city educational authorities took over the Committee's activities along this line.[48] It was chiefly responsible, too, for the formation of an immigration branch of the Legal Aid Society of Buffalo, and instrumental in organizing a Legal Aid Bureau in 1912.[49]

The Committee also extended its activities to the Brooklyn area in 1911, when it opened a special office there in April of that year. The domestic education experiments were introduced into the Flatbush section supplementing the work of the public schools. At the same time, the Committee carried on a campaign to acquaint the native-born American neighbors of the immigrants with many of the latter's problems.[50] In Manhattan, the Committee arranged for classes in English for Greeks and Poles in 1911 and 1912, and prepared a special course in citizenship for foreigners in cooperation with the New York City school authorities. This was introduced into the night schools in January 1913. Members of the Committee regarded this experiment as an effort to coordinate the educational systems of the country with the naturalization process which, if successful, could be introduced into other cities.[51] A pamphlet entitled, *How to Secure First-Papers,* was published by the group in English-Spanish, English-Italian, English-Russian, and English-Greek editions in an effort to stimulate interest

48 The League reported having made over 12,000 such visits by its agents before the city authorities took over its activities. *Cf. Report, December 1, 1909–February 1, 1913, op. cit.,* pp. 12-13.

49 *Ibid.,* pp. 7-8.

50 *Ibid., Report, December 1910–March 1911, op. cit.,* p. 40.

51 *Ibid., Report, Dec. 1, 1909–Feb. 1, 1913, op. cit.,* pp. 13-14.

in naturalization. Fully 14,000 copies of these were distributed through the public night schools, libraries, national and ethnic societies, and individuals.[52]

The New York-New Jersey Committee was instrumental also in having the New York State Bureau of Industries and Immigration call a conference of railroad lines to discuss a plan for a national transfer system to secure through booking and delivery of immigrants. Through its influence, too, a national conference of immigration, land, and labor officials took place in Washington, D. C., in December 1911. The conference resolved itself into a permanent body and agreed to become a national clearing house on such matters as the distribution of land and immigrants.[53]

Thus, with a broad program of education and organization both on a municipal and state-wide scale, the New York-New Jersey Committee of the North American Civic League for Immigrants assumed rapidly the leadership in the campaign to assimilate (or as it later was designated, to Americanize) the immigrant. Largely as a result of its more centrally located headquarters, and because of the great influence of its supporters, the Committee was successful in arousing a considerable and favorable interest in the immigrant and his problems among the native-American elements. With the mother organization actively engaged in carrying on similar efforts in the New England area, and the Immigrants' Protective League publicizing the immigrant problems in the Chicago region, the three organizations had laid the foundations for a strong concerted movement to assimilate and to Americanize the immigrant, and had pointed the way to eventual governmental support of such a policy.

52 *Ibid., Report, Dec. 1910–Mar. 1911, op. cit.,* pp. 10-11.

53 *Ibid.,* pp. 11-12.

# CHAPTER III

## THE MOVEMENT STRENGTHENED THROUGH STATE ACTION

THE first decade of the 20th century had witnessed the gradual rise of interest in the question of the immigrant and his assimilation. Action had followed discussion. Organization had replaced individual interest in the problem. Cities had been led to broaden their night school programs to include some sort of work for the benefit of their adult immigrant residents. By the end of the year 1910, two of the most powerful of the future ' Americanizing' groups had obtained a numerous and influential membership, completely devoted to the problem of the assimilation of the immigrant.

The second decade of the new century was to witness this interest continue on a rising scale until it finally expressed itself in the form of vigorous activity, not only on the part of individuals and groups, but on the part of municipal, state, and federal agencies as well. All combined to strengthen the growing movement to win over the immigrant to a better understanding of what was generally publicized as the good old-fashioned ' American ideals'.[1]

Many factors combined to bring about this situation. Not the least of these were the revelations uncovered by the Federal Immigration Commission, which made known the results of its findings to the Congress of the United States during the first year of the new decade. By Section 39 of the immigration act of February 20, 1907, Congress had acceded to the demands of the immigration restrictionists by authorizing the appointment of a Federal Immigration Commission "to make full inquiry, examination and investigation by sub-committee or otherwise into the subject of immigration". This the Commission had accomplished after a four year thorough study

1 For author's interpretation of just what was meant by 'Americanism' and other terminology used by the Americanizers, cf. Chapter X, pp. 269-271.

of the sources of recent immigration to the United States from Europe, the general character of the incoming immigrants, the methods employed in America and abroad to prevent the immigration of persons classed as undesirable under the law, the general status of the more recent immigrants as residents of the United States, and the effect of such immigration upon the institutions, industries and people of the United States.[2]

The work had been undertaken with great care. As a result, an important and valuable accumulation of material upon all phases of the immigrants' condition in America had been obtained. In a monumental work of forty-two volumes, the Commission presented the results of its findings to Congress in 1911. To the great satisfaction of the immigration restrictionists, the Commission's *Report* bore out their general analysis of the immigrant situation.

After contrasting the 'old' immigration with the 'new' and noting how the former had mingled freely with the native Americans becoming assimilated quickly despite a large proportion of non-English-speaking groups, the Commission pointed out that the movement which had sent these people to America was largely one of settlers who came from the most progressive sections of Europe for the purpose of making their homes in America. According to the *Report,* the 'old immigrants' readily learned English, while the second generation almost completely forgot the ethnic origins of their parents. Not so the 'new' type of immigrant. These people, the Commission felt, were definitely of a different mentality and

---

2 U. S. Immigration Commission, *Abstracts of the Immigration Commission with Conclusions and Recommendations and Views of the Minority,* I, 9-13. Members of the Commission were: Senators William P. Dillingham of Vermont, Henry Cabot Lodge of Massachusetts, Anselm J. McLaurin of Mississippi, and later Asbury C. Latimer of South Carolina, and LeRoy Percy of South Carolina; Representatives Benjamin F. Howell of New Jersey, William S. Bennett of New York, and John L. Burnett of Alabama; also, Charles P. Neill of Washington, D. C., Professor Jeremiah W. Jenks of New York, and William R. Wheeler of California, appointed by the President.

actuated by motives of another sort. Noting the contrast, the Commission stated:

> On the other hand, the new immigration has been largely a movement of unskilled laboring men who have come, in large part temporarily, from the less progressive and advanced countries of Europe in response to the call for industrial workers in the eastern and middle western states. They have almost entirely avoided agricultural pursuits, and in cities and industrial communities have congregated together in sections apart from native Americans and the older immigrants to such an extent that assimilation has been slow as compared to that of the earlier non-English-speaking races.
>
> The new immigration as a class is far less intelligent than the old, approximately one-third of all those over 14 years of age when admitted being illiterate. Racially they are for the most part essentially unlike the British, German, and other peoples who came during the period prior to 1880, and generally speaking they are actuated in coming by different ideals, for the old immigrants came to be a part of the country, while the new, in a large measure, comes with the intention of profiting, in a pecuniary way, by the superior advantages of the new world and then returning to the old country.[3]

The Commission added that although it was impossible from existing data to determine whether the immigrant population was relatively more or less criminal than the native-born population, the proportion of more serious crimes such as homicide, blackmail, and robbery, as well as the less serious offenses, was greater among the foreign-born.[4] It added, too, that it was difficult to measure correctly the tendency of the newer ' races ' to become Americanized or assimilated into the American people. " If, however, the tendency to acquire citizenship, to learn the English language, and to abandon native customs and standards of living may be considered as

3 *Ibid.*, p. 14.

4 *Ibid.*, p. 33.

factors, it is found that many of the more recent immigrants
are backward in this regard, while some others have made
excellent progress ". A similar situation was noted in regard
to the process of naturalization. The tendency to become
naturalized citizens among those who had been in the country
five years or longer was not very strong, although more pronounced in some ethnic groups than in others. The Commission admitted, however, that this result might be influenced by
language considerations and to the fact that naturalization
was accomplished with greater difficulty than formerly.[5]

The Federal Immigration Commission placed itself on record
definitely as favoring immigration restriction. While, in the
opinion of the members, the American people should welcome
the oppressed of other lands as in the past, the group felt that
exceedingly great care should be taken to see that immigration
in the future was such both in quality and quantity that the
process of assimilation was not rendered too difficult. They
recommended further that economic and business conditions
touching the prosperity and economic well-being of the American should be the primary consideration governing legislation
concerning the admission of aliens.[6] " The investigations of
the Commission show an oversupply of unskilled labor in basic
industries to an extent which indicated an oversupply of unskilled labor in the industries of the country as a whole, a
condition which demands legislation restricting the further
admission of unskilled labor. It is desirable to make the restriction such that a sufficient number be debarred to produce
a marked effect upon the present supply of unskilled labor, and
as far as possible those excluded should be those who come
to this country with no intention of becoming American citizens, or even maintaining a permanent residence, but merely
to save enough by the adoption, if necessary, of low standards
of living to return permanently to their home country. As far

5 *Ibid.*, p. 42.

6 *Ibid.*, p. 45.

as possible the aliens excluded should also be those, who, by reasons of their personal qualities or habits, would make the least desirable citizens." [7]

The Commission closed its summary of the immigrant situation by definitely recommending restriction of immigration because economic, moral, and social considerations demanded such a program, and then added: " A majority of this Commission favor the reading and writing test as the most feasible single method of restricting undesirable immigration." [8]

The reaction to the publication of the Commission's findings was marked and widespread. Unquestionably, it strengthened the cause of the immigration restrictionists in their campaign against the admission of the ' dregs of southern and eastern Europe '. Undoubtedly, too, it was partially responsible for the enactment of legislation concerning the immigrant in certain of the so-called immigrant states. If the Commission's findings bore out the conclusions which the restrictionists had held in regard to the immigrant, they also bore out the need for the sort of action for which the Americanization groups had been agitating during the preceding three years. Unquestionably, the Commission's findings publicized the need for remedial action far more successfully than the North American Civic League for Immigrants and its affiliated Americanization groups could have ever hoped to do in as short a period of time.

New York State took the lead in providing governmental machinery to bring about the rapid assimilation and Americanization of its immigrant residents through the enactment of legislation in 1910 which created a special Bureau of Industries and Immigration to accomplish this goal. In addition, three other bills were passed regulating private bankers,

7 *Ibid.*, p. 48. Representative William S. Bennett of New York dissented from the above specific recommendation claiming that it was a selective test for which no logical argument could be found as the result of the material uncovered by the *Report.*

8 *Ibid.*, p. 48.

steam-ship ticket agents, and notaries public, all aimed at preventing much of the abuse which had beset the immigrant from these agencies in the past.[9]

The new Bureau was clothed with the power to carry out the state's new immigrant policy by assuring to every immigrant, unfamiliar with the language, country, laws, and customs of America, a hearing in which he could state in his own language his complaints or difficulties and have an impartial inquiry made into the matter. The Bureau was to serve as mediator in bringing together the disputants in cases concerning immigrants. It was also to enforce the existing laws to prevent crime, fraud, and the exploitation of the immigrant. The newly created agency was authorized to recommend

9 State of New York, Bureau of Industries and Immigration, *First Annual Report of the Bureau of Industries and Immigration for the Twelve Months Ended September 30, 1911*, Albany, 1912, p. 11. The Bureau indicated the feeling governing its policy as follows: " Believing that an alien's first impression, his first experiences on arriving and his first contact with American institutions, are the most lasting; that if his property rights and liberty are not respected on arrival he cannot be expected to respect those of people resident here; that if he has not been given a square deal he will later visit his early experiences upon his newly arrived brothers; the State has undertaken so far as its facilities permit, to make these early experiences forces for real civilization. The word which these humble arrivals send back to their own countries inspires or discourages their countrymen. Their understanding of liberty and justice, as shown to them in this country, goes a long way to win freedom and enlightened governmental action for their less fortunate brothers in their own country, or the reverse. It is therefore no longer an individual matter, but a community matter, and it is New York State's obligation to the progress of civilization in both the old and new countries to assure the alien a fair start and a safe road to travel.

" Believing that whatever makes one alien a better producer and larger consumer; whatever makes him an understanding, independent and thoughtful citizen; whatever puts him in possession of his own land, or gives him honest employment and self-respect; whatever puts into his life a love for his adopted State and makes him feel a man among men and lessens the distinction between alien and American; whatever teaches him to work with and stand by his fellow workmen; that all of these make directly and powerfully for stability and progress; the State has undertaken to assure these, so far as possible, to its resident aliens, as well as to its citizens, and thereby to carry out the guarantee of its constitution and of the treaty provisions of the Federal government." *Ibid.*, pp. 15-16.

further remedial legislation if necessary, and to undertake studies and investigations of living and labor conditions, and submit the results of such studies as recommendations for improvements. In addition, the Bureau was authorized to publish and distribute information which would facilitate assimilation.[10]

The Bureau of Industries and Immigration was opened on October 3, 1910, with Miss Frances A. Kellor as chief investigator, assisted by four special investigators to care for the Italian, Polish, Yiddish, and Hungarian speaking immigrants. Special district headquarters were set up at Buffalo to care for the Buffalo-Rochester area and another at Brooklyn. A legal counsel was appointed in 1911 to care for the legal aspects of the Bureau's work.[11]

The Bureau sent out its investigators to gather evidence for its studies and made its recommendations accordingly. Special advice and protection were rendered to the immigrants in line with the Bureau's instructions. It assumed immediately the functions of a coordinating agency for all problems concerning the immigrant in the state of New York. Special announcements were sent to the press concerning its functions and activities, while all foreign-speaking groups and organizations were informed of its services.[12]

For the next ten years of its existence, the Bureau carried on the work of preventing fraud, running down those who preyed upon the ignorance of the newcomers, and carrying on its investigations of general immigrant conditions. Through its numerous services and advisory functions, the Bureau was able to build up a spirit of good will on the part of the immigrant which unquestionably aided the Americanization process.

10 *Ibid.*, p. 17.

11 *Ibid.*, p. 23. The Bureau functioned on an appropriation of $9,700. The original appropriation called for $41,000, but this was reduced to the former sum by Governor Charles Evans Hughes.

12 *Ibid.*, pp. 28-30.

It cooperated in every possible way with the newer Americanization groups which were formed as the new decade advanced, and formed one of the chief agencies in the advancing Americanization drive.[13]

With the activities of the New York Bureau a visible evidence of what could be accomplished by Americanization groups in their drive to obtain governmental support of the movement to assimilate the immigrant, the same little group which had been chiefly responsible for the legislation leading to its creation prepared to obtain similar action on the part of the state of New Jersey. A special bill was drawn up by the New York-New Jersey Committee of the North American Civic League which provided for the appointment of a State Immigration Commission. The bill was presented to the 1911-1912 session of the New Jersey legislature and was passed early in 1911. Under the provisions of the bill, a commission of three was to be appointed by the governor " to make full inquiry, examination and investigation into the conditions, welfare, distribution and industrial opportunities of aliens in this State." [14] William Fellowes Morgan of Short Hills, Robert A. Franks of Hoboken, and Robert L. Fleming of Jersey City, were appointed by Governor Woodrow Wilson to serve on the Commission.[15]

Unfortunately, the bill creating the Commission carried with it no appropriation to finance its activities. As a result, the work carried on by it during the year 1912 was made possible only through funds provided by public-spirited citizens and by the New York-New Jersey Committee of the North

13 For further activities of the Bureau of Industries and Immigration, cf. Annual Reports, 1912-1925.

14 State of New Jersey, Report of the Commission of Immigration of the State of New Jersey, Trenton, 1914, p. 9; also, New York–New Jersey, Committee of the North American Civic League for Immigrants, Report, December 1, 1909–February 1, 1913, op. cit., p. 8.

15 Report of the Commission of Immigration of the State of New Jersey, op. cit., p. 3. For text of bill, cf. State of New Jersey, Laws of 1911, Chapter 362.

American Civic League.[16] Later on, the 1913 legislative session appropriated $5,000 to defray the costs of the Commission, but the appropriations committee failed to include this amount or any other sum in the general appropriations bill. The Commission was thus forced to rely on the same sources of financial support that it had had during the previous months of its existence. In the report which it issued, it pointed out acidly that the failure of the New Jersey legislature to provide it with adequate funds contrasted sharply with the action of the New York legislature, which had voted $41,000 for its permanent Bureau of Industries and Immigration.[17]

The Commission held its first meeting at Hoboken on December 27, 1911. It employed the services of two regular investigators and several others as their services were needed. It held a grand total of 15 meetings and 27 hearings, and examined 87 witnesses on all phases of the immigrant problem in the state.[18]

The New Jersey Commission found that conditions existing among the immigrants in its state were substantially the same as those uncovered by the New York State Immigration Commission and made somewhat similar recommendations. It felt that there were certain matters affecting aliens which no exising agencies were qualified to handle, and therefore recommended that a state bureau of immigration be created as the most effective means of correcting the prevalent evils and of promoting the well-being of the state's new residents.[19]

The Commission also recommended state regulation of transportation of immigrants and their protection from swindlers, the regulation of private employment agencies, the estab-

16. *Ibid.*, p. 201. The New York–New Jersey Committee gave $5,000, while William Fellowes Morgan and 15 others gave gifts varying from $1,180 to $50 for a grand total of $9,915, the total expenses of the Commission.

17 *Ibid.*, p. 9.

18 *Ibid.*, p. 10.

19 *Ibid.*, pp. 130-132.

lishment of employment bureaus under the State Department of Labor, the appointment of a state board of arbitration, and a strict regulation of private banking.[20] It recommended further the compulsory attendance of illiterate minors at school, the introduction of adequate courses in citizenship into the public night schools throughout the state where not already in existence, the appointment of a federal naturalization commission to investigate the entire problem of naturalization, and mandatory action on the part of boards of education to furnish the education desired when petitioned by 20 or more adults for instruction in English.[21] Unfortunately, no action was taken by New Jersey in support of its recommendations.

While the New York-New Jersey Committee was actively urging the appointment of the New Jersey Immigration Commission, the parent organization, the North American Civic League for Immigrants, had drafted a similar bill for the appointment of a similar immigration commission for the Commonwealth of Massachusetts. The bill was presented to the legislature of that state during the session of 1913, and received its approval on May 2 of that year.[22]

The Massachusetts Commission, according to the terms of the act creating it, was ordered to make a full investigation of the status and general condition of immigrants within the Commonwealth, including their ways of living, distribution, occupations, educational opportunities, and business opportunities and facilities, as well as their relation to the industrial, social, and economic conditions of all the people of the Com-

20 *Ibid.*, pp. 134-135.

21 *Ibid.*, pp. 136-137. The Committee also recommended that greater attention be paid by school authorities to the establishment of special classes for immigrant children, and that the New Jersey Board of Education cooperate with the Philadelphia Board of Education in an effort to secure special classes during the seasonal work period in the fruit and berry sections of New Jersey. *Cf.* pp. 136-137.

22 North American Civic League for Immigrants, *Annual Report, 1912-1913*, pp. 9-10.

monwealth. Further authorization was granted it to procure information regarding such laws and agencies of the federal government and of other state governments as affected immigrants after their admission to the United States. All investigations were to be carried out "with a view to obtaining information for the enactment of such laws as will bring non-English-speaking foreigners, residents or transient, into sympathetic relation with American institutions and customs." [23]

The Commission held its first meeting on June 6, 1913, and conducted a total of 40 meetings in all. Special hearings were held at Worcester, Fall River, New Bedford, Holyoke, Springfield, Lowell, North Adams, Lynn, Maynard, and Boston. It conferred with health authorities, the Board of Labor and Industries, the Bureau of Statistics, public officials, clergymen, educators, social workers, and representatives of the foreign-born. It made personal inspections of foreign neighborhoods, and employed agents to make special investigations. It hired Miss Grace Abbott, director of the Immigrants' Protective League of Chicago, as its executive secretary. Approximately $12,500 of the $15,000 appropriated was spent by the Commission.

The Massachusetts body found conditions throughout the state much the same as those uncovered by the New York and New Jersey Commissions. Unsanitary living conditions, evidences of fraud, illiteracy, and a general attitude of indifference to the problems of the immigrant on the part of the native American elements manifested themselves everywhere. It recommended therefore that legislation be provided for better housing conditions, that the regulation of the practice of medicine to eliminate quacks be assumed by the state, that there

---

[23] Commonwealth of Massachusetts, *Report of the Commission on Immigration on the Problem of Immigration in Massachusetts*, Boston, 1914, p. 3. Members of the Commission served without compensation and consisted of Bernard J. Rothwell, Emily G. Balch, and William H. O'Brien of Boston, Frederick C. McDuffy of Lawrence, and Frank E. Spaulding, supt. of schools, of Newton.

be official court interpreters, state regulation of banking to protect the immigrant's savings, and that an employment bureau be set up under the supervision of the Board of Labor and Industries to aid in the distribution of immigrants. It also recommended that better opportunities be given the immigrant in the way of agricultural advantages.[24]

Stressing the importance of education as fundamental in the process of Americanization, the Committee worked out an elaborate twelve-point program in regard to immigrant education which would assure the immigrant at least the fundamentals of the English language and a proper understanding of the principlles of 'Americanism'. Compulsory half-day schools for illiterate minors in towns which had twenty such, and the compulsory maintenance of evening schools for illiterates between 17 and 21 in all cities and towns where there were fifteen or more were also recommended. Special library facilities were suggested as an aid to immigrant education.[25]

24 *Ibid.*, pp. 18-21.

25 *Ibid.*, pp. 15-17. The Commission's twelve-point program read as follows: 1. a more careful adaptation of the methods of teaching and of the course of study on the part of public school authorities in order that immigrant children would not lose respect for their parents through their Americanization; 2. the establishment of compulsory half-day schools for illiterates between fourteen and seventeen in all cities and towns where there were as many as twenty such; 3. the maintenance of evening schools which should be compulsory for illiterates between 17 and 21 in all cities and towns where there were fifteen or more of such; 4. the maintenance of evening schools at least forty weeks each year; 5. to assure better enforcement of attendance of illiterate minors at evening schools, an annual census should be made which should include all between the ages of 5 and 21 in schools; and that the State Board of Education secure from the Federal Bureau of Immigration the names and addresses of all immigrants between those ages destined for Massachusetts and distribute these to the local attendance officers and that the Board exercise such supervision over the enforcement of compulsory attendance law as would best secure its efficient operation; 6. that special evening classes for immigrants be conducted by the State Board of Education in labor camps; 7. that normal schools should maintain, when practicable, model evening schools for immigrants, in order that experimerts could be conducted by educational experts

The Commission recommended the creation of a permanent board of immigration to serve as a clearing house and as an information bureau to investigate complaints of exploitation and fraud, to have oversight over the conditions surrounding the arrival and release of immigrants, and to accumulate information in regard to the immigrant population of the state and to place such at the disposal of immigrant agencies. It then drafted bills to cover its recommendations and attached them to its report. Unfortunately, no action was taken upon its recommendations until 1915, when the Department of University Extension of the Massachusetts Board of Education began its program in support of immigrant education.[26]

While three of the eastern states were engaged in considering the problem of the Americanization of the immigrant, yet another state, one of the far-western group, California, joined the new movement through the creation of a special commission to investigate the immigrant question within the confines of that commonwealth in 1913. The new agency, which took the name California Commission of Immigration and Housing, differed from the commissions appointed in the three eastern states to investigate the problem of the immigrant in that it

---

in the neglected field of immigrant education; 8. that the State Board of Education appoint a deputy Commissioner of Education and such agents as might be necessary to supervise and direct these evening classes and part-time classes for immigrants; 9. that the State pay to cities and towns a portion of the total amount upon a graduated scale for expenses involved in teaching such evening and part-time schools upon the approval of the State Board of Education; 10. that public schools in foreign districts maintain neighborhood centers to offer to immigrant children and other children as wholesome substitutes for 'dangerous commercialized recreation' and to the older residents, recreation and fellowship, as well as assistance in considering in the light of their own experience America's international, national, and municipal problems; 11. that responsibility for approval of private schools be vested in the State Board of Education; 12. that a larger appropriation for the Free Public Library Commission be made in order that it could extend its traveling foreign-library feature of its work.

26 *Ibid.*, p. 22. *Cf.* Massachusetts Board of Education., Extension Division, *First Annual Report, 1915, passim.*

was created as a permanent body rather than as a temporary one.[27]

In creating the new agency, the California legislature hoped to benefit the state by expediting the distribution and assimilation of the immigrants within the state through the means of the new Commission. It felt that these results could be accomplished by protecting the immigrant from exploitation, by guiding and aiding him in his adaptation to American standards of living, and by encouraging his education in the English language and particularly in the duties of citizenship. In addition to its aid to the immigrant in these ways, the Commission was authorized to investigate and study housing conditions in the state, since it was felt that the whole problem of assimilation was so closely related to the question of housing and sanitation.[28]

The California body was given full power to make inquiry, examination, and investigation into the condition, welfare, and industrial opportunities of all immigrants arriving in the state and remaining there. It was also ordered to collect information on the need and demand for labor in the agricultural, industrial, and other productive fields, including public works, and to gather information with respect to the supply of labor afforded by such immigrant groups. Futher duties assigned to the Commission included ascertaining the occupations for which immigrants were best adapted; bringing about the intercommunication between them and the several activities requiring labor which would best promote their respective needs; investigating and determining the genuineness of any application for labor that might be received and the treatment accorded those secured; cooperating with the state, municipal, and private employment of immigrants so as to aid in the distribution and employment of immigrants; and carrying out and

27 State of California, Commission of Immigration and Housing, *First Annual Report*, Jan. 2, 1915, p. 7.

28 *Ibid.*, pp. 7-8.

devising methods which would tend to prevent or relieve congestion and obviate unemployment.[29]

Specific powers in regard to the education of the immigrant were given to the Commission which illustrated the importance placed on this activity as an aid in the Americanization process. It was ordered to cooperate with the proper authorities and organizations, federal, state, county, municipal, and private, with the object of bringing to the immigrant the best opportunities for acquiring education and citizenship. It was also ordered to cooperate with the superintendents of public education and with the several boards of education throughout the state to ascertain the necessity for and the extent to which

---

29 *Ibid.*, p. 8. Other powers given to the Commission included: the inspection of all labor camps in the State, all employment agencies, and contract agencies dealing with immigrants, the investigation of the banking relations existing among immigrants and laborers, institutions established for the temporary shelter and care of immigrants, and of such philanthropic societies as were organized for the purpose of securing employment for or aiding in the distribution of immigrants, and the methods by which they were conducted; the investigation of the sanitary and safety conditions under which the immigrants were employed and the places where immigrants were landed within the state, at the docks, ferries, railroad stations, trains, boats, etc., and to investigate any and all complaints in regard to frauds, extortion, incompetency, and improper practices by notaries public and other public officials; the investigation of relations existing between immigrants and steamships, railroads, ticket agencies and agents, pawnbrokers, interpreters, etc., to report evidences of fraud, crime, extortion, or other improper practices to the proper authorities, and to bring to bear all authority in its power to see that justice be rendered; to encourage the establishment of legal aid societies to further bring to the immigrant the best protection of the state; similar steps were to be taken in *re* violations of the laws pertaining to the payment of wages, modes of payment, child labor, the employment of women, factory inspection laws, weekly day of rest laws, white slave traffic, building protection laws, and health, sanitation, tenement house and other housing laws; to investigate and study the general economic, housing and social conditions of the immigrants with the state for the purpose of introducing remedial action by the various state agencies; to enter into tenement houses, and other buildings to secure compliance with the governmental ordinances, etc. The Commission was also given the right to examine the records of the various city departments charged with the enforcement of such laws and regulations and to secure from them reports and copies of their records at any time. *Cf.* pp. 8-9.

instruction should be imparted to the immigrant, as well as to devise methods for the proper instruction of adult and minor aliens in English and other subjects. Included among these latter were the duties and rights of citizenship and the fundamental principles of the American system of government.[30]

The Commission was instructed to cooperate with the proper authorities and with private agencies to put practical devices for training for citizenship and for encouraging naturalization into operation. It was to promote the instruction of the immigrant in this fashion as soon after his arrival as practicable. Special attention was to be given to the education of both children and adults in labor camps and other localities where regular schools were not easily accessible. Additional duties consisted of cooperating in the organization and encouragement of playgrounds and recreational facilities, and in establishing settlement houses and social centers in the cities and towns of the state.[30]

The California Commission of Immigration and Housing was appointed by the governor in 1913, and set up headquarters at San Francisco with branch offices at Los Angeles and at Sacramento.[31] It set to work at once to carry out the instructions embodied in the act which created it. As a result of the investigation, the existence of horrible living conditions was discovered which the Commission set about to remedy in conformance with its powers. Action was pursued immediately to prosecute the guilty violators of the housing laws of the state.[32]

A survey was made of the naturalization process at work in California at the same time. The results revealed great neglect of the opportunity to acquire citizenship and very little appre-

30 *Ibid.*, p. 1. Members of the Commission were: Simon J. Lubin, president, Edward J. Hanna, vice-president, Mary S. Gibson, and Paul Scharrenburg, secretary. The Commission served without compensation except for traveling expenses.

31 *Ibid.*, p. 11.

32 *Ibid.*, p. 11.

ciation of the value of citizenship when acquired. The Commission placed most of the blame for the situation upon the state itself in as much as most of the instruction had come from private sources. The survey proved that California continued the same careless methods of making citizens that prevailed in the east.[33]

Finding that 18% of the foreign-born children were not attending school and that there was great need of efficient truancy supervision, the Commission made arrangements to send the names and addresses of newly arrived immigrant children of school age to the local authorities. Its survey revealed the need for special instruction in English for foreign children otherwise advanced in their studies.[33] As for the large number of illiterate adult aliens in the state, the Commission pointed out the need for the creation of a thoroughgoing program by the state for the education of the adult immigrant. Only Los Angeles had made any effort to meet the needs of its immigrants through classes in English and civics. Realizing the need for such instruction, detailed surveys were made in San Francisco, Sacramento, and Los Angeles, and valuable data obtained for use in drawing up a definite program of action. The need of special home teachers to go into the homes of the immigrants was stressed, and a law which would provide for this necessary adjunct to the immigrant education program drawn up. The Commission also investigated the labor camp situation and reported widespread conditions of illiteracy. It drew up a bill to provide educational facilities in such places under the direction of the State Board of Educa-

---

33 *Ibid.*, pp. 99-100. The Commission praised the initiative and activity of the Los Angeles school authorities and courts which had worked out a naturalization system whereby citizenship papers were granted to all aliens who could present diplomas from night schools of the city in English and citizenship conducted by the department of education for adult immigrants. Impressive ceremonies were held when the citizenship papers were given with addresses by prominent citizens. Entertainment followed. The Commission urged the adoption of the method.

tion.[34] The Commission's recommendations in this respect however were not enacted into law until two years later.

The new body investigated the relationship of the immigrant to the law, and found widespread opportunities existing for fraudulent practices. The usual conditions uncovered by the three eastern immigration commissions were also found in California, with parasites and hangers-on, dishonest bankers, corrupt lawyers, and court-interpreters profiting at the expense of the newcomers.[35] The commission delved into the unemployment situation and as the result of its findings recommended that a state bureau of labor and exchange be created, the passage of more stringent laws to regulate private employment agencies, the passage of definite laws governing sanitation and housing in labor camps, and the placing of such enforcement in the hands of a competent bureau under the administration of the Commission.[36]

The California Commission thus embarked upon a vigorous and progressive program during its first year of existence. Through the experience it had obtained it coordinated its work with that of other departments of the state government and with local governments in a strong effort to solve the problem of the assimilation and the Americanization of the immigrant. In the labor camps, inspection arrangements were made with the Industrial Accident Commission and the Industrial Wel-

34 *Ibid.*, p. 101.

35 *Ibid., passim.*

36 California Commission of Immigration and Housing, *Report on Unemployment* (Supplement to First Annual Report), Dec. 9, 1914, pp. 6-7. The Commission also recommended a complete revision of existing housing laws so that these could be broadened to include family dwellings as well as tenements and lodging houses with the enforcement of such placed in the hands of a Bureau of Housing under the Commission or under a reorganized Board of Health. It recommended, too, the appointment of a special committee to investigate the possibility of 'out-of-work' insurance, methods of dealing with the unemployable and vagrants, public works projects during periods of depression, the encouragement of rural credits, and the creation of a State Land Bureau to aid prospective purchasers with information.

fare Commission for the inspection and reporting of conditions of immigrants in such places. The California legislature
adopted its suggestions in 1915 and gave it direct powers of
enforcement concerning violations of the state tenement
house and labor camp sanitation laws, making it possible to
accomplish results in these fields with a minimum of effort.
The handling of cases in the Commission's Complaint Bureau
became well systematized, so much so, that the Commission
was able to accomplish much in bringing the immigrants into
contact with American social and economic life. Through the
standardization of the work in these fields, the new body reported, the possibility of placing more emphasis upon the field
of education resulted, thus strengthening " the most constructive feature of any program for the assimilation of the immigrant ".[37] The Commission saw the enactment into law in 1915
of the bill which it had proposed to the legislature providing
for the appointment of home teachers to visit the homes of
the immigrants as an aid in the Americanization process.[38]

During 1915, the Commission continued its efforts on
behalf of immigrant education by campaigning for the establishment of evening classes in English and citizenship in conjunction with the California State Board of Education. It
presented a formal program for the consideration of the people
of California, which stressed the necessity for the Americanization of the immigrant, and the need of accomplishing this
at the expense of the state. During the campaign for a nation-

[37] California Commission of Immigration and Housing, *Second Annual
Report*, Jan. 2, 1916, p. 7.

[38] *Ibid.*, p. 7.  The Act provided boards of education of any school district might employ ' home teachers ' to work in homes of immigrants instructing pupils and adults in matters relating to attendance at schools, the
preparation therefor, to sanitation, English language, household duties, and
in American citizenship. The Commission felt the new law to be of greatest
importance to Americanization through its unique approach to the immigrant
mother. *Cf.* California Commission of Immigration and Housing, *The Home
Teacher, the Act, with a Working Plan and Forty Lessons in English*,
c. 1915.

wide Americanization movement which was inaugurated that year,[39] the Commission enlisted the aid of the various women's clubs, local civic groups, the D.A.R., and other organizations in support of the campaign. For the next six years, the California Commission of Immigration and Housing was to carry on the campaign for Americanization of the immigrant, and to take a leading place among the agencies at work to accomplish this desired goal.[40]

While California had sought to meet the problem of the immigrant through the creation of a new permanent governmental agency to deal with the various aspects of the problem, Pennsylvania became the first state to carry on an inquiry into the immigrant question through an already existing agency. Whereas New York, Massachusetts, and California had made special appropriations for the purposes of their immigrant commissions, Pennsylvania allowed the general appropriation for regular departmental work to cover the expenses of the investigation.[41]

Under the provisions of the act of assembly, approved June 2, 1913, which created the new Department of Labor and Industry, the Pennsylvania legislature had made provision for a Bureau of Statistics and Information to make inquiry and investigation into the conditions, welfare, and industrial opportunities of all aliens arriving and residing in the state, to gather information with respect to the supply of labor afforded by such aliens, to ascertain the occupations for which aliens might be best adapted, and to bring about communication between aliens and the several industries requiring labor. The Bureau was instructed to publish such statistical details and general information concerning these matters which were re-

39 See below, Chapter V.

40 California Commission of Immigration and Housing, *Second Annual Report, op. cit.*, pp. 118-122.

41 Commonwealth of Pennsylvania, Department of Labor and Industry, Bureau of Statistics and Information, " Report of the Division of Immigration and Unemployment ", *First Annual Report of the Commissioner of Labor and Industry*, I, 1913, p. 228.

vealed by its investigations.[42] The basic consideration prompting this legislation was a desire on the part of the legislature to prevent exploitation of the immigrant, to give some intelligent direction to the process of Americanization at work within the boundaries of the commonwealth, and to develop a state policy toward the solution of the problem of immigration in harmony with the policies developed by the federal government.[43]

Under its general powers, the Bureau of Statistics and Information was required to keep in touch with labor in the state, especially in relation to commercial, industrial, physical, educational, social, moral, and sanitary conditions of the wage-earners of the commonwealth including its immigrant population. Although the powers granted the Bureau were limited primarily to investigation and inquiry, emphasis was placed upon the necessity of ascertaining existing conditions and tabulating and publishing the results for the information of the public.[44]

Although given authority to bring about communication between aliens and the industries requiring the use of their labor, no machinery had been created for the execution of this important power so that no practical steps could be taken along this line. Recognizing this, the Bureau concentrated its attention in the direction of an investigation and inquiry into the industrial, educational, and social conditions of immigrants in the state. The scope of the investigation was very extensive including the relation of the state to the immigrant, of industry to the immigrant, and of the immigrants among themselves. Main features receiving emphasis were the types of legislation affecting the conditions of aliens, the means em-

42 *Ibid.*, pp. 223-224.

43 Commonwealth of Pennsylvania, Department of Labor and Industry, "Report of the Division of Immigration of the Bureau of Employment", *Third Annual Report of the Commissioner of Labor and Industry of the Commonwealth of Pennsylvania*, 1916, p. 1147.

44 Commonwealth of Pennsylvania, *First Annual Report of the Commissioner of Labor and Industry, op. cit.*, pp. 223-224.

ployed to obtain and retain immigrant labor including labor camps and employment agencies, the extent of educational facilities for aliens, and housing conditions among the immigrants. As the result of its findings, the Division believed that not only had a substantial body of information been collected but that a general view of the entire existing situation among the state's immigrant groups had been obtained.[45]

Utilizing the information revealed by the United States Immigration Commission as well as data issued by private agencies, the Division sent circular letters to all communities and agencies affected in order to receive additional information and statistics. Community studies were then made in all cities, boroughs, and other communities where any large proportion of the population was foreign-born. Comprehensive inquiry was made into the general housing and sanitary conditions, the various agencies dealing with immigrants, the educational facilities provided by local officials, the special provisions made by the more important industries, and other features of a distinctly community interest.[46]

The results of the survey sustained the findings made by the other state immigration investigating bodies. The usual evidences of discrimination, of unsanitary and unwholesome housing, and of inadequate educational facilities were revealed as almost universal in those areas of the state containing a considerable immigrant population. Impressed by the lack of educational facilities for the immigrant, the Division recommended that legislation similar to that passed by New Jersey on behalf of the education of its immigrants be passed by the state legislature.[47] It recommended further the creation of a bureau of employment and immigration within the Department of Labor and Industry. Such bureau it suggested should

45 *Ibid.*, pp. 223-224.

46 *Ibid.*, pp. 227-228.

47 *Ibid.*, pp. 261-262. H. H. Wheaton, chief of the Division, urged state responsibility for this type of education. He felt it would enhance the social and industrial efficiency of the immigrant and would aid in his assimilation.

have a special director and be granted the power not only to bring about better relations between workers and employers, but to encourage the distribution of native and immigrant labor throughout the state. The Division felt that the new bureau should be given general inspectional and investigational powers over all matters concerning the welfare and condition of the immigrants within the commonwealth.[48]

As a result of the Division's findings and recommendations, the Pennsylvania legislature approved a bill on June 7, 1915, which regulated employment agencies, and conferred upon the Commissioner of Labor and Industry definite and extensive powers relative to aliens living within Pennsylvania.[49] The same session also created a Bureau of Employment which received the duty of enforcing the provisions of the new act.[50] The new agency immediately took up the work of the old Bureau of Statistics and Information. A survey of the immigrant conditions in the western part of the state resulted in an even better understanding of the many problems confronting the immigrant. Methods of improving the houses of workers were recommended to many of the large scale industries. Special efforts were taken to improve the sanitary conditions of the labor camps. An active campaign to arouse general interest in the problem of Americanization and the education of the immigrant was inaugurated. By the end of the year 1915, the new Bureau of Employment had taken a very active place among the agencies at work in support of the Americanization of the foreign-born.[51]

---

48 *Ibid.*, p. 282.

49 Commonwealth of Pennsylvania, *Act 397 of the Legislature of 1915.*

50 Commonwealth of Pennsylvania, *Act 373 of the Legislature of 1915. Cf.* Pennsylvania Department of Labor and Industry, "Report of the Division of Immigration of the Bureau of Employment", *Second Annual Report of the Commissioner of Labor and Industry*, 1915, II, p. 548.

51 Pennsylvania Department of Labor and Industry, "Report of the Division of Immigration of the Bureau of Employment", *Second Annual Report of the Commissioner of Labor and Industry, op. cit.*, II, pp. 548-551.

One other state showed its interest in the question of Americanization of the immigrant during this period. Rhode Island followed the example of its sister state, Massachusetts, by creating a special Immigration Commission at the January session of its 1914 legislature. The bill, which received the approval of the governor on May 6, 1914, provided for the appointment of a commission to inquire into the condition, welfare, and industrial opportunities of all immigrants and aliens resident in the state. The new body was authorized to obtain information for the enactment of such laws as would bring non-English-speaking foreigners into sympathetic relations with American institutions and customs, provided however that such investigation subjected the state to no financial expense. The Commission was ordered to make a full and final report to the governor, including its recommendations, on or before January 15, 1915, but apparently no such report was ever made. Evidently, the failure of the legislature to appropriate funds to cover the expense of the Commission impeded the functioning of the Commission considerably, if not actually causing the Commission to discontinue its investigation.[52]

Thus the beginning of the second decade of the new century witnessed the spread of interest in the problems of the immigrant and in his possible Americanization to the legislatures of six of the states, each of which took action of one sort or another in support of the program outlined by the North American Civic League for Immigrants and its affiliated groups. The Americanizers had been successful in their efforts to obtain governmental support of their pet project. Henceforth they could depend upon each of the new agencies set up by the states to support their further efforts to arouse the country to an appreciation of the magnitude of the problem.

52 State of Rhode Island and Providence Plantations, *Acts and Resolves Passed by the General Assembly of the State of Rhode Island ... at the January Session, A. D. 1914*, Chapter 1078, p. 136. No evidence of the findings of the Commission has been found by the author.

# CHAPTER IV

## INDUSTRY AND FEDERAL AGENCIES JOIN THE MOVEMENT

WHILE the period 1910-1914 saw the inauguration of active state programs in support of measures to assimilate the foreign-born, it witnessed also the first attempts of industrial interests to win over the immigrant to a better appreciation of the country's ideals, and the beginning of an interest on the part of the federal government in the Americanization of the immigrant.

As early as 1910, the Board of Managers of the North American Civic League for Immigrants had seen the wisdom of attempting to arouse the industrialists of New England in the problem of the assimilation of the foreign-born. They recognized that a great economic blunder had been made through the mishandling of the immigrant in the past, and felt that if proper steps were taken to educate the immigrant workers through classes in English and citizenship, the danger of industrial disorders and economic unrest might be lessened considerably. The officers of the League reasoned that if the immigrant were equipped with a proper knowledge of the American language and the traditional American way of life, he would be more appreciative of the good old-fashioned American ideals, including the *laissez-faire* maxims concerning economic activity.[1]

In an effort to stimulate action along this line, the League arranged for a conference of New England industrial leaders which met on March 19, 1910 at the Hotel Vendome in Boston. In each case, the men present were closely identified with the great manufacturing interests of New England. Addresses were made by Charles Nagel, the Federal Secretary of Commerce and Labor, Judge Charles De Courcey of the Supreme

[1] North American Civic League for Immigrants, *Annual Report, 1911-1912*, pp. 6-7. *Cf.* Note 1, Chapter III, above.

Court of Massachusetts, Lucius Tuttle, president of the Boston and Maine Railroad, Bernard J. Rothwell, president of the Boston Chamber of Commerce, and Samuel B. Capen, prominent New England industrialist

A thorough discussion of the immigrant situation followed the speeches, whereupon the meeting placed itself on record as being unanimous in its praise of the work which the League had been carrying on in protecting and educating the immigrant, and recommended heartily continued support of the League's program both as a means of " self-preservation " from the menace of immigrant " radical " action, and because of its economic value to every industrial section in which it operated. The group held that it was desirable to secure the early cooperation of both representatives of labor and of the manufacturers in support of the League's efforts, and appointed a special committee to consider means by which the interests represented at the meeting could promote more vigorous action. The committee, which consisted of L. A. Coolidge, treasurer of the United Shoe Machinery Company, Henry Hornblower, of the banking firm of Hornblower and Weeks, and Charles K. Darling, clerk, U. S. Circuit Court, Massachusetts District, began to function immediately upon the conclusion of the conference. A circular containing a powerful appeal for action in support of the League was issued and distributed widely in an attempt to organize the industrial interests solidly behind an active program of Americanization of the immigrant worker.[2]

Later in the year, December 1, 1910, another meeting of representatives of the industrial interests of New England took place at the Algonquin Club in Boston on the occasion of a dinner tendered to Senator William P. Dillingham of Vermont, chairman of the Federal Immigration Commission. The latter outlined the work accomplished by the Commission and presented the more important results of its findings. Stressing

2 North American Civic League for Immigrants, *Annual Report, 1909-1910*, pp. 36-37.

the necessity for immediate action on the part of the native American population in support of a program to assimilate the great numbers of immigrants then entering the country, the Senator pleaded with the audience for vigorous support of the work then being carried on by the North American Civic League for Immigrants. " All these newcomers need help. They need to be interested in American institutions, and it can only be done through a society of this nature, and by cooperation of churches, societies, and individuals by team work." [3]

The response to the Senator's speech was enthusiastic and altogether appreciative of the work which the League had been carrying on. At the same time, considerable enthusiasm was aroused over the possibility of cooperation between the League and the industrial interests in bringing the immigrants into the " right relations " with the American people and with American institutions. As a result of the meeting, a New England Industrial Committee was formed, consisting of fifteen men prominent in the New England industrial world, to devise ways and means of aiding the League with its work.[4]

A special sub-committee of the new Committee, composed of Messrs. Coolidge and Hornblower of the original industrial committee, and Frederick C. McDuffie of the Work and Everett Mills, worked out a campaign to rally industrial opinion behind the League. Believing that nothing adequate in the line of " protection " could be expected in the large industrial centers until business men initiated reforms as a business measure, the Committee set apart a district along the Merrimac River Valley, which included the cities of Lawrence, Lowell, Haverhill, and Manchester, as an experimental center. According to the Committee, the same phenomena had appeared in each city: unrest, friction between labor and capital, ' economic conditions different from what the agitators, rational and irrational, were calling for ', and crowded colonies full of un-Americanized

3 North American Civic League, *Annual Report, 1910-1911*, p. 25.

4 *Ibid.*, pp. 25-26.

foreigners.[5] Evidently, the recent I.W.W. outbreaks in the New England section had aroused fear of an increase in radicalism among the immigrant working-class population of that area.

The Committee appointed Frank L. Shaw, formerly of the Federal Immigration Commission, to act as a special industrial secretary. A budget was provided for his use. Shaw made his headquarters at Lawrence, and proceeded to investigate the industrial conditions of the area for the information of the League. His findings confirmed the worst fears of the Committee in regard to the increasing radicalism of the immigrant worker,[6] so much so, that a special call was sent forth for financial aid to meet what the Committee considered the serious conditions in New England. As a further aid to meet the existing " industrial threat " in that region, the League published a new *Message,* an industrial one, entitled, *Respect the Law and Preserve Order,* which pointed out to the foreigners the desirability of allying themselves with the orderly part of the communities in which they lived. The pamphlet was published in Greek, Italian, Polish, and English, and was widely distributed throughout the Merrimac Valley. Reemphasizing the importance of such leaflets, the League pointed out " that if patriotic people, whether identified with labor or capital, realized how useful such leaflets are in the hands of an uninformed foreigner, they would see that this circle of influence was greatly widened." [7]

In view of the Merrimac Valley findings of the Industrial Committee, the League instituted a campaign in the spring of 1912 to awaken the various chambers of commerce and boards of trade to a realization of their duties as conservators of the " best interests " of their communities, this in conform-

5 North American Civic League, *Annual Report, 1911-1912, op. cit.,* pp. 6-7.

6 *Ibid.,* p. 7. For text of Shaw's report, *cf.* pp. 40-42.

7 *Ibid.,* p. 9; for text of *Message, cf.* pp. 29-30.

ance with the League's belief that the industrial future of
the country depended largely upon the education of the adult
alien workers in industry. The response was reported as having been both eager and earnest, with many of the organizations showing a strong desire to assist the League in its work
and to make use of its advice and counsel in solving local problems. Particularly active was the Boston Chamber of Commerce of which, D. Chauncey Brewer, the League's president,
was the executive head. The Boston group held an immigration meeting at the Hotel Somerset in Boston on February
29, 1912, at which a large gathering of business and industrial
representatives was addressed by Brewer, Bernard Rothwell,
vice-president of the Chamber, and Colonel Sweetsea, who
had been the officer in charge of the militia at Lawrence during the recent strike outbreaks. The need for an increase in
vigilance in regard to the immigrant situation was stressed
The cooperation between the League and the Boston Chamber
of Commerce remained very close and active thereafter.[8]

The Chamber of Commerce of Portland, Me., appointed a
special immigration committee to cooperate with the League as
the result of a dinner held in that city shortly thereafter, while
the business organizations of Hartford, Springfield, Willi-
mantic, Peabody, Haverhill, Worcester, Providence, Detroit,
and Cleveland, perfected plans to carry out the general lines
of work laid down by the League. Thus the Americanizers had
succeeded in arousing an interest in their campaign among
the various commercial and industrial bodies of the New England area; they had inaugurated a movement which was to
spread to the Middle Atlantic States and the middle west until
practically every chamber of commerce or similar organization
of every municipality of significance containing an alien population had a special immigration committee taking a vigorous
and active part on behalf of the Americanization of the immigrant.[8]

8 *Ibid.*, p. 42; for further information on the activities of the various chambers of commerce, *cf.* Chapter VI below.

Illustrative of the fears of the League in regard to the supposed increase in radicalism among the immigrant working class was the analysis made by President Brewer of the industrial disorders which broke out in the early part of 1912 and were quelled with the aid of the Massachusetts militia. Holding that such incidents showed the reason for the League's creation better than any other argument, Brewer stated:

> Its [the League's] literature and earlier reports have consistently and repeatedly called upon the public of the industrial states to address itself to the serious problem confronting it because of marvelous social and economic changes. Figures have been given that could be easily verified, and conclusions have been frankly stated. In brief, and to repeat, these are:—
>
> 1. That unless strenuous and adequate endeavor were made to prevent disaster, the presence of a great foreign population, knowing nothing of self government, in the midst of a commercialized and apathetic population, meant ruin;
>
> 2. That less than nothing was being done to meet the peril;
>
> 3. That certain positive tendencies were aggravating the situation. Among these attention has been called to:—
>
> > a. The lax and abominable naturalization laws—badly administered and used by politicians to further their personal ends;
> >
> > b. Respect for law decreasing in ratio with, if not as a result of, the increased participation of labor in state and Federal legislation—a fact that concerns labor as directly as it does capital;
> >
> > c. Criticisms of local authorities, the lower courts and law officers entrusted with the protection of life and property;
> >
> > d. Growth of that type of socialism which is synonymous with treason;
> >
> > e. Encouragement of the sort of free speech which ignores legal restraints.

Now we have the Lawrence upheaval and many minor disturbances to justify the League's warnings, and scores of instances to illustrate the vicious tendencies which have been briefly catalogued.

As we go to press it looks as if a threatened conflagration had been checked. Meanwhile it is a question if the fire is all out. A smouldering blaze in the dry thatch which is screened by the tall grass, may do endless damage.

It will be well for the public not only to learn of its peril through recent experiences but also to stamp out any errant flames which are feeding out of sight." [9]

Again in his *Report for 1912-1913*, Brewer stressed the concern which the League felt over the industrial disorders of the period. Stating that the industrial states had been reaping the harvest of the country's immigration policy during the past year, he added:

At the time when the League's last Report went to press viz.—April 1, 1912—the Lawrence disorders were still the subject of public comment. Since that date more than fifty strikes, most of which have borne revolutionary earmarks, have disturbed New England; Patterson has brought new fame to New Jersey; and Little Falls to New York.

As none of these incendiary movements would have the sinister form which makes them dangerous, had it not been for the mishandled non-English-speaking population, it is hoped that the sharp object lesson of 1912-1913 will bring about corrective action." [10]

Brewer went on to dwell upon the need for educating the immigrant and for instilling in him an appreciation of the old American ideals. He felt that both labor and capital had been sufficiently impressed with the recent outbreaks to give cordial attention to the League's program. " Volleys in the streets— ribald attacks on courts and departments of public order—

9 North American Civic League, *Annual Report, 1911-1912*, p. 5.

10 North American Civic League, *Annual Report, 1912-1913*, pp. 5-6.

and impassioned appeals to frenzied, if misguided mobs, are having an educational value." [11]

In pursuance of its purpose of instituting a campaign among the employers of alien labor to show them that adherence to the League's program and principles was not only a patriotic move but also an economic necessity, the League sent out explanatory letters to nearly all the large manufacturers of New England. The response, which was considered extremely favorable, no doubt resulted from psychological reaction to the labor troubles in the various industrial sections. At the same time the League's Industrial Committee continued its efforts to educate the employers of alien labor along the lines laid down by the League. Its work was for the most part described as successful " to the extent little short of wonderful ".

The Committee reported one astonishing feature, however, in the short-sighted attitude assumed by some manufacturers, who seemed to feel that in gaining a temporary ascendency over the foreign-born strikers they had won a signal victory and could rest safely upon their laurels. Realizing the need for winning the cooperation of employers such as these, the Committee reported " if this last mentioned class of manufacturers can be brought to feel the patriotic necessity of making good citizens out of their alien employees, whether strikes are in progress or not, in order to build a foundation for their country and their business on which their prosperity may safely depend, then, and not until then, will victory be really won; and not until then will the Committee feel that its *raison d'etre* no longer exists." [12]

The Industrial Committee continued to press its educational campaign among the industrial interests, performing thereby valuable supplementary aid to the efforts of the North American Civic League. For the next decade, the Committee served the very unique purpose in the New England region as a vital

11 *Ibid.*, pp. 14-15.

12 *Ibid.*, pp. 14-15.

force working in opposition to all efforts to win over the immigrants to a program of radical action while at the same time sponsoring a vigorous program of Americanization. Praising the work of the Committee, the League stated, " its members are men who loom large in the business world and to whom the mission of the League appealed with two-fold force. Their influence has been most valuable in enlisting the aid of business men throughout the North Atlantic States." [13]

The North American Civic League for Immigrants continued to push its program throughout the pre-war years. Officers of the League spoke to selected audiences in Worcester, Springfield, and Holyoke, and addressed manufacturing groups in New Haven, Bridgeport, Hartford, and Philadelphia, as well as a host of other cities as the years went by. Special agents of the League addressed chambers of commerce, church organizations, boards of trade, and manufacturing groups in many of the New England towns. In every instance, a vigorous effort was made to whip up and sustain an interest in the immigrant and the need for his rapid assimilation. When the Americanization drive reached its heights during the ' war years ', the movement found a receptive populace in New England largely due to the spade-work already accomplished by the North American Civic League.[14]

While the mother organization was making its concerted drive to rally the industrial interests behind its program of Americanization, the New York-New Jersey Committee of the North American Civic League continued its program along the lines indicated.[15] The Committee tended to broaden its activities more and more upon a national scale, however, until it became eventually the spearhead and guiding genius of the attack upon the unassimilated status of the immigrant. As early as May 1911, the Committee indicated that it was moving

13 North American Civic League, *Annual Report, 1911-1912*, p. 42.

14 North American Civic League, *Annual Report, 1912-1913*, p. 15.

15 See above, Chapter III.

in this direction when it arranged a conference to discuss a plan for organizing an immigration council as a clearing-house of information regarding work for immigrants in New York City. This was accomplished in March 1912, with the assistant secretary of the League serving as temporary secretary of the council,[16] but it was not until the spring of 1914 that the group determined to carry on its activities upon a national scale.

The Committee's members felt that their program in New York and New Jersey had been for the most part successful. They now felt the time appropriate to extend their program to the entire nation. They therefore changed the name of their organization to the Committee for Immigrants in America, and converted it into a practical clearing house for information, literature, plans, standards, methods, experts, and aid of all sorts relating to the Americanization of the immigrant. For the duration of its existence, the Committee for Immigrants in America stimulated and aided other organizations engaged in immigrant work, created new organizations, and secured the passage of laws when needed. It became eventually the general consulting headquarters for immigrant and Americanization work throughout the country.[17]

As the first step in the newly reorganized Committee's campaign for the Americanization of the immigrant upon a national scale, the Committee for Immigrants in America brought the problem to the attention of Franklin K. Lane, Secretary of the Interior, in April 1914. It suggested that the Bureau of Education undertake to sponsor programs on behalf of the education and Americanization of the immigrant in so far as possible. The response to the Committee's suggestion was very cordial

16 New York–New Jersey Committee of the North American Civic League for Immigrants, *Report, December 1, 1909–February 1, 1913, op. cit.,* p. 19.

17 Committee for Immigrants in America, *Memorandum to the Advisory Commission of the Council of National Defense Concerning the Committee for Immigrants in America, National Americanization Committee, and Affiliated Organizations,* Oct. 12, 1917, p. 5.

for both Secretary Lane and Commissioner of Education, P. P. Claxton, had gone on record as favoring the new movement to Americanize the immigrant.[18] Lane referred the Committee to Claxton to work with the latter in setting up a Division of Immigrant Education in the Bureau of Education. Because no funds were available for the work, and no expert services at the command of the Bureau, the Committee for Immigrants in America provided the necessary money as well as a complete staff of investigators and other experienced personnel to allow the Division to function. The Division soon became the nucleus for all types of educational activity concerning the foreign-born. One of the Committee's staff members was appointed in charge of the new Division with the title of Specialist in Immigrant Education.[19]

18 Claxton had registered his approval of a program of immigrant education on a nation-wide scale as early as November 1, 1913, when he recommended such a program in his letter to Secretary Lane recommending the publication of the abstracts of the papers read at the New York–New Jersey Committee's conference on immigrant education. After pointing out the great contrast in the environment of the immigrant, his lack of knowledge of American political and civic life, etc., he wrote: "The millions of adult men and women, of children older than the upper limit of the compulsory school attendance age, must be looked after; they must be prepared for American citizenship and for participation in our democratic, industrial, social, and religious life. For the enrichment of our national life as well as for the happiness and welfare of individuals we must respect their ideals and preserve and strengthen all of the best of their Old World life they bring with them. We must not attempt to destroy and remake—we can only transform. Racial and national virtues must not be thoughtlessly exchanged for American vices.

"The proper education of these people is a duty which the nation owes to itself and to them. It can neglect this duty only to their hurt and to its peril. No systematic effort has ever been made to work out the best methods therefor. We have little definite usable knowledge of the varying characteristics of the several races. We are ignorant even of the surest and quickest way to teach them to speak and understand English. To work out the several phases of this vital problem of the education of immigrants and their children should be the task of this bureau, and the bureau will gladly undertake it whenever sufficient funds are made available for that purpose ". Letter from Claxton to Secretary Lane, Nov. 1, 1913, "Education of the Immigrant", U. S. Bureau of Education, *Bulletin*, 1913, No. 51, pp. 5-6.

19 Committee for Immigrants, *Memorandum to Advisory Commission, op. cit.*, pp. 7-8.

The Federal Bureau of Education had already shown its interest in the movement to educate the adult immigrant by publishing the papers and addresses read and discussed at a public two-day conference on the education of the immigrant held in New York City, May 16 and 17, 1913, and sponsored by the New York-New Jersey Committee of the North American Civic League for Immigrants. The conference, the first of its kind, proved such a success that Commissioner Claxton recommended that the papers read and discussed by the twenty-eight speakers be incorporated into one of its official bulletins for general distribution throughout the country. Practically every phase of the immigrant education program was discussed by authorities from all parts of the United States.[20]

Now, with the funds furnished by the Committee for Immigrants in America, the Bureau of Education set to work on its new program on behalf of the education of the foreign-born. A trained sociologist and investigator was assigned to work with the Pennsylvania Department of Labor at Harrisburg to

20 U. S. Bureau of Education, "Education of the Immigrant", *Bulletin,* 1913, No. 51. For text of speeches and papers, *cf.* pp. 7-52. Speakers included: Mrs. Annie L. Hansen, of the North American Civic League; Miss Winifred Gibbs of the New York Assn. for Improving the Condition of the Poor; Miss Helen Kinne of Columbia Teachers' College; Miss Mabel H. Killredge of the Assn. of Practical Home Making Centers of New York City; Joseph Mayper of the New York Bureau of Industries and Immigration; Jane E. Robbins of the Society for Italian Immigrants; William H. Maxwell, supt. of New York City schools; John H. Haaren, asst. supt. of New York City schools; Cecil A. Kidd, Edward W. Stitt, and Joseph W. Wade, district supts. of New York City schools; Robbins Gilman, headworker of University Settlement House; Margaret Knox, Arthur J. Roberts, Robert B. Brodie, Isador Springer, Albert Lowinthal and Michael J. Isaacs, principals in New York City schools; Warren C. Eberle of the North American Civic League; Annie Carroll Moore of the New York Public Library; Rosamond Kimbell; Albert Shiels, dist. supt. of New York City schools; James C. Byrnes, secretary of the Board of Examiners, New York Board of Education; Edith L. Jardine, general secretary of the International Institute of the Y. W. C. A., and Arthur V. Taylor, supervisor of evening schools of Newark, N. J.

ascertain the prevalence of adult illiteracy among the immigrants of that state, and to consider methods of preparing immigrants for citizenship, and for participation in American industrial, social, and civic life. Upon the completion of this project, the Bureau began in 1914 a national investigation of facilities for the education of aliens, which revealed the generally chaotic condition then existing in this phase of education.[21]

The Bureau found that few established and well-approved standards existed and that practically all methods of conducting such educational classes were in the experimental stage. Policies, except that of federal noninterference, were known only to cities and states where evening schools for immigrants had been maintained for a number of years. Public agencies and private ones of various kinds were endeavoring to treat the problem each in its own way, without any definite effort to cooperate with other agencies, and with no fixed policies. " Immigrant education was considered at this time as primarily a matter for local attention and jurisdiction. The spectacle of cities working out methods independently and adopting fads in immigrant education without the coordinating influence of even a clearing house of information was so common as hardly to excite comment. State supervision, and especially state aid, had not been seriously considered." [22]

H. H. Wheaton, the Bureau's specialist in immigrant education, who had been in charge of the national investigation, presented the results of his survey in time for their inclusion in the Commissioner of Education's *Annual Report* for the year 1914. His findings so impressed Commissioner Claxton that the latter included among his recommendations to Secretary Lane provision for the investigation of the education

21 P. P. Claxton, *Report of the Commissioner of Education for the Year Ended June 30, 1914*, I, 1915, p. xxiii.

22 H. H. Wheaton, "Education of Immigrants", *Report of the Commissioner of Education for the Year Ended June 30, 1916*, I, p. 339.

of adult illiterates and the dissemination of information as to the best methods of teaching such people to read and to write, and of extending the meagre education of those who had been denied the advantages of the schools in their childhood and youth.

Claxton cited the revelations of the census of 1910 which indicated that there were approximately 5,500,000 illiterates in the United States over the age when they could be expected to make a beginning in the public schools, and that there were many millions barely able to read and write the English language at all. He emphasized the findings of the Division of Immigrant Education which indicated that state, local communities, individuals, and benevolent societies were ready to cooperate heartily with the federal government in any reasonable plans which might be devised and presented by his Bureau for that purpose.[23] Unfortunately, no financial action was taken on his proposals. The Division remained dependent upon the financial support of the Committee for Immigrants in America for its work on behalf of Americanization and the education of the immigrant, a situation which existed until July 1, 1919.[24]

For the next four years, the Division of Immigrant Education of the Federal Bureau of Education devoted most of its time and energy to calling attention to the importance of the Americanization problem. Eventually, through issuing bulletins, circular letters, and press releases, it became gradually

[23] *Report of the Commissioner of Education for the Year Ended June 30, 1914*, I, *op. cit.*, p. xxviii.

[24] Letter from Frank Trumbull, chairman of the Committee for Immigrants in America to Commissioner Claxton, dated New York City, Apr. 1, 1919. During the four year period 1914–July 1, 1919, when the law of 1917 prohibiting the federal government from accepting financial aid from private organizations became effective, Trumbull estimated a total of $87,247.80 was disbursed by the Committee for the Americanization work of the Bureau in addition to other facilities furnished. *Cf.* National Archives, Independent Agencies Archives, Federal Security Agency: Office of Education, *Accession 106*, "Americanization War Work, 1917-1918".

a focal point and general clearing house for all matters concerning Americanization and the immigrant problem.[25]

While the Bureau of Education was inaugurating its work of stimulating and publicizing immigrant educational activities supported financially by the Committee for Immigrants in America, the Federal Bureau of Naturalization entered the Americanization movement by joining forces with the public schools in the spring of 1914 to sponsor a system of citizenship classes throughout the nation.[26] The Bureau had been vested with authority to determine whether or not candidates for citizenship were or were not fit for that status, and had considered taking steps to sponsor classes in citizenship as early as 1910. No action was taken by the Bureau at that time. Stimulated, however, by the action of the public school authorities of Hartford, Conn., which had organized such classes through conferences with the naturalization officers and Judge James P. Platt of the United States District Court, and the formation of similar classes in other parts of New England, at Rock Island, Ill., and elsewhere throughout the nation, the Bureau began to consider the problem seriously in the latter part of 1913.[27]

Discussions were held in the Bureau's headquarters in the fall of that year and in the early part of 1914, with the result that on April 20, 1914, a plan was submitted " for dignifying in the eyes of the public the proceeding of admission to citizenship and placing it upon that high plane which it has always held in the minds of those who thoroughly appreciate and

25 For brief account of the growth of the Bureau of Education's Americanization activities, cf. Claxton's "Reply to Memorandum of Elliot Dunlap Smith in Regard to Conflict Between Federal Agencies for Americanization", National Archives, Independent Agencies Archives, Federal Security Agency: Office of Education, *Accession 106*, "Americanization War Work, 1917-1918 ".

26 Raymond F. Crist, " The Growth of the Federal Americanization Movement ", *Foreign-Born*, I, No. 1 (Nov. 1919), p. 17.

27 " Report of the Commissioner of Naturalization ", *Reports of the Department of Labor*, 1916, pp. 461-462.

value citizenship." Local conferences were held and citizenship classes formed in many of the larger cities containing large immigrant populations to inaugurate the program. After conferences with the Assistant Secretary of Labor on the project, and at his instance, a representative of the Bureau visited the cities of Chicago, St. Louis, Milwaukee, St. Paul, Minneapolis, Philadelphia, and New York, in the summer of 1914 and the following winter. This agent held discussions and conferences with public school officials, representatives of the judiciary, government officials, business organizations, and individuals, upon a proposed nation-wide plan for citizenship preparedness through the Americanization of the resident alien body.

This cooperative movement on the part of the Bureau of Naturalization with the public schools was not only heartily endorsed by educators, but the Bureau was urged by them to take the lead in this education so vital to citizenship, and to formulate a course of instruction adaptable to the candidates for citizenship. Conferences with judges of the courts brought forth their unanimous endorsement and assurances that they would recognize the cooperation of the school authorities with the Bureau at the time the petitions for naturalization were being heard by the courts for the admission to citizenship.[28]

Pleased by the reception of the Bureau's new program, Commissioner of Naturalization Raymond F. Crist stated that as the result of the Bureau's new actions, the elimination of the known evils attending some of the private organizations seeking under the guise of instruction to exploit the ignorance of the candidates for citizenship as an easy means for a lucrative income would result. Claiming that the Bureau could use its influence to stimulate citizenship more effectively, perhaps, than any other agency, Crist commented:

> It was seen that the influence of the Bureau for the betterment of citizenship could be extended to every hamlet in the United States through the expansion and extension of the

28 *Ibid.*, 462.

influence of the naturalization laws. This plan proposed the organization of the public schools with the Bureau of Naturalization into an active unit for the development of American ideals of citizenship in the student body; the assembling together on stated occasions in different metropolitan and other centers, of naturalized citizens and candidates for citizenship; the conduct of patriotic exercises, including, addresses, and singing national anthems; and a public conferring of citizenship.[29]

At the same time that the Bureau was making plans for the cooperative venture with the public schools, it carried on correspondence directly with the authorities of the different cities and with those interested in naturalization. Los Angeles, in particular, drew the Bureau's praise because of the progressive work it had undertaken in connection with preparing its aliens for citizenship. The Bureau rounded out the year 1914 still in the process of preparing its program for the education of the immigrant for American citizenship. The year 1915 was to see it inaugurate its program on a large scale and to render very valuable support to the growing Americanization movement.[30]

Thus the period 1910-1914 witnessed a marked heightening of interest in the Americanization of the immigrant largely due to the industrial strikes and disorders of the period. The North American Civic League for Immigrants had begun the process of lining up the industrial interests in support of the movement, while its daughter organization, the New York-New Jersey Committee, undertook to push the movement on a national scale. Both the Federal Bureaus of Education and Naturalization had entered the lists and had begun plans for the sponsoring and strengthening of the movement. The stage was set for a grand campaign of action in support of Americanization, when the opportune moment should arrive.

29 *Ibid.*, p. 462.

30 *Ibid.*, pp. 462-463.

# CHAPTER V

# WAR IN EUROPE ACCELERATES
# THE MOVEMENT

In the previous chapters it has been noted how the period 1910-1914 saw the gradual rise of an increased interest in the problem of the assimilation of the immigrant. This period, it will be recalled, witnessed the inauguration of active steps to aid that process, not only through the efforts of the organized Americanization groups, but through various state agencies and the Federal Bureaus of Education and Naturalization as well. For the most part, however, the movement had not yet succeeded in capturing the American public generally. Despite the active propaganda of the North American Civic League for Immigrants, the Committee for Immigrants in America, and the two federal bureaus, the public remained largely indifferent.

The year 1915, however, was to witness a changeover in this respect. From an attitude of indifference to the immigrant, the public changed to one of active interest; so much so, that the whole question of Americanization began to assume the proportions of a national crusade—that traditional mode of action which Americans had followed in the past when once aroused over a problem.

Unquestionably, the great factor responsible for this change of interest was the effect of the European War upon America. This first began to make itself felt toward the end of the year 1914. The fierce display of force on the other side of the Atlantic heightened undoubtedly not only the fears of those who felt that America might eventually become embroiled itself, but the nationalistic feelings of practically all Americans. An intense patriotism and devotion to all things 'American' gripped the nation, while a suspicion of all things alien in nature or which might be considered as a threat to the security of the nation began to grow in intensity as the conflict continued. Propagandists for both sides helped to confuse the situation from the very start and to cast suspicion upon the actions of the respective warring powers toward the United States.

From suspicion of the enemy state, or prospective enemy state, to suspicion of the aliens living in America who had been former residents of that country was a fairly easy process. A natural corollary was a further transference of suspicion from such immigrants to immigrants generally. In this respect, the British and the French fared well, while the Germans and Austrians fared badly. Whereas the British could bank on the language factor to eliminate much of the suspicion which might be cast at their nationals in the United States, and whereas French immigration to the States had been practically nil, the Germans and Austrians had millions of their former subjects residing in the United States,—all foreign-language speakers and all apt to be viewed with suspicion by an aroused American public. The Allied Powers had very little to lose from the growing suspicion of the foreigner in the United States; the Germans and their allies had a great deal.

The European War, too, brought forth a response from the immigrant population of America which must have shocked the indifferent American public, heretofore very little concerned about the aliens within its midst. To the Lithuanian, Czech, Pole, Slovak, and many other nationalities represented in the United States, the War offered an opportunity for the long-cherished independence hopes of those peoples for their fellow-countrymen at home. It was but human and natural that they should become interested actively in the national aspirations of their subjected homelands, and begin propagandizing efforts. Such activity seemed to many Americans to be a violation of the nation's hospitality to say the least.

Propagandizing tactics were not limited to the minor foreign-speaking groups resident in the United States. The numerically strong and powerfully influential German-language groups took part in such activities as well. It was because of the activities of this latter group, no doubt more than any other, that many Americans began to fear that the immigrant situation might get well out of hand. It was quite one thing to find Czechs and Lithuanians agitating for the establishment of seemingly inoffensive little republics. It was quite another to find certain German-Americans engaged actively in pro-German activities throughout the United States. For regardless of which of the great powers might have been chiefly responsible for the outbreak of World War I, the German Empire was *the* threat in most Americans' minds, a possible enemy, and had been so considered for some time.

From the actions of such immigrant groups on behalf of their former mother-lands developed a counteraction on the part of the so-called native Americans which took the form of an anti-Hyphen movement. To these Americans, a ' Hyphen ' was one who put the interests of his former homeland before those of his adopted country. Many of the German-Americans were so designated. Conspicuously in the forefront of the drive to crack-down on these people and to eliminate the menace of the hyphenated American was former President Theodore Roosevelt. Others of prominence engaged actively in denouncing their activities, while President Wilson, himself, spoke in opposition to " Hyphenated " actions.

With such an atmosphere of suspicion and distrust of the immigrant becoming increasingly evident as the European struggle progressed, it is very understandable that the efforts of the Americanizers should find a much more receptive audience than they had ever found before. The time was ripe for a campaign of crusading proportions to win over the nation to the necessity for concerted action along the lines of assimilation or Americanization (for the latter term began to replace the former as the more appropriate one to describe the process which would mould the immigrant into a full-fledged American with undivided loyalties). That such a crusade was not long in forming was inevitable. That it received such a favorable response was indicative of the change which had come over America as a result of the outbreak of hostilities abroad.[1]

The Federal Bureau of Naturalization was responsible for laying the plans which blossomed eventually into the full crusade in the summer of 1915. The Bureau proposed a novel scheme to the mayor of Philadelphia in December 1914, as a means of centralizing training in cooperation with the public schools of the nation. The agency suggested that the mayor hold a reception for the newly naturalized citizens of that city as a means of publicizing its program. The mayor agreed, and plans were made to hold the reception on May 10, 1915.[2]

Such a reception was not exactly new, for as early as July 4, 1910, Rochester, N. Y., had given a banquet and reception

[1] Commenting on the rise of the Americanization movement, Miss Frances A. Kellor, one of the key workers in the crusade, stated: " The war found America with its native and foreign-born peoples living far apart. The foreign-born were united each in their own racial solidarity, with their own economic systems and quite independent of native American assistance; the native born were pursuing their own way toward success and happiness quite unconscious of the separateness of the many races." Claiming native Americans never fully appreciated what the declaration of war in Europe meant to almost one-third of the population, she added: " The restlessness and anxiety were not, however, all on the side of the immigrant. Americans, too, grew uneasy when they began to read of the war activities of some of the foreign-born in America.... They began to ask why aliens had not become Americanized; why America did not come first in their interests; and why naturalized citizens were returning to serve in the armies of their home countries. As the war progressed, a widespread apprehension grew among many Americans as to what the foreign-born ultimately might do. In some quarters, because the apparent un-Americanism of the few was taken to represent the attitude of all, this fear began to develop into a deep-seated resentment against the whole of the foreign-born population. The breach between native and foreign-born was gradually widening and antagonism on both sides was increasing when America's entry into the war called for united action on the part of all, irrespective of race, creed, color, or class." Cf. Frances A. Kellor, *Immigration and the Future*, New York, 1920, pp. 49 and 52.

[2] " Report of the Commissioner of Naturalization ", *Reports of the Department of Labor, 1916, op. cit.*, p. 464.

in honor of its newly naturalized citizens attended by public officials and other notables of the city as a token of its recognition of the need for a more intelligent attitude toward the immigrant.[3] But the importance of the Philadelphia reception lay in the definite bid which was being made on a national scale for support of the Bureau's citizenship plans. Arrangements were made to have the President of the United States give the principal address.[4]

At the same time, the Bureau perfected steps in March 1915, for a survey of the entire country by correspondence and through its field officers to ascertain the efforts and accomplishments of the public school authorities in the direction of the education of foreigners over 18 years of age. The inquiry further asked what percentage of foreigners were candidates for citizenship in these classes, what scope of instruction was offered by the public schools, and what other organizations were interested in the preparations of the foreigner for citizenship. The survey was carried on throughout the United States by the entire Naturalization Service and continued uninterruptedly until the inauguration of the Bureau's cooperative work with the public schools in the autumn of 1915.[5]

Immediately preceding the Philadelphia reception, the federal agency announced in the columns of the press the launching of its nation-wide cooperative educational campaign " for the betterment and strengthening of the citizenship of the entire nation, through the aid of the public schools." To the delight of the Bureau, the public response and endorsement given to both the reception plans and the educational announcement went beyond its expectations.[6]

In the meantime, Baltimore had shown its interest in the new movement by holding a ' New Voters' Day ', sponsored by

3 Edwin A. Rumball, " Rochester's Civic Banquet ", *Survey*, XXIV (July 16, 1910), p. 604.

4 " Report of the Commissioner of Naturalization," *op. cit.*, p. 464.

5 *Ibid.*, p. 463.

6 *Ibid.*, p. 464.

the City Club at which Secretary of State, William Jennings Bryan, and former President William H. Taft spoke on citizenship.[7] Taking advantage of the opportunity presented by this new publicity, the Committee for Immigrants in America established a quarterly periodical entitled *The Immigrants in America Review*, with the hope of vitalizing " American public opinion into the adoption of a national policy with reference to admitted aliens." [8] The *Review* served this useful propagandizing mission for the next year and a half.

The Philadelphia reception was held finally as planned and became the occasion of Wilson's ' Too Proud to Fight ' speech. As such it tended to cloud the true nature of the occasion. The President, however, did inject into the speech his dislike and suspicion of the activities of the hyphen. He stressed the idea that America did not consist of groups, and that those who thought of themselves as belonging to a particular national group in America had not yet become Americans. On the other hand, he praised the immigrants for their idealism and strength of courage. " You dreamed dreams of what America was to be, and I hope you have brought the dreams with you. No man who does not see high visions will ever realize any high hope or undertake any high enterprise, and just because you brought the dreams with you, America is more likely to realize the dream

7 " Record of Progress ", *Immigrants in America Review*, I, No. 2, (June 1915), p. 81.

8 Committee for Immigrants in America, *Immigrants in America Review*, I, No. 1 (Mar. 1915), p. 3 [the first issue of the *Review*]. The *Review* continued to be issued until June 1916 under the guidance of Miss Frances A. Kellor as editor. The periodical became a virtual storehouse of information on all phases of the Americanization crusade, and forms a valuable guide to the Americanization efforts during this period. Others intimately connected with the *Review* were: Royal Dixon, managing editor; members of the advisory board: Mary Antin, Emily Balch, Winston Churchill, Herbert Croly, editor of the *New Republic*, Martha Foote Crowe, Henry P. Fairchild, Felix Frankfurter, Virginia C. Gildersleeve, Frederick C. Howe, Dr. Woods Hutchinson, authority on public health and sanitation, Walter Lippmann, S. S. McClure, Mrs. William Vaughn Moody, Jessie B. Rittenhouse, author and poet, Charles P. Steinmetz, Graham Taylor, sociologist and Edmund J. Wheeler. *Ibid.*, p. 1.

you brought. You are enriching us if you came expecting us to be better than we are." [9]

As a result of the address of the President and the newspaper publicity and discussions resulting from the meeting, a wave of patriotic sentiment was aroused which extended throughout the nation. During the entire month of May, patriotic and enterprising individuals proceeded to associate themselves together in the organization of committees whose main objects were to maintain this newly aroused interest. " Some looked to a national recognition of the naturalization proceedings while others by celebrations, and all in various ways, strove to make impressive in the eyes of the public the steps attendent upon naturalization. Those occupying positions of official responsibility, as well as others prominent in the industrial, religious, social and political world, responded to the influence of this national wave of interest in citizenship created by the reception in Philadelphia. Americanization Committees, led by the mayors and other officials, were formed in cities

9 For the complete text of Wilson's speech, cf. "Address of President Wilson Delivered at Convention Hall, Philadelphia, May 10, 1915 ", *Immigrants in America Review*, I, No. 3 (Sept. 1915), pp. 30-32. A description of the reception follows: "At the Philadelphia reception 5,000 newly naturalized citizens occupied the front seats in a great convention hall, 8,000 older citizens sat behind and above them, a chorus of 4,500 voices, itself as composite racially as the thousands it faced, rose in semi-circles at the rear of the platform, and on the platform, sat national, state and city officials, judges, mayors, college presidents, law-makers, officers from navy yard and fleet, and distinguished citizens, among whom nearly every man in the audience could find a fellow-countryman. Great flags draped each of the twenty main pillars; festoons of bunting hung from the high arched roof and terminated in a gigantic canshaped decoration over the heads of the choir. Facing the new citizens, and topped by a wreath thirty feet in diameter, were the words, in electric lighted letters: 'Welcome to a government of the people, by the people, for the people'. And among the speakers, at the front of the platform, sat the gray-haired mayor of Philadelphia, who had himself reached New York a penniless immigrant fifty years ago, and the President of the United States." Cf. *Survey*, XXXIV (June 19, 1915), p. 261. For further details of the citizenship reception, cf. U. S. Department of Labor, *Proceedings of the Naturalization Reception Held at Philadelphia, Pa., May 10, 1915, passim.*

throughout the land to take some cognizance of the naturalization proceedings." [10]

Included among these "patriotic and enterprising individuals" weie members of the Committee for Immigrants in America. Desirous of using the newly aroused interest to strengthen the program for Americanization which it had been conducting, the Committee for Immigrants in America began a campaign for Americanization—a word hitherto not used by the group for publicity purposes—urging that July 4, 1915 be made a national Americanization Day, a day in which all peoples in America would be brought together in their towns and cities in a great nationalistic expression of unity and faith in America. The Committee hoped to impress the foreign-born with the necessity for a whole-hearted loyalty to their adopted country, and at the same time to arouse the interest of the native-born in the problems of their foreign-born neighbors. [11]

Accordingly, the Committee organized the National Americanization Day Committee in May 1915, to make this campaign effective. The new committee, composed of 59 citizens from all parts of the United States, represented various social, philanthropic, and industrial interests throughout the nation. It issued a statement to the effect that its chief aims would be " to promote a national movement to bring American citizens, foreign-born and native alike, together on our national Independence Day to celebrate the common privileges and define the common loyalties of all Americans wherever born." [12] It also issued a pamphlet written by Miss Frances

10 " Report of the Commissioner of Naturalization ", *op. cit.,* p. 464.

11 Committee for Immigrants in America, *Memorandum to the Advisory Commission of the Council of National Defense, op. cit.,* pp. 6-7.

12 National Americanization Committee, *A Call to National Service,* New York, 1916, p. 2. Listed as officers of the new Committee were: Frank Trumbull, chairman, Percy R. Pyne, 2nd., banker and president of Pyne, Kendall and Hollister Co., New York City, vice-chairman, Mrs. Edward T. Stotesbury, wife of the prominent banker and member of J. P. Morgan & Co., vice-chairman, William Sproul, U. S. Senator from Pennsylvania, and banker and financier, vice-chairman, William Fellowes Morgan, treas-

Kellor stressing the need and desirability for a domestic policy in regard to the immigrant and outlining a seven-point program in order to achieve it.[13] Miss Kellor stressed in particular the great role which American industrial organizations could assume in working out this policy. Emphasizing the point if industry could solve the industrial problem connected with

---

urer. Executive Committee: Mrs. Vincent Astor, Frances A. Kellor, Peter Roberts of the Y. M. C. A., Mrs. Cornelius Vanderbilt, Felix A. Warburg, banker and financier. Other Committee members included: Mary Antin, Nicholas Murray Butler, P. P. Claxton, Federal Commissioner of Education, T. Coleman DuPont, president of the E. I. duPont de Nemours Powder Co., Thomas A. Edison, John A. Fahey, vice-president of the Associated Press, John H. Finley, former president of C.C.N.Y. and then Commissioner of Education of the State of New York, James Cardinal Gibbons, Roman Catholic Archbishop of Baltimore, Myron T. Herrick, diplomat and director of New York Life Insurance Co., Frederick C. Howe, Charles H. Ingersoll, Jacob H. Schiff, banker and financier, General Leonard Wood, and many others. For full list of members, cf. *Memorandum . . . Council of National Defense, op. cit.*, p. 7.

13 Committee for Immigrants in America, *Immigrants in America, Program for a Domestic Policy*, New York, 1915. The seven point program read as follows: 1. Direct expeditious and safe distribution of admitted aliens to destinations, with suitable train, terminal and transfer facilities and municipal facilities for directing immigrants within the city—comprising the subject of transportation; 2. Security of employment and adequate, coordinated, regulated labor market organization through which admitted aliens might find work, with equal opportunity to engage in occupations by which they might earn their living—comprising the subject of employment; 3. Maintenance of American standards of living, by removal of discriminations in localities, housing, sanitation, over-crowding, rentals, and supplies—comprising the subject of living; 4. Opportunity for intelligent, safe investment of savings with such information, organization, and legislation, as would accomplish this, including banking institutions, loan funds, agricultural colonies, and workingmen's home projects—comprising the subject of savings and investments; 5. Reduction of illiteracy and advancement of knowledge of the English language and civics, extension of public social facilities and industrial training—comprising the subject of education; 6. Higher and more simplified standard of naturalization requirements, uniform state naturalization laws, simplification of processes and increase of facilities for naturalization and for coordination of educational requirements with educational facilities—constituting the subject of naturalization; and 7. National cooperation in the care of public charges, increased facilities for locating deportable persons, and better coordination of state and national work—constituting the subject of public charges. *Cf.* pp. 1-3.

immigration there would be no need for clumsy poorly-prepared laws, she advocated that government, industry, and philanthropy should get together for each was important in the formulation and execution of a sound Americanization policy. Government might be effective where philanthropy could not, and *vice versa,* while industry could institute experiments and solve problems where others failed. She added significantly:

> However well government, business, and philanthropy may conceive and launch a national policy, its ultimate success will depend upon the average American citizen. He and he alone can eliminate race prejudice and class distinction, hold out the hand of friendship, perform such personal services as will disarm the exploiter, and enable the immigrant to express his best self. Such a citizen is the natural foe of the I.W.W. and of the destructive forces that seek to direct unwisely the expression of the immigrant in the new country, and upon him rest the hope and defense of the country's ideals and institutions.
>
> For the first time in many years this country is free from the absorbing demand made by the entrance of hundreds of thousands of immigrants yearly. Now is the time to take up the conditions of the nearly thirteen million foreign-born in this country and to formulate and execute the measures necessary for the welfare of the country. Now is the time to establish adequate machinery for dealing intelligently and efficiently with increased immigration after the war. In the meantime, the unguided childworkers, the children out of school, the illiterate parents, the thousands of unnaturalized, the unemployed, the congested cities and deserted farms, the isolated colonies, the padroni, the precarious institutions for savings and investments,—these and many other matters require national consideration and action.
>
> Thousands of organizations and individuals are at work upon it [Americanization], but largely without a *national* goal or consciousness. The need now is not *more* work for the *Italian* or the *Jew* as such, not more interest in school facilities for the *Greek* or *Finn,* not merely the *importation*

of more *peasants* from farm lands, but the conscious effort to forge the people in this country into an American race that will stand together for America in times of peace or of war. Every effort should be bent toward an Americanization which will mean that there will be no ' German-Americans ', no ' Italian quarter ', no ' East Side Jew ', no ' Up-town Ghetto ', no 'Slav movement in America ', but that we are one people in ideals, rights and privileges and in making common cause for America. We are far from that ideal citizenship today, how far the European war has brought vividly home to us. Many of us believe that the time has come for a national movement for the Americanization of aliens within the country." [14]

With such a program in mind, the National Americanization Day Committee set about perfecting plans to make July 4, 1915, a day of significance in the relations existing between native and foreign-born Americans. It decided that receptions to the newly naturalized citizens, their friends, and their families, would be the best means for carrying out its ideas. Although this had been done before in isolated cases (such as the Rochester civic banquet of 1910), the Committee felt that a joint effort was needed on the part of the entire nation to extend officially through its city officials recognition and welcome to the new citizens. By so doing, they reasoned, America would make the newcomers feel for the first time the friendly aims of the government in place of the repression, discrimination, and injustices hitherto dealt out to them.[15]

The Americanization group found it no small task in the space of six weeks at the beginning of the summer to gather together a national committee of 54 representative members, set it to work, collect sufficient funds, and organize a uniform movement from the Atlantic coast to the Pacific. Many cities felt the idea frought with possible danger in that various na-

14 *Ibid.*, pp. 1-8.

15 Kellor, "National Americanization Day—July 4th", *Immigrants in American Review*, I, No. 3 (Sept. 1915), p. 19.

tionalities might clash at the proposed meetings, or that propagandists might obtain a hearing. Luckily, such fears were unfounded. The Committee believed that this was itself a tribute to the foreign-born Americans, for in many cities the national colors and songs of the various nationalities were used without one instance of disturbance of any sort. Although fearful that the immigrants might not respond to the Committee's appeal, when the big day finally arrived, reports from all sections of the country showed that even more than the native-born they had entered into the spirit of the occasion. No section of the country failed to respond to the rallying call; even New Orleans in the deep south held a most successful celebration.[16]

The Committee for Immigrants in America, as sponsoring agency, gladly turned over its equipment, facilities, and staff to the new Americanization Day Committee, whose executive committee of ten bore the full burden of carrying on the campaign. Through the courtesy of Frank Trumbull, the Committee's chairman, who donated the prize, a contest for the best statement of the meaning of Americanization Day and for the best program was started. The contest was given wide publicity especially in the foreign-language newspapers, thanks to the American Foreign Language Newspaper Association. An attractive poster was also designed and distributed calling attention to the prize contest.[17]

The Americanization Day Committee arranged for Commissioner of Immigration, Frederick C. Howe, to send out a personal letter to each of the mayors of the cities of the nation asking their support in observance of July 4 as Americanization Day. Howe stressed the point that every community could take part in giving the newcomers a national consciouness and in making them feel that their interests and affections were deeply rooted in America. " The significance of such a recep-

16 *Ibid.*, pp. 19-20.

17 *Ibid.*, p. 20.

tion given on the Fourth of July is obvious ", Howe wrote.
" Should they become national in scope, they should have
great civic value. I am sending you this information with the
thought that you may desire to appoint a mayor's committee
for the organization of such a reception in your city in connection with whatever exercise may be held on the Fourth
of July." [18]

Howe's appeal was followed by letters from the Commissioner of Education, P. P. Claxton, to various school authorities asking for their cooperation in the organization of suitable
exercises, circulating announcements, programs, and other
types of publicity. The New York State Commissioner of
Education, John H. Finley, writing in the department's *Bulletin*
also appealed to New York educational authorities for similar
cooperation. [19]

The Americanizers reported that the response was instan-
taneous and exceedingly favorable. The chief question remaining was just how fast the Committee could draw up programs,
design emblems, suggest speakers, prepare schedules, and
answer the hundreds of questions that the local committees

---

18 "Americanization Day, a New Idea for July 4 ", *Survey*, XXXIV
(May 25, 1915), p. 189. Credit for the idea was given to the city of Cleveland by the Commissioner of Immigration. The latter city held a ' sane
4th of July celebration in 1914. A special ' sane 4th committee ' assumed the
responsibility for a program arranged by a committee representing all local
patriotic and civic organizations. " Through the clerks of naturalization, the
names and addresses of aliens admitted to citizenship during the preceding
year were secured, and invitations for the reception were sent to each.    At
the reception, each new citizen on entering the auditorium and showing his
ticket, was presented with a small American flag and also a seal button of
the city with the word ' citizen ' upon it. A platform decorated with the
flags of all nations was reserved to seat the new citizens. The audience itself
was secured by general publicity through the newspapers, which gladly gave
publicity to the idea. The program opened with national airs. This was
followed with the unfurling of a large American flag, the singing of the
*Star Spangled Banner* and the reciting in unison of the 'pledge of allegiance'.
Officials representing the nation, state, and city, made addresses, followed
by a speech of appreciation by one of the prominent foreign-born citizens."
*Cf.* Letter of Frederick C. Howe, *ibid.*

submitted for solution. To certain cities, strategically located, the Committee sent representatives to explain the work and outline the procedure involved in making the receptions a success. In this way, Boston, Detroit, St. Paul, Minneapolis, St. Louis, Pittsburgh, and other important cities were able to work out complete programs of action.[19]

In spite of the rapidity with which the movement proceeded in many cities, the Americanization Day Committee felt that one last appeal to the whole country was needed. To accomplish this, a poster was designed showing the advantages of citizenship in the acquirement of an education and a home and extending a welcome by Uncle Sam to the immigrant. Railroad stations were selected as the best possible centers of publicity for this. The Committee persuaded the railroads to set aside their general regulations prohibiting the posting of such material. Sixty-two of the railroads cooperated with the Committee in advertising the Americanization Day plans, and approximately 38,524 such posters were placed in stations and railroad shops. 7,612 more were posted by various industries employing immigrants, while another 6,430 were sent to various cities for their celebrations.[20]

As another means of arousing interest, the Committee sponsored exercises and civic lessons on Flag Day, June 14, and sent invitations to the parents of immigrant children to attend the exercises. The sending of the Liberty Bell from Philadelphia to the California Exposition was made the occasion for including the foreign-born in the official exercises which greeted its passage through the various cities along the route of shipment. The Committee claimed that this would scarcely have been thought of had it not suggested to the authorities concerned that the foreign-born be invited to attend.[20]

The campaign had begun on May 22, and closed on July 3, during which time approximately 179,250 units of information

19 Kellor, " National Americanization Day ", *op. cit.*, p. 20.

20 *Ibid.*, pp. 20-22.

were distributed from the Committee's offices in New York City and from the Bureau of Education in Washington. Six news releases were sent out setting forth the idea and progress of the work, and these were widely used by the newspapers. Posters, emblems, suggestions for programs, and a host of other material of value, were also distributed. In return, the Committee received thousands of newspaper clippings showing the widespread educational work accomplished. Many newspapers in cities where no celebrations were held carried news items and favorable editorials concerning the Americanization Day plans. The Committee reported that the Associated Press had been particularly cooperative and helpful.[21]

The Committee's efforts received the endorsement of the President of the United States. Woodrow Wilson, in a letter to Chairman Trumbull, expressed his interest in the movement and sent his best wishes for the success of the venture. Theodore Roosevelt also endorsed the movement and gave wide publicity to the crusade through his article on Americanization Day which appeared in the *Metropolitan Magazine's* July 1915 issue. The Committee reprinted the article and distributed it broadcast.[22]

In addition to its published material, the National Americanization Day Committee prepared data and suggestions for

21 *Ibid.*, p. 22.

22 *Ibid.*, p. 22. The text of Wilson's letter, dated Cornish, New Hampshire, June 30, 1915, follows:

" My dear Mr. Trumbull:

" I have read with care your letter of June 28th in regard to Americanization Day, and I am greatly interested in this nation-wide movement. I wish that my time would permit me to send you a message as you request, but I can only ask you to be good enough to convey my warmest greetings to all assembled on that day and my very best wishes for their prosperity and welfare as citizens of our beloved country.

" May I congratulate you upon the prospect of a most successful movement?

" Cordially and sincerely yours,

Woodrow Wilson."

hundreds of speakers and distributed such material to the various committees. The data enabled the speakers to translate to the audiences something of the meaning of the crusade to both Americans and to the immigrants. The data consisted of material designed to explain the need for Americanization Day, why it should be held on Independence Day, what American citizenship was, what the Americanization of the foreign-born meant to America, what Americanization meant to the foreign-born, and the best ways of bringing it about. The facts were presented in a brief for speakers which enabled them to state the deplorable conditions revealed by the various state immigration commissions. Such speakers appeared at the celebrations both for the native Americans and for the foreign-born. The Committee was kept busy outlining programs, selecting music, suggesting features for parents, and helping local committees in all manner of ways. Through the generosity of Mrs. Cornelius Vanderbilt, Tiffany and Company of New York City designed four different citizenship buttons which were distributed at some of the celebrations. These were later used very extensively at naturalization ceremonies in the Chicago area.[23]

The most difficult task confronting the Committee was that of awakening an intelligent interest and response among the ' old American ' stock. Many of these thought of immigrants, if at all, chiefly as industrial cogs. Many, too, had allowed ' racial ' prejudices to prevent the immigrant from entering into an enjoyment of their social life. Moreover, most Americans had come to regard the 4th as a mere day of pleasure and of sport. " It was symbolic of the day ", the Committee reported, " that in some localities, Americans forgot to decorate their home with the Stars and Stripes while the shacks of nearby immigrants carried them." [24]

23 *Ibid.*, pp. 22-23.
24 *Ibid.*, pp. 19-20.

When the Fourth arrived finally, not less than 150 cities observed it as Americanization Day, as a day to foster in the hearts of the new citizens and immigrants a spirit of higher patriotism and of loyalty to their adopted land. Particularly successful celebrations were held in Seattle, Boston, Kalamazoo, and Washington, D. C. At Pittsburgh, more than 10,000 adults, chiefly aliens, heard almost 1000 school children sing patriotic airs as they formed a huge American flag. In Indianapolis, speeches in eleven different languages on the duties of American citizenship were given by newly made American citizens. Trenton, N. J., received thirty-five of her immigrants into citizenship, while Milwaukee held a special celebration during which church bells rang, street traffic was stopped, and citizens and immigrants gathered to sing and to take part in the ceremonies. Jackson, Mich., typified the melting pot idea by holding a flag pageant. These were but a few of the many ways in which the various cities of the nation showed their interest in the Americanization idea. " Emphasis in almost every city celebration was laid on the fact that while European nations were locked in deadly combat, the sons of these same nations in America through common interests and loyalties could live in peaceful neighborliness." [25]

To Miss Frances Kellor, who had taken an active part in the campaign, the success of the movement for an Americanization Day celebration seemed due not so much to the creation of the new Committee, but rather to the wisdom of that Committee in acting as a clearing house for existing organizations that were ready for such work, but which lacked the central idea and organizing power. In this respect, the Committee played a useful part in coordinating the joint efforts of city officials, chambers of commerce, industrial corporations, schools, churches, Y.M.C.A.'s, Y.W.C.A.'s, civic and fraternal groups, and patriotic organizations. In many of the churches, special Americanization Day sermons were preached, while

25 "Americanization Day in 150 Communities," *Survey*, XXXIV (July 31, 1915), p. 390.

in some instances, where cities did not hold receptions officially, the churches took charge of the arrangements. All in all, Miss Kellor held, " Americanization Day offered one of the finest illustrations of the cooperative patriotism of widely varying organizations throughout the country." [26]

As for the lasting results of the Americanization Day celebration, the Committee reported these to have been far-reaching and widespread. Not only were the existing agencies, already actively engaged in work on behalf of the movement, stimulated to greater effort, but circles heretofore completely indifferent to the problem of the immigrant began to engage in Americanization activities.[27] The Committee later claimed optimistically that in some communities the effect of the celebration changed for all time the relationship of American-born and foreign-born men and women, " for once the barriers had been let down, the Americans found the immigrants much like themselves, with the same sorrows, aspirations, hopes, and joys, and the same patriotism and loyalty to America ".[28]

[26] Kellor, " National Americanization Day ", *op. cit.*, p. 24. In the same article Miss Kellor explained that the idea of Americanization Day originated from the desire in the hearts and minds of thousands of Americans to have July 4th, 1915, express their gratitude for the peace and prosperity of the nation, for the safety of their loved ones, and for the maintenance of national ideals and honor. In search for adequate means for such expression, she stated, the nation was divided, with many believing that a peace expression or demonstration would best express it, others that national defense should characterize the day's celebration, while still others felt that a nationwide expression of patriotism would more widely meet the need of the hour. In answer to this need for general expression the National Americanization Day Committee was organized to give special significance to the July 4th celebrations throughout the country. " Its work was an answer to the desire of Americans to more fittingly express on this day, when the whole world was at war, their patriotism and loyalty to America." To the Committee, nothing seemed more fitting and more necessary than that American-born citizens and the foreign-born and future citizens alike should be brought together in common observance of the day and in a common understanding. *Ibid.*, p. 18.

[27] Kellor, " By-Products of Americanization Day ", *Immigrants in America Review*, I, No. 3 (Sept. 1915), pp. 16-17.

[28] Kellor, " National Americanization Day ", *op. cit.*, p. 19.

Among the more specific activities mentioned by Miss Kellor as a direct result of the Americanization Day effort were: the campaign of the Detroit Board of Commerce to increase the registration of the non-English-speaking immigrants in the public evening schools; the authorization of citizenship classes in connection with the elementary evening schools by the Boston School Committee; the installation of systems of teaching English in a number of industries employing immigrant labor, the active cooperation of chambers of commerce in many places with the public schools in support of immigrant classes in English and citizenship, the organization of a school for naturalization in Wilmington, Del., and the formation of permanent Americanization Day Committees in many localities, each pledged to carry on further plans for the Americanization of the immigrant.[29] Noting the fact that some mayors issued special proclamations for the first time, Miss Kellor wrote: " If Americanization Day did not succeed in reaching the entire country, it did succeed in setting in motion a far-reaching campaign for national solidarity as important in its way as the building of battleships, and the organization of standing armies; a campaign tending alike to peace and defense, and the surest guarantee of both." [30]

The Federal Bureau of Naturalization felt that its efforts to arouse a better interest in the problem of the citizenship-training of the immigrant had been largely successful, and took full credit for inaugurating the Americanization campaign which had reached such successful heights in the Americanization Day celebration of 1915. So well pleased was the Bureau, that its deputy commissioner of naturalization was authorized to make a tour of the United States to present the plans of the

29 Kellor, " By-Products of Americanization Day ", *op. cit.*, pp. 16-17. For comments of officials and others of prominence on Americanization Day, *cf.* "Americanization Day ", *American Leader*, VIII, No. 4, (Aug. 26, 1915), pp. 240-246.

30 Kellor, "Americanization through Art ", *Immigrants in America Review*, I, No. 3 (Sept. 1915), pp. 6-7.

Bureau, address gatherings of educators, and confer with public-school authorities and other prominent citizens upon the details necessary for unified action on its proposed program to be inauguarated in the autumn of 1915. The under-secretary visited Chicago, Pittsburgh, Kansas City, Omaha, Denver, Salt Lake City, Los Angeles, Oakland, San Francisco, Seattle, Tacoma, Spokane, Bismarck, Duluth, St. Paul, Minneapolis, Albany, Philadelphia, Boston, New York, and a score of smaller places. As a result of these conferences, definite plans were matured and approved by Secretary of Labor Lane, as head of the Department, for carrying on the work. To the Bureau, the nation-wide cooperative work announced through the columns of the public press in May 1915, had become a reality with the opening of the new school year.[31]

At the close of the Americanization Day campaign, there was so much demand for Americanization work, methods of procedure, and appropriate material for speeches, that the National Americanization Day Committee decided to remain in existence and to continue to direct all the public, social, civic, philanthropic, and welfare work of the Committee for Immigrants in America, both through government and through voluntary agencies. In so doing, it changed its name to that of the National Americanization Committee under which title it functioned until its dissolution in 1919.[32]

The Committee thereupon set to work upon a permanent campaign for the Americanization of the immigrant. From its headquarters in New York City, it defined Americanization as the union of the many peoples of the country into one nation

---

[31] "Report of the Commissioner of Naturalization" *1916, op. cit.,* pp. 464-465. In the meantime, the Bureau completed its survey of the educational programs in regard to the immigrant begun in March 1915. The results indicated good work being done in many of the larger cities and uneven efforts elsewhere. Practically unanimous support of the Bureau's plans was given. *Cf.* pp. 463-464.

[32] Committee for Immigrants in America, *Memorandum to the Advisory Commission of the Council of National Defense, op. cit.,* p. 7.

and the use of the English language throughout the nation, the establishment of American standards of living in every community of the country, a common interpretation of American citizenship, and a recognition of foreign-born men and women in the human, social, and civic as well as the industrial aspects of American life. It elaborated further to explain that this definition of Americanization involved equal responsibility for native and foreign-born residents. For the native American it meant responsibility for the abolition of race prejudice, for a better understanding of the meaning of America, for the recognition of the fact that American citizenship meant equal opportunities and privileges as well as equal obligations. For the foreign-born it meant the responsibility for learning and using the language of the country, for becoming literate, for becoming efficient citizens, and for loyally supporting the best ideals and traditions of America in return for the rights America guaranteed to all residents of the country. The Commission recognized that Americanization was a complex process, produced by many agencies, and one that could not be accomplished swiftly. However, it believed that the English language, American citizenship, and American standards of living were without question the first steps in the right direction to achieve this goal.

It then stated that the work of the Committee would be confined to these main lines of effort: First, an " English Language First " movement to get immigrants into the night schools where they could learn English, to promote night schools for immigrants in every town that was an immigrant center, and to sponsor correspondence courses through lesson leaflets. Second, an " America First " campaign to facilitate the naturalization of foreigners by establishing civics classes where there were night schools, by making a direct connection between them and the naturalization courts, by adopting standardized courses of study in all schools that prepared for citizenship, by attaching greater importance to the ceremony of the taking of the oath of allegiance, by interesting the American community in every new group of foreign-born citizens by means of official citizenship receptions, and " by not only emphasizing to the foreign-born the necessity of undivided loyalty to America, but by bringing home to the American-born the common interests and privileges of all American citizens ". Third, a " Conservation First " movement to safeguard the labor supply and improve relations between employers and immigrant workmen, to direct the attention of employers to the fact that immigrant workmen were peculiarly subject to industrial accidents and to industrial misunderstandings with consequent labor troubles because of their ignorance of the English language, to point out to these same employers the forces that retarded Americanization with recommendations for their improvement, and to acquaint business men and bankers with the fact that immigrant workmen were ofttimes property holders and had investments in America which should be safeguarded and encouraged in as much as they tended to create permanent home ties in America. Fourth, an " American Standard of Living " campaign to carry American standards to the immigrant sections of American cities, to make the immigrant's home an American home, to recommend to state and city departments, industries, *et al.,* methods of carrying into immigrant sections American ideas and standards of cleanliness, ventilation, hygiene, sanitation, and the like, and finally to cooperate with health departments in making it impossible for ignorance of American customs, climate, and conditions to lower the standards of public health. As part of this latter point, the Committee stressed the necessity of acquainting the American populace with the fact that it was impossible for the immigrants to observe standards of living which they did not know and which had never been interpreted to them.[33]

33 The above mentioned program and the role of the Committee were both explained in detail in a pamphlet issued in March 1916. Describing itself as a clearing house for all information concerning the Americanization of the immigrant, the agency outlined the work which the various civic groups

The National Americanization Committee launched its "America First" campaign at a dinner at the home of Vincent Astor in New York City on October 15, 1915. Speakers emphasized the necessity for support of the Committee's program as well as for preparedness on both the military and civilian side. It was only too apparent that the Committee was making a strong bid to have its Americanization program made a part of the general preparedness campaign which had seized the country as the result of America's increasing diplomatic difficulties with Germany.[34] Shortly thereafter, the Committee prepared and issued a syllabus on civics for public school work, which was printed by the Federal Bureau of Education. It

---

could play in helping the movement along. Included were schools, courts, municipal departments and bureaus, colleges, patriotic organizations, women's clubs, etc. Of significant interest were the suggestions made by the Committee *re* chambers of commerce, industries, labor organizations, and ethnic societies. In regard to the first, the Committee suggested they serve as clearing houses for Americanization activities, working out follow-up systems for employers with reference to night school records, presenting to cities and boards of estimate the importance of Americanization work. Industries were urged to support the night school authorities in getting the men to school and keeping them there, to distribute leaflets through pay-envelopes especially in places where the establishment of night schools was delayed, to adapt a policy of preferring men who were in attendance at night schools and were making an effort to learn English, to follow up the night school progress of such men, to promote American citizenship through the use of slips in pay envelopes, noon hour talks, and posters, and to stabilize and promote the community and social efficiency of immigrant workmen through proper organization of industrial relations work inside the plant, as well as a healthy and happy community life outside the plant. Labor organizations were urged to translate American industrial conditions and ideals to the foreign-born workers, to interpret the principles of labor organization, and to encourage American standards of living and American investments. Ethnic societies were urged to interest 'racial' leaders in the Americanization of their less fortunate fellow countrymen from abroad, to translate to America the artistic, intellectual, and spiritual tendencies and capacities of their particular 'racial' groups, and to give direction to the work of Americanization so that the best of the native qualities might be retained in the process of Americanization. *Cf.* National Americanization Committee, *A Call to National Service*, New York, Mar. 31, 1916, pp. 3-6.

34 Editorial, "The Campaign for Better Citizenship", *American Leader*, VIII, No. 9 (Nov. 11, 1915), p. 520.

also prepared a course to train men and women to become leaders in Americanization work, and appealed to approximately 150 colleges to take the initiative in training these individuals.[35]

The Committee realized that in urging Americanization through the use of the English language and preparation for citizenship it was preaching a gospel largely incapable of fulfillment because of the weakness of existing facilities for the preparation of citizenship, and because of the fact that thousands of immigrant communities had no night schools or classes for such a program. Moreover, many boards of education had yet to be educated to the need for such classes, while hundreds of thousands of immigrants lived in remote construction camps with scanty educational facilities if any at all. The Committee, therefore, devised a series of simple lessons in citizenship as a means of attempting to aid the process of Americanization where normal facilities for such education were lacking. The lessons were issued in pamphlet form, and were designed to put into the pay envelopes of the immigrant laborers. Stressing the traditional American ideals, these were printed in each of the various languages and formed an exceedingly simple set of instructions on the requirements for citizenship and on the laws of health and social conduct. The Committee reported their enthusiastic acceptance by employers of immigrant labor. Some of these reported that to many of their workmen the lessons formed their first contact with the aims of American citizenship.[36]

To carry out its *English First* campaign, the National Americanization Committee decided upon an experiment. The Board of Education of Detroit had become increasingly aware of the tremendous problem besetting it in the form of a population which consisted of 75% foreign-born. Realizing that Detroit

35 *Ibid.*, pp. 517-520.

36 "Citizenship through the Pay Envelope", *Immigrants in America Review*, I, No. 3 (Sept. 1915), p. 12.

employers would have more influence on their help than any other force, the Committee appealed to the Detroit Board of Commerce for help in the matter. The two agencies, thereupon, joined forces to sponsor an *English First* movement in the Michigan metropolis in the fall of 1915.[37]

With the aid of the Committee's agents, the Board of Commerce contacted employers of immigrant labor and all agencies working with the immigrant in the city and sold them the idea of convincing non-English-speaking workmen of the advantages of learning English. The employers chose different methods to bring the night schools to the attention of their men. Some put the matter in charge of a ' Safety First ' committee; others deputized a special executive officer to look after the work. On September 8, the men were assembled in many factories at noon and given talks on the relationship of night school work to their chances of getting and keeping a job. Practically every factory and shop of the city displayed large posters furnished by the National Americanization Committee, while small notices concerning the night schools were placed in the pay envelopes. Large handbills giving the location of the schools were circulated among the men. A number of the employers made a careful canvass of their plants and kept records of the returns on the night school question. The Employers' Association seconded the appeal of the Board of Commerce by sending out a special letter to all employers on its list urging their active cooperation.[38]

The Detroit Board of Commerce suggested that employers, in addition to aiding in advertising the night school opening among their men, also give the night school experiment sustained support by following up the night school attendance

37 Esther Everett Lape, " The 'English First' Movement in Detroit ", *Immigrants in America Review*, I, No. 3 (Sept. 1915), pp. 46-50. For complete account of the crusade in Detroit, *cf.* National Americanization Committee, *Americanizing a City, the Campaign for the Detroit Night Schools Conducted in Co-operation with the Detroit Board of Commerce and Board of Education, August–September 1915*, New York, Dec. 15, 1915.

and the progress of their men in such classes. A number of
concerns not only adopted this suggestion, but declared that
they would make it imperative for their men to attend night
school. One factory announced that all its non-English-speaking employees must attend night school or the classes conducted in the factory or face dismissal. Others gave their men
notice that they preferred to employ men going to night school
and those making an effort to learn English.[88]

In conducting the campaign, the Detroit Board worked
through every agency which might serve its purpose. The
Ford Motor Company's moving picture department made moving pictures of a line at the Employers' Association Bureau
showing the turning away of the men unable to understand
English, thus emphasizing how indispensable a knowledge of
English was in obtaining employment. The film was shown
in the various theatres of Detroit and elsewhere. Editors of
newspapers both American and foreign-language cooperated
in publicizing the campaign and in offering suggestions. Pastors of foreign-language churches cooperated, while social
agencies aided in advertising the campaign in the foreign districts, and fraternal and civic bodies aided the efforts of the
employers.[88]

The results were phenomenal. Registration in the night
schools rose to over 153% over the attendance of the previous
year. Moreover, employers, civic groups, church officials, and
a score of others, had Americanization brought to their attention in a fashion which the Board felt could not have been
accomplished in any other way. Both the Board and the National Americanization Committee felt that their campaign
had been a success. The experiment of full-fledged Americanization had been tried and at least on the surface undertaken
successfully. The Detroit experiment was to be repeated time
and time again in the future.[88]

38 *Ibid., passim.*

The National Americanization Committee had realized already the important role which industry could play in the Americanization drive. It had made an analysis of conditions existing among the immigrants in those industries upon which preparedness depended and had suggested measures to diminish strikes and sabotage.[39] Now, as the result of the Detroit experiment, the Committee recognized that effective Americanization work among aliens inevitably meant active steps through the medium of the industrial plants of America, for here in this important economic area seemed to lie the real " melting pot ". Members of the Committee felt that ' industrial Americanization' was the great need of the day and the work of the future. Unless employers made this their great patriotic duty, i. e., to establish industrial justice for the alien and for the American workmen alike, there could be "no enduring Americanization and no sound nationalism ".[40]

The Committee therefore set about, again on a national scale, to interest the employers of immigrant labor in Americanization. The Detroit experiment had shown their willingness to cooperate if given the opportunity. The group felt consequently that its best approach would be through the cooperation of the Chamber of Commerce of the United States, to which most of the industries employing immigrant labor were associated in one way or another. The Committee brought the matter to the attention of John H. Fahey, then president of the Chamber (also a member of the National Americanization Committee), who agreed whole-heartedly to the suggestions of the Committee. Fahey recommended to the Board of Directors of the Chamber that an Immigration Committee be appointed to encourage the Americanization of the immigrant with special emphasis being placed upon its new phase, " Industrial Americanization ". The Directors approved the

39 Editorial, " The Campaign for Better Citizenship ", *op. cit.*, pp. 517-520.

40 Committee for Immigrants in America, *Memorandum to the Advisory Commission, op. cit.*, pp. 8-9.

plan in December 1915, and voted the new Immigration Committee a small appropriation. The latter was very generously enlarged by the Committee for Immigrants in America and the National Americanization Committee. The new agency of the Chamber then set itself up as a center of Americanization activities for local chambers of commerce, trade associations, and industrial plants, and made plans for carrying the crusade to the attention of these groups. It did not begin to function, however, until the beginning of the new year, 1916.[41]

In the meantime, the National Americanization Committee continued its drive to win over the general public through utilizing the services and prestige of the Federal Bureau of Education. The latter agency distributed over 150,000 " America First " posters as a means of publicizing the night school movement and of attracting the immigrant to attend. The posters set forth in English and seven foreign languages the advantages of attending night school and learning the English language. The Bureau reported that the response to the posters was definite and conclusive, for not only was a perceptible increase in attendance noted, but a positive demand for night schools came from many sections where such facilities had never been maintained. A considerable number of communities established night schools as a result, and a keen interest in the Americanization movement was developed among American citizens.[42]

The Americanizers had used the year 1915 very well indeed. Benefiting from the general uneasiness and suspicion en-

41 *Ibid.*, pp. 8-9. Members of the Immigration Committee of the Chamber of Commerce of the United States were: Frank Trumbull, chairman, Frances A. Kellor, asst. to the chairman, William Fellowes Morgan, treasurer, J. F. Donechaud, Gano Dunn, Richard H. Edmonds, Marion E. Hay, Alexander Hilton, W. F. Hypes, Herbert Myrick, Raymond B. Price, Julius Rosenwald, Bernard J. Rothwell, Bolton Smith, Felix M. Warburg, A. C. Weiss, Walter F. Willcox, and B. L. Winchell.

42 H. H. Wheaton, " Education of the Immigrants " *Report of the Commissioner of Education for the Year Ended June 30, 1916*, I, *op. cit.*, pp. 350-351.

gendered by the European War and the rise of a spirit of American patriotism and nationalism, the advocates of a strong domestic policy for the Americanization of the foreign-born were able, through excellent publicity and well-thought-out campaigns, to convince a substantial portion of the American populace of the urgent need for action along the lines first advocated as early as 1908. The following year, 1916, was to see a continuance of the crusade and the even firmer entrenchment of the feeling that America's best interests and safety necessitated the complete Americanization of her immigrant residents as rapidly as possible.

# CHAPTER VI

## AMERICANIZATION ENDEAVORS DURING THE YEAR 1916

THE new year, 1916, opened auspiciously for the Americanizers with the holding of a National Conference on Immigration and Americanization on January 19 and 20 at Philadelphia. The Conference had been called by the National Americanization Committee in the belief that through such a conference the work of Americanization might be given a better national outlook, and that certain standards might be worked out to adapt the work to the " national needs and opportunities of the present through the mutual understanding and cooperation that would result." The Committee had asked for the cooperation of all agencies interested in the assimilation of the immigrant by sending representatives to the Conference.[1]

The National Conference met to devote itself explicitly to the problems which had arisen as a result of the past year's

1 Editorial " National Conference on Immigration and Americanization ", *Immigrants in America Review*, I, No. 4 (Jan. 1916), pp. 10-11. The Committee in its letters to the various agencies and mayors, etc., asking them to send representatives to the Conference, stressed the important role which Americanization could play in the national preparedness effort. After explaining that the Conference would deal with citizenship, the education of the immigrant adults, housing, American standards of living, and the like, the Committee added : " This Committee appreciates your interest and cooperation, which made 'Americanization Day' a country-wide success and which launched the enthusiastic movement for making our many people into one nation. It believes that Congress and this country will not be ' prepared ', if we consider only military necessities and not the complicated questions of social and economic preparedness so essential to good industrial relations, expanding trade conditions, the living conditions of our own people, and a strong national spirit. The most important part of this social and economic preparedness naturally falls to the state and city governments and the Committee asks your co-operation by requesting that you send representatives to this first national conference on Americanization, and that you will give the matter such publicity as you may deem advisable." *Cf.* Editorial, *Immigrants in American Review*, II, No. 1 (Apr. 1916), p. 38.

work. Addresses were delivered on practically every phase of the Americanization problem, including sanitation and health, and analyses of the difficulties of the situation made by such people of prominence as Frank Trumbull of the Chamber of Commerce of the United States, John Price Jackson, Commissioner of Labor and Industry of Pennsylvania, Governor Martin G. Brumbaugh, Commissioner of Education, P. P. Claxton, Albert Shiels of the New York City Department of Education, Robert Bliss of the American Library Commission, Peter Roberts of the Y.M.C.A., Louis F. Post, Assistant-Secretary of Labor, social workers Grace Abbott and Mary Antin, former President Theodore Roosevelt, and many others.[2]

In the eyes of the National Americanization Committee, what had been accomplished as a result of the conference was a three-fold success, because, for the first time, philanthropic, business, civic, and educational organizations had been brought together to discuss the problem of Americanization as it affected them all; for the first time, Americanization had been recognized as a national movement requiring uniform standards of approach and procedure; for the first time, government and private organizations of all kinds and creeds had pledged themselves to cooperate in carrying out Americanization as a national endeavor.[3] It was, therefore, with enthusiasm that the Committee prepared to carry on with its program, knowing that proper contacts had been made and sympathetic response had been engendered in strategic circles throughout the nation.

Reaching out into yet another channel, the National Americanization Committee solicited the aid and help of that very influential group, the rapidly growing women's clubs and organizations. The Committee felt that these groups could do much to educate sentiment in support of the movement and to

2 Editorial, " National Conference on Immigration and Amercanization ", *Immigrants in America Review*, II, No. 1 (Apr. 1916), p. 39; for text of speeches, *cf.* pp. 40-46.

3 *Ibid.*, p. 46.

influence boards of health, boards of education, housing committees, and other groups in the work of Americanizing the foreign-born particularly the foreign-born women. The response from the ladies was enthusiastic and keen. Mrs. Percy V. Pennypacker, president of the General Federation of Women's Clubs, endorsed the plan presented by the Committee and agreed to make Americanization a part of her executive work. Suggestions by the National Americanization Committee on civics and education were adopted by the chairmen of the Committees on Civic and Education Departments. State federations took up the work, with those of New York, Pennsylvania, Ohio, and Michigan, in the lead. Both the New York City Federation and the Chicago Women's Club appointed special committees which engaged actively in Americanization work along the lines of aid to libraries and night schools, in particular, and by sponsoring special classes in civics.[4] Mrs. Pennypacker sent out a circular letter to the various state federations and clubs urging them to take an active part in the Americanization of Immigrant women, together with copies of the pamphlet, *Americanization, What Women's Organizations Can Do,* which had been prepared by the National Americanization Committee for that purpose. At the same time, the Committee urged upon all women interested in the social and civic welfare of their communities the importance of their undertaking definite Americanization work.[5]

The National Americanization Committee also secured the aid of the National Society of the Daughters of the American Revolution. The latter pledged their cooperation and used the service of their extended machinery to bring to individual women throughout the country an appeal to take part in the development of the Americanization movement. The national

4 Editorial, "Americanization Work of Women's Clubs", *Immigrants in America Review,* I, No. 4 (Jan. 1916), p. 64.

5 Anne Rhodes, "Americanization through Women's Organization", *Immigrants in America Review,* II, No. 1 (Apr. 1916), pp. 71-73.

chairman of patriotic education, Mrs. James G. Dunning, sent
out letters to the regents of the various chapters of the D.A.R.
requesting the stimulation of public school work, library work,
and industrial cooperation on behalf of that "portion of the
immigrant tide least often thought of and planned for—the
immigrant woman" to the end that American standards of
living and learning might be made possible to them and to
their families and homes.[6]

Both the Women's Clubs and the D.A.R. were "stirred"
to enthusiastic action, the Committee reported, with the result
that new impetus was added to the Americanization movement
from this source and fresh activities engaged in. Night school
classes were encouraged and developed. Graduation exercises
were attended by the groups and a patriotic air engendered in
the proceedings. New editions of the already current Citizenship Manual of the D.A.R. were projected. The Federal
Bureau of Education was urged to produce a standard system
of teaching English and citizenship, home economics, and
other subjects of value to the immigrant. As a result of this
support of Americanization efforts, both organizations reported
having received a stream of letters daily asking for help in
forming programs of study and for advice in meeting local
situations. Practically every state group responded to the call
of the national chairmen, while many examples of enthusiastic
work carried on by local groups were received. The national
heads of both organizations sent letters of progress to the
local committees and clubs as a stimulating aid to further
effort.[7]

Having engaged the various women's organizations in action
along the lines of Americanization, the National Americanization Committee next turned its attention to arousing interest in the problem of bettering the environmental conditions
surrounding the immigrant. It felt that in this area in particu-

6 *Ibid.*, pp. 71-73.

7 *Ibid.*, pp. 71-73.

lar serious conditions existed that would have to be remedied before true Americanization could take place. A number of surveys of small industrial towns in respect to housing facilities and sanitary conditions were made in April 1916. Realizing, however, that it could not possibly reach all the thousands of such towns directly, and feeling that there was a great need for a country-wide movement to improve conditions, the Committee began to lay plans for some practical way of bettering the immigrant housing situation. It was felt that minimum requirements for an American home should be defined for the immigrant workmen and communities, and that employers must be impressed with the fact that improved housing meant better health, stronger men and women, and community happiness which would result in greater contentment and efficiency. The Committee decided to accomplish these results through inaugurating an Americanization campaign which should have housing as its central note. To stimulate interest, a special 'housing competition' was launched on February 1, at a luncheon given by Mrs. Vincent Astor at her home in New York City. Mrs. William B. Cutting made the competition possible by donating the Committee's competition fund.[8]

The competition was divided into two parts, a housing contest and a railroad-car contest. The first had as its object the securing of plans for workingmen's homes suited to industrial towns of not more than 35,000 population. Prizes in this part of the competition totaled $1,800, with the first prize $300, the 2nd $100 for each of four problems involved in the contest, and an additional prize of $200 for excellence of construction. Competitors were asked to supply plans for single families, boarding houses, and family houses. The object of the car competition was to furnish a satisfactory substitute for the freight cars used to house construction gangs along the railroads. The prizes in this latter phase of the competition

8 Editorial, "The Immigrant Housing Competition", *Immigrants in America Review*, II, No. 1 (Apr. 1916), p. 55.

included $300 for the first, $200 for the second, and $100 for the third.[9]

The response to the preliminary announcement of the competition in the public press and the interest expressed by many different groups proved to be so spontaneous that a special Housing Committee was formed to take care of the correspondence and publicity in connection with the campaign. The National Americanization Committee realized from the start that the educational side of the work would far outweigh the actual competition in final importance. It reported being especially pleased with the cooperation and publicity given to the contest by architectural and engineering groups.[10]

The competition closed on July 1. As a result of the contest, many evidences of interest were reported on the part of employers and small industrial communities of exactly the kind that could profit from the results of the competition. Advance news of the competition was sent to many of these towns, and in many cases editors seized eagerly upon the story of the competition to comment on the needs of their own communities. The Committee felt that its competition had aroused the right kind of interest which it believed was necessary to make the movement nation-wide in scope, and that it had achieved its object, namely, to interest the persons in whose power it lay to put the results of the competition to direct practical use. A movement had been set afoot which it hoped might become in time a widespread experiment in making American standards of living prevail in those industrial communities having foreign-born residents.[11]

The Committee continued to propagandize on behalf of its program during 1916 by distributing pamphlet literature, including a professional course for service among immigrants. The latter recommended topics for study and desirable reading

9 *Ibid.*, pp. 55-57.

10 *Ibid.*, p. 56.

11 *Ibid.*, p. 56.

material.[12] Another pamphlet issued by the group gave suggestions on how to carry through a successful Americanization program for the coming Fourth of July. Profiting from its experience of the preceding year, the Committee outlined a program which took into full consideration the matters of finance, publicity, committees, the press, the churches, and many other factors necessary to make the venture a complete success. Programs of correct procedure were given in the pamphlet, including flag ceremonies, pledges of allegiance, pageants, parades, and citizenship receptions.[13] A supplementary pamphlet, already mentioned, *Call to National Service,* was brought out in the spring of 1916. It outlined briefly the activities of the Committee, the need for Americanization, and the role which every group—racial, social, civic, industrial, and business—could play in the movement.[14]

In the meantime, the New York Department of Education had brought out a new citizenship syllabus which the National Americanization Committee engaged in distributing. The syllabus, considered quite an improvement over the existing aids in training for citizenship, was planned to be used as a textbook in the night schools of the state.[15]

The activities of the Americanizers had until this time aroused no opposition. Now, however, in 1916, strong suspicion of the motives of the propagandists and of the National Americanization Committee, in particular, began to express itself in one important quarter, that of organized labor. Labor's reactions to the Americanization movement were of a decidedly mixed nature. Recognition of the need for educating the im-

12 Committee for Immigrants in America, *Professional Course for Service among Immigrants,* New York, 1916.

13 National Americanization Committee, *Americanization Day—Fourth of July,* 1916.

14 National Americanization Committee, *A Call to National Service,* New York, Mar. 31, 1916. See above, Chapter V, pp. 126-127.

15 Committee for Immigrants in America, *Citizenship Syllabus,* Albany, 1916 [pamphlet published by the New York Department of Education].

migrant in regard to American institutions and ways of life and in a knowledge of the English language was universal. Doubts, however, as to the motives of certain of the Americanizers, and demands that the movement, in order to be successful, should be accompanied by reforms in labor conditions, unionization, and increases in wages, were expressed by certain of the labor leaders.

Samuel Gompers, head of the American Federation of Labor, writing in the August 1916 issue of the *American Federationist,* summarized the feelings of Labor on this score:

> It is not reasonable to expect an intelligent understanding of American ideals or patriotism among those whose daily lives are filled with industrial injustice and who meet with nothing but abuse and exploitation. Any serious attempt to Americanize the foreign-workers who have been crowded into our industrial centers and our mining districts must concern itself also with the problem of Americanizing employers, trusts, and corporations. Before the employes of the United States Steel Corporation can have an opportunity to understand the ideal for which America stands, the United States Steel Corporation must first express that ideal in its dealings with its employes. So long as that corporation hires armed thugs to beat into submission workers who have the manhood to make a fight for their rights, that corporation will remain an institution destructive to the American spirit and an obstacle to the work of Americanizing aliens within our country. The United States Steel Corporation, as well as many other institutions with similar methods and standards, has taken away from aliens who have already been wronged through being lured to this country through false pretenses, opportunities to earn a decent living, to give their families decent homes, food, and clothing and the things necessary to make life worth while; and gravest of all it has robbed them of their ideals, their faith in mankind, and proper respect for their own personalities.[16]

16 Samuel Gompers, "Americanizing Foreign Workers", *American Federationist,* XXIII (Aug. 1916), pp. 689-690.

Frank P. Walsh, of the United Mine Workers, challenged
the motives of the National Americanization Committee
sharply when the latter refused to endorse and urge the use
of American trade and labor unions as Americanization
agencies by claiming these were outside the Committee's sphere.
In a letter to Frank Trumbull, chairman of the Committee,
Walsh claimed he was forced to draw only one conclusion
after their refusal and a study of the literature issued by the
Committee:

> I am forced to believe that the last thing your committee
> desires is the Americanization of the immigrant, and that in-
> stead you are attempting to set up a paternalism that will
> bring the workers of this country even more absolutely under
> the control of the employers than they are at present.
>
> Among the active members of your committee are many
> large employers who are relentlessly resisting any movement
> that threatens to free their employes from industrial tyranny
> and gross economic exploitation and by thus freeing them to
> Americanize them in the only true sense in which that word
> can be used.

Walsh stated that he could not find the merest suggestion in
the program offered by the Committee that offered relief to
the wage-earner from the wretched conditions that prevailed
on the New York Subway, largely financed by Edward Stotesbury, one of the Committee's members, or among the em-
ployes of the Pennsylvania Railroad, deprived of their freedom
by an elaborate spy system and armed guards, which corporation was headed by Samuel Rea, as president, another of the
Committee's members. Others of the Committee cited by
Walsh as not having treated labor fairly in the past included
Jacob H. Schiff, director of Western Union, Charles H.
Mackey of Postal Telegraph, Howard Elliott, president of the
New Haven Railroad, Frank Trumbull, executive head of the
Illinois Central Railroad, and Elbert H. Gary, president of
the United States Steel Corporation. Nor did Walsh see any

indication on the part of the Committee to strike at the system which " permits the idle few to amass high fortunes through their control of natural resources and thereby exact a heavy toll in rents and other unearned revenues from the foreign-born workers who inhabit the tenements of the cities and are dependent for food and shelter on the natural resources thus controlled and plundered by men who perform no service." Continuing, he saw little hope of such action when some of the Committee's most active members, Mrs. Vincent Astor, Mrs. Cornelius Vanderbilt, and Mrs. Edward Stotesbury, were the most notorious recipients of unearned income obtained through the exploitation of land and other natural resources.

On the contrary, I find much positive evidence that your efforts are primarily directed to strengthening the chain of industrial tyranny in this country. You propose to sanctify and confirm oppression by waving the American flag in the the face of its victims and by insidiously stigmatizing as un-patriotic any attempts they may make to throw off the yoke of the exploiting interests you represent.

You cite with approval the policy of employers who have used compulsion to force workmen into night schools where they may learn English. You would have employers extend their arbitrary control over the lives of the workers' leisure hours, dictating to them what they shall do in the evening and threatening them with the loss of their opportunity to earn a living — that is, with starvation for themselves and their familes, if they do not obey.

And it is admitted by you that this hateful use of arbi-trary power by the employer is for the purpose of defeating the efforts of strike agitators, preventing strikes, and in-creasing the economic value of the worker to his employer.

You admit frankly that your problem is the ' economic problem of giving the immigrant a chance as a piece of benevolent paternalism ' and it does not seem to occur to you that the arbitrary control over the lives of others which permits this paternalism is, together with the economic exploitation and injustice which accompany it, the greatest foe of those things which our forefathers loved and for which America stands.

Walsh did not doubt that the Committee would be friendly to slight wage increases in industries where exploitation had gone to the limit and revolt of workers seemed imminent, but he likened such action to those who kept livestock well fed and healthy in order that they might work the harder and bear their burdens less complainingly. Disagreeing with the action of the Committee, Walsh claimed the use of trade unions was not outside the Committee's sphere. "If you are determined wilfully to neglect the American trade and labor union as an Americanization influence of first importance, I cannot avoid the conclusion that docile subserviency, not Americanization, is what you desire." [17]

Secretary Paul Scharrenberg, of the California State Federation of Labor, viewed the progress of the Americanization movement with tongue in cheek. Claiming that the trade union movement was the most potent factor in the Americanization of the immigrants, Scharrenberg stated in an address at Los Angeles to the Convention of the California State Federation of Labor, that the aliens needed more than patriotic talks. In many cases, their living conditions were far worse than those they left on the other side. It was for this reason that they were disappointed in their homes and ambitions and had turned from the spirit of Americanism and surrendered to the spirit born of actual conditions of their lives—a spirit of revolt against society. "The patriotic address, the flag-waving exercises, the 'welfare work', however well meant and however successful their appeal to the emotions, leave untouched the real need to realize in practical ways the promised opportunity for liberty and full development upon the highest plane of

17 Frank P. Walsh, "Americanization and Liberty Eliminated", *United Mine Workers' Journal*, XXV, No. 39 (Feb. 3, 1916), p. 7. Evidently impressed with the arguments presented by Walsh, the Committee included labor unions as agencies for Americanization, *cf.* Chapter V, Note 31, p. 127.

social justice and equality." Claiming that the labor union was the only movement of fundamental reform in the condition of labor, Scharrenberg went further and added that it was the only movement that made for Americanization by making for the establishment in the daily lives of the people of that condition which labor regarded as the essence of Americanism, the opportunity for full social justice. " What a hollow mockery is all talk of Americanization unless the ' Americanizers ' see to it that sufficient leisure is provided to enable the immigrant to take advantage of the educational opportunities offered. In this particular field of endeavor—shortening the work day—the labor union has been the pioneer and has maintained the leadership right up to date." [18]

Indicative, too, of the reaction of organized labor to the efforts of the Americanizers was the series of editorials which appeared in the *United Mine Workers' Journal* during the year 1916. Recognition was given to the need for the education of the immigrants and the necessity for their assimilation, but emphasis was placed on the elimination of many of the existing evils in the treatment of labor, on increasing wages, and on the usefulness of the trade union as an Americanizing medium. Typical of the trend of thought of this important labor journal was the editorial which appeared in the July 6, 1916 issue, which read as follows:

> We assert here, as we have claimed in previous articles, that the labor union is the greatest factor toward the assimilation, the Americanization, of the workers from abroad. In the labor union halls we find means to make them understand the problems of the workers; we soon find that they have long recognized our problems as theirs. That only lack of understanding each other ever stood between us; and this we find means to overcome.
>
> However, we cannot but recognize how much simpler would be our task if all the workers could be taught to under-

---

18 Paul Scharrenberg, " Immigrants Need More Than Patriotic Talks ", *United Mine Workers' Journal*, XXVII, No. 5 (June 1, 1916), p. 6.

stand, to speak, and to read the one language, and as the English language does and should predominate in this country, we can only see advantage in any program calculated to make possible for foreign-speaking workers instruction in the language of this country.

Possibly this movement for ' Americanization ' was never initiated with intent to better the conditions of the workers. But if in this movement we see the possibility of advantage that may accrue it behooves us to give it our support.

We have said that we know how to reach our foreign brothers when we meet in union labor halls. Yes, but before we are able to meet with them there, often incalculable damage has been done to our cause and to theirs, owing, as we have said before, to the want of mutual distrust made possible by the fact that we cannot talk a common mother tongue.

Whatever might be the motives of those who are advocating Americanization of the foreign workers through education in the English language, we can only see possible advantage to all the workers of this country in the success of this program.[19]

The attitude taken by the *United Mine Workers' Journal,* namely that through the Americanization movement nothing but possible advantage could accrue to the cause of labor, became the dominant attitude of labor in regard to the movement, particularly when state and federal agencies began to play an ever more important role during the ' War ' years. Criticism of the Americanizers ceased from this quarter as the movement gained momentum after 1916.[20]

While the National Americanization Committee continued to spearhead the drive for the Americanization of the immigrant, the newly appointed Committee on Immigration of the Chamber of Commerce of the United States began to play an active part in the campaign.[21] It had made a survey of the

---

19 Editorial, "Americanization", *United Mine Workers' Journal,* XXVII, No. 10 (July 6, 1916), p. 5; also, *ibid.,* XXVII, No. 28, pp. 4-5.

20 See below, Chapter IX, pp. 261-264.

21 See above, Chapter V, pp. 131-132.

field of immigration and found that the usual immigration problems of admission and restriction and of the distribution of the labor supply had been upset by the conditions abroad. It found an insistent demand for practical Americanization work to strengthen the country's unity, as well as for measures which would interest the foreign-born resident in remaining in the United States at the close of the war. To meet these demands, the Committee on Immigration adopted a six-point program of work to consist of:

1. The preparation of a Service Bulletin with suggestive programs of work, so that constructive campaigns to secure the use of the English language and to promote better citizenship might result.
2. The organization of 'America First' dinners on Washington's Birthday, February 22, 1916, under the auspices of the local chambers of commerce, to discuss industrial and labor conditions, and how best to bring together American and foreign-born residents.
3. The sponsoring of an inquiry into the probable effects of the war on immigration and emigration by means of questionnaires to be sent out to railroads and steamship agencies and other sources of information.
4. The distribution by individual industries through the medium of chambers of commerce of a 'pay envelope series' of twelve civic lesson leaflets for better citizenship, printed in English and in foreign languages.
5. The following up of proposed legislation on immigration matters so that definite action might be recommended.
6. The making of immigration surveys for local chambers of commerce and industries in isolated communities, so that practical Americanization work might be undertaken.[22]

22 *Report of the Committee on Immigration of the Chamber of Commerce of the United States of America, 5th. Annual Meeting* [of the Chamber, not of the Committee], Washington, Jan. 31–Feb. 1 and 2, 1917, p. 3. The Committee announced the reasons for its formation as follows: "The nationwide Americanization movement is part of the present day trend toward humanizing industries. It aims to take what is commonly called welfare

Accordingly, the Committee inaugurated its program with the publication of its service *Bulletin,* which first appeared as of April 1, 1916, and was published as a monthly bulletin on the first of each month thereafter. In addition to serving the purpose of acting as a channel whereby the Committee could reach each of the local chambers with the need for Americanization and of industrial Americanization in particular, the *Bulletin* noted month by month the progress of the movement throughout the country.[23]

The Committee on Immigration, through the cooperation of the National Americanization Committee and the Committee for Immigrants in America, made surveys of industrial plants and communities in 244 industrial towns in Connecticut, Illinois, Delaware, Kansas, Indiana, Maryland, Michigan, Missouri, New Jersey, New York, Ohio, Pennsylvania, Rhode Island, and Virginia, during the year to learn the conditions which surrounded the immigrant workmen in these states. Data gathered included the number of foreign-born adults and minors, the use of the English language and its preference or necessary use in business, the facilities for learning English, the opportunities for citizenship, the number of naturalized, the methods of securing labor, housing conditions, sanitation facilities, the conditions of women and children, the number

---

work out of paternalism and make it a part of legitimate business organization everywhere. There is no agreement among American employers now as to the extent and manner of its organization or where it really belongs. There are no recognized standards. What we need is to extend scientific methods to the human phase of industrial organization and give welfare work a more definite place and recognized standards. The engineer as the consulting mind of industry must be a leader in this work but the Chamber of Commerce must be the clearing house by which men may know what is being done and why some experiments fail and others succeed. The Immigration Committee of the Chamber of Commerce is acting as such a clearing house and standardizing agency for local chambers of commerce and industrial industries. These considerations induced the Chamber of Commerce of the United States of America to appoint an Immigration Committee in December 1915 ". *Ibid.,* p. 2.

23 *Ibid.,* pp. 3-4.

of immigrant savings and investments, the number and type of recreational facilities, and the general community life of the immigrants. A summary of this information was sent to the local chambers of commerce and other commercial bodies as well as to industries and local organizations with definite recommendations for practical Americanization work. Among the conditions recommended to the local chambers and to the large industrial plants as requiring attention were: the heavy turnover in industries employing immigrant workmen, the generally inadequate housing facilities, the congestion due to the 'boarder' system, unsanitary conditions created by the growth of mushroom towns, the lack of American influences in the homelife of the immigrant workingmen, the need for facilities for learning English and American social ideals, and the need for insuring to the immigrants equal opportunities with the native-born for work and recreation.[24]

The Chamber's Committee reported a nation-wide interest in " industrial Americanization ". This it defined as a program of action which would result in the establishment of the fundamental principles of Americanism in the relationship of men in all industries protected by the ' American flag '. The minimum requirements for such a program seemed to the Committee to consist of American citizenship and undivided allegiance, a common language, an American standard of living, one American industrial standard, a home stake in America, reasonable stability of population, and industrial justice—the same standard for both employer and employed. To bring this more clearly to the attention of the local chambers, the Committee arranged through the chambers of commerce of fourteen cities a series of Industrial Americanization Conferences at which local conditions were presented, principles of work discussed, and methods of Americanization outlined.[25]

24 Chamber of Commerce of the United States of America, Committee on Immigration, *Bulletins,* 1 to 46, Apr. 1, 1916–Aug. 20, 1918.

25 *Report of Committee on Immigration, op. cit.,* pp. 4-5.

Many cities followed up the suggestions offered, and a number of improvements were reported as having been made in various industries as a result. New Haven, Conn., made an industrial and social survey of its city. Youngstown, Ohio, secured the services of a paid secretary to organize and direct the Americanization work, and created a council on immigration among the leaders of the foreign-born residents to distribute information on health, sanitation, police regulations, thrift, and housing. It also organized Americanization activities in industrial plants throughout the city and stimulated the development of trade schools. Akron, Ohio, raised $2,000 among its leading industries to establish free night schools to teach the adult immigrant English and civics. Boston initiated a vigorous campaign among its industries to secure 1,000 more new citizens, while the local chamber actively supported a bill for a permanent state board of immigration. Buffalo cooperated with the Civic Association in its city-wide work, including the taking of a census of plants employing foreign-born workers. The Chamber secured also an additional appropriation of $7,000 from the city for night school work.[26]

Chicago, through conferences with various interested agencies arranged by the Association of Commerce, succeeded in arousing city-wide interest in Americanization and enlisted the Board of Education to the extent of opening day schools for aliens unable to attend night school. Hoboken, N. J., pursued actively a campaign directed by the Board of Trade to increase enrollment in the evening schools, secured publicity for the campaign in the newspapers, and distributed a pamphlet, entitled *Foreign-Born Residents Should Be Reminded,* freely among the citizens of the city. It undertook also an industrial census of its immigrant workers. St. Louis, through its Business Men's League, adopted a program providing for a citizenship and educational census of the foreign-born workmen in its industrial plants, made arrangements for the continuation

26 *Ibid.,* p. 5.

of the public evening school facilities during the spring months, and organized a city-wide Americanization campaign in the autumn of 1916. Wilkes-Barre, Pa., organized the first Americanization conference of a coal district on May 1, through its chamber of commerce, which included a luncheon conference for employers on Americanization by industries, a meeting of educators and others interested in educational work for the adult immigrant, and a public evening meeting for the workers of the district addressed by speakers in both English and foreign languages. As a result of the conference, Americanization activities were stimulated throughout the entire anthracite region.[27]

In many cities, the Committee on Immigration found considerable interest in the problem of immigration and a desire to undertake Americanization activities, but no organization to carry on the work. In such places it suggested the appointment of Americanization or immigration committees and placed its facilities at their disposal. Suggestions were sent out for local work and for meetings, and arrangements made to employ speakers. Through the Committee's efforts, local chambers of commerce in thirty-one cities appointed Americanization or immigrant committees.[28] In six other cities, Buffalo, Chicago, Hartford, Conn., Newark, Passaic, N. J., and Pueblo, Col., the work was assigned to some standing committee. Notable achievements were reported by many of these committees including establishment of classes in industrial plants, organization of special citizenship classes, organization of neighborhood associations in immigrant districts for Americanization in the homes, holding of special night school cam-

27 *Ibid.*, pp. 5-7.

28 *Ibid.*, p. 7. The cities were Akron, Boston, Bridgeport, Conn., Denver, Detroit, Easton, Pa., Elizabeth, N. J.. Evansville, Ind., Fall River, Fargo, N. D., Granite City, Ill., Hammond, Ind., Hoboken, Jamestown, N. Y., Kalamazoo, Kansas City, Mo., Los Angeles, Manchester, N. H., Minneapolis, Niagara Falls, New Haven, Patterson, Pittsburgh, Providence, Rochester, N. Y., Syracuse, Spokane, St. Louis, Wilkes-Barre, Pa., Youngstown, Ohio, and Yonkers, N. Y.

paigns, and arranging shop meetings under the auspicies of the committees of the local chambers and of the local boards of education.[29]

The Committee on Immigration, by means of its monthly *Bulletin,* outlined a program for an evening school campaign which should include a survey of industrial conditions and other practical suggestions on education, citizenship, sanitation, and housing. At the same time, it carried on a considerable amount of general educational work, which consisted of addresses on various aspects of industrial Americanization, the publication of special articles, and the distribution of manuals and reports. Cooperating with the National Americanization Committee, it helped distribute a series of leaflets, containing brief lessons in civics, in pay envelopes. It sent these to 700 chambers of commerce, and to about 1,000 different industries employing immigrant labor. The leaflets were printed in English, Italian, Polish, Lithuanian, Hungarian, and Slovak, and were meant to meet the need for a simple method of carrying to the immigrant workmen simple information about their immediate needs. The Committee also sponsored its ' America First ' dinner on February 22 in twenty-four cities at which employers and representatives of the foreign-born industrial forces met in many cases for the first time.[30]

In an effort to organize the interest of employers in the work and to attempt to secure some agreement on standards and methods of action, the Committee sponsored special industrial Americanization conferences. Two such conferences were held in New York City, which brought together the industrial leaders at the first, and the engineers interested in industrial organization at the second. A third conference was planned and held especially for publishers and editors. In addition to these activities, the Committee constituted itself into a service department and information bureau upon all matters affecting the immigrant and industry. The agency felt that there was a real demand for setting up standards in Americanization

29 *Ibid.,* pp. 8-9.

work, consequently, it devoted a considerable amount of its time to meeting requests from local groups and business organizations concerning the proper methods of Americanization. Through such activities as these, the Committee felt that it aided the progressive movement toward the standardization of the principles of industrial Americanization and the improvement of methods to bring about this desired end.[30] Because of its active work and influence, the Committee on Immigration of the Chamber of Commerce of the United States rapidly became one of the most powerful forces in support of the Americanization drive.

While the National Americanization Committee and the Immigration Committee of the Chamber were busily active in support of the Americanization movement during 1916, the Federal Bureau of Naturalization, under the direction of Raymond F. Crist, continued its citizenship drive along the lines laid down in 1914. During the period, September 1915 to July 1916, the Bureau distributed approximately 12,931 copies of its influential pamphlet, *Proceedings of the Naturalization Conference* held at Philadelphia, 15,014, copies of a new pamphlet entitled, *Outline Course in Citizenship*,[31] and 3,527 copies of the pamphlet entitled, *Syllabus of the Naturalization Law*,[32] all for the use of school teachers in connection with their

---

30 *Ibid.*, pp. 9-10; *cf. Bulletin*, No. 1 (Apr. 1, 1916). List of places holding dinners: San Diego, Cal., Colorado Springs, Col., Winsted, Conn., Washington, D. C., East Chicago, Ind., Portland, Ind., Kansas City, Kan., Shreveport, La., Holyoke, Mass., Kalamazoo, Mich., Detroit, Great Falls, Mont., Lewiston, Me., Rahway, N. J., Ithaca, N. Y., Little Falls, N. Y., Rochester, N. Y., Rome, N. Y., Fargo, N. D., Akron, O., Marietta, O., Pittsburgh, Spokane, and Wheeling, W. Va.

31 U. S. Bureau of Naturalization, *An Outline Course in Citizenship to Be Used in the Public Schools for the Instruction of the Foreign- and Native-Born Candidate for Adult-Citizenship Responsibilities*, Washington, 1916.

32 *Ibid., Syllabus of the Naturalization Law, an Aid to the Public School Teachers in the Instruction of Aliens in the Requirements of the Naturalization Law*, Washington, 1916.

Americanization work.[33] In doing so, the Bureau was very careful to point out that it was not attempting to assume the role of educator, but was merely serving as an aid to the public schools of the entire country in their citizenship programs. The Bureau maintained that its position was one of aiding in making public in succinct form the approved methods of instructing the foreigners in the citizenship classes, in enlarging the attendance of the foreigners at these classes, and in pursuing in the classroom its uniform policy of facilitating the naturalization of all foreigners desirous of becoming American citizens.[34]

The Federal Bureau had learned early that the greatest difficulty was experienced in securing the enrollment of adults other than those who came voluntarily. In spite of the support rendered the Bureau's efforts on the part of many agencies through the publication of notices in the public press and in public places, through appeals in the various immigrant languages, through the efforts of alien organizations, employers of labor, labor organizations, and others, and the publicity aroused by the Bureau of Education's colored posters, the naturalization agency felt some more practical plan was needed, one with a personal touch to it to bring in the vast numbers not responding. It, therefore, undertook to call upon each alien candidate for citizenship to go to the public schools for instruction through letters addressed to him and to his wife. It also requested the teachers to secure the aid of the student body in the classes for adult foreigners to prevail upon their countrymen and friends to enroll. Finally, it asked that the names and addresses of the foreign-born parents of the children in the public schools be obtained, and that personal invitations be sent to those who would be so benefited to attend them. The Bureau believed that with the full development of these avenues

33 "Report of the Commissioner of Naturalization", Reports of the Department of Labor, 1916, p. 453.

34 Ibid., pp. 458-459.

of activity, every alien in every community in time would be approached and invited to attend the public schools.[35]

Nevertheless, the federal agency reported difficulty in securing regular and continued attendance at such classes. It found that the average attendance compared very poorly with the enrollment in many of the large centers. Feeling, therefore, that some material betterment should result beyond a more or less crude ability to speak and write English, the Bureau advocated through its correspondence with the supporting organizations that prizes be offered for papers and debates upon different subjects of Americanism by students. It also continued to urge public recognition of citizenship through the presentation of certificates of graduation and naturalization and the awarding of prizes, believing these to be legitimate inducements which could be offered by the public schools and the public to secure higher proficiency and a larger attendance. The Bureau felt gratified to find that a large measure of support was given to all of its suggestions.[36]

Further investigations of the Bureau revealed great need of a standard course of instruction to occupy a certain period of time in its mastery by the foreign-born, including illiterates. For quite some time, the Bureau had been urged to prepare such a course by reason of its authority over all matters concerning naturalization. To meet this need, therefore, the Bureau compiled an *Outline Course in Citizenship* for the use of the public schools. Although it provided a standard course in citizenship instruction, the Bureau considered the pamphlet as merely a step in the advance toward standardization of methods. The *Outline* dealt with the duties of citizenship in an elementary fashion calculated to hold the interest of the alien. In compiling it, the Bureau used much of the material and suggestions furnished by the many schools throughout the nation, considering as it did, the entire public school system of

35 *Ibid.*, p. 466.
36 *Ibid.*, p. 467.

the United States as a vast national committee working with
it in the standardization of this branch of instruction.[37]

Requests had been received by the Bureau for the compilation
of the naturalization law for the use of public school teachers
along with the preliminary forms supplied by the Bureau to
the foreigners. Such a syllabus was prepared to meet this need,
and distributed widely among the teachers of citizenship classes.
Requests had been made, too, for the preparation of a textbook
on citizenship for use in the naturalization classes. To meet
this appeal, the Bureau wrote to the various superintendents
of schools engaged in the work, requesting that they send in
copies of courses of instruction then in use and any other materials of value. From the material accumulated, the Bureau
proceeded to construct its textbook. The book did not make
its appearance, however, until 1917.[38]

To further attendance of immigrants at citizenship classes,
the federal agency prepared individual school cards for each
immigrant who applied for citizenship papers, and sent these
to the school superintendents, hoping in this way to have the
school authorities follow through and see that the applicants
entered classes for proper training.[39] In this connection, it reported that splendid cooperation had been received from the
public school authorities in support of its general program.
From the original 38 cities and towns that had first responded
enthusiastically to the appeal of the Secretary of Labor of July
20, 1915 in support of the Bureau's program, the number of
towns and cities that agreed to cooperate with the Bureau in
carrying on citizenship classes increased to 93 in September,
to 217 in October, to 290 in November 1915, and rapidly
thereafter until the number reached 613 by July 1, 1916 and
over 1,000 by the end of 1916.[40]

37 Ibid., p. 467.

38 Ibid., p. 468.

39 Ibid., pp. 469-470.

40 Ibid., p. 476.

Turning its attention to the immigrant wife in the citizenship betterment program, the Federal Bureau wrote a special letter personally addressed to the wives of the 49,094 petitioners and declarants during the year, telling them of the advantages which would result from their attendance upon the public schools. The name of each wife was sent also upon an individual card to the public school in the community where the candidate lived hoping through acquaintance with this institution to enable her to get some conception of the meaning of the American home and to aid her in establishing American standards of living.[41]

The Bureau of Naturalization aided the Americanization movement by sponsoring a Citizenship Convention in Washington, D. C., during the week of July 10, 1916. Raymond F. Crist, Commissioner of Naturalization, presided. Addresses were given on many aspects of the problem by representatives from the public schools, superintendents of schools, and prominent figures in American life including the President of the United States. The Convention was attended by government officials, representatives of the legislative, executive and judicial branches of the government, as well as the staff and field officers of the Bureau. The two-fold object of the Convention was to consider the problems and advancements during the past year in the education of the immigrant in citizenship by the public schools, and to discuss the textbook for such candidates which the Bureau had in preparation. From the Bureau's standpoint, the Citizenship Convention was the crowning event of the year and of the two and one-half years of preparation which had led to the unification of the public schools with the federal government in a joint program of citizenship education. The agency hoped the convention would

41 *Ibid.*, pp. 474-475. In this connection, the Bureau reported many cities throughout the country were teaching home care, sewing, cooking, and domestic arts and science to the foreign-born women of their communities through the medium of the public schools. The Bureau also reported an intense interest on the part of the immigrant wives in these classes, many of them bringing their babies to the schoolroom with them and learning to read, write and cook, while the children slept in an adjoining room.

be but the first of a series of similar gatherings where "annually the feast of reason may be partaken with profit by an increasing number and mark a steady annual development of instruction, the broadening of the potentiality of effort, a drawing together of the candidates for citizenship with the prospective candidates for citizenship and the public schools of the country in this Nation-wide Americanization undertaking." [42]

For the remainder of the year, the Bureau continued its activities on behalf of its citizenship program. Unlike the Federal Bureau of Education, which propagandized actively on behalf of the Americanization movement through the publication of literature and posters for general distribution, the Bureau of Naturalization confined its activities to dealing directly with the school authorities through its field representatives, and with giving occasional advice and suggestions through the same means to local civic groups. In this fashion, the Bureau aroused steadily an interest in Americanization activities among the high schools and school boards of the country, thereby aiding the spread of classes in English and citizenship for the immigrant groups of many of the smaller cities and towns.

The year 1916 also found the Bureau of Education continuing its support of the Americanization movement through its Division of Immigrant Education. As has already been pointed out, the Division had been supported financially by the Committee for Immigrants in America, so that for all practical purposes the activities of the Division formed a very valuable

---

42 *Ibid.*, pp. 503-505. Addresses were given by President Woodrow Wilson, Robert S. Coleman, chief naturalization examiner of St. Paul, Josephus Daniels, Secretary of the Navy, Samuel Gompers, J. Henri Wagner, chief clerk of the Bureau, E. A. Freeman, dist. supt. of schools of Grand Rapids, Mich., Commissioner of Education P. P. Claxton, Mrs. Cora Stewart of the Kentucky Illiteracy Commission, J. M. Berkey of the Pittsburgh schools, L. R. Anderson, supt. of schools, Portland, Ore., William B. Wilson, Secretary of Labor, M. J. Downey, supt. of Boston evening schools, I. Walton Schmidt of the Detroit Board of Commerce, Andrew H. Melville of the Univ. of Wisconsin's Extension Division, and Commissioner of Naturalization, Raymond F. Crist.

and influential supplement to the work which the Committee and its affiliate, the National Americanization Committee, had undertaken under their own names. During the year, the Division had made decided progress toward making itself the national clearing house for all types of information on the Americanization movement. It had done much, too, toward establishing standards and methods in the education of the immigrants, and toward welding into one united force all the agencies dealing educationally with the Americanization movement.[43] Approximately 96,958 circulars, newsletters, schedules of standards and syllabi were distributed, 29,400 news releases on the progress of the movement, 57,000 enrollment blanks, 9,265 'American First' posters, 5,719 pamphlets and bulletins, and a large quantity of other material to aid the movement, were sent out during the year. Special exhibits were shown in ten state and national conferences, including the annual meetings of the National Educational Association and the Chamber of Commerce of the United States.[44]

In his report for 1916, the Commissioner of Education, P. P. Claxton, renewed his recommendation for some provision for the investigation of the education of adult illiterates and of the foreign-born. To his appeal of 1914, he added the plea: " Within the last two years the people of the country have become conscious of the special need for more adequate provision for preparing for American life and possible citizenship the large number of persons who came to this country from southern and eastern European countries. It is especially important that they be given opportunity for learning the language of the country that they be induced to take advantage of this opportunity. States and cities must provide the means for this, but the task of working out effective plans and of assisting States and cities in putting them into operation belongs to the Nation

[43] *Report of the Commissioner of Education for the Year Ended June 30, 1917*, I, pp. 62-63.

[44] *Ibid.*, p. 63.

as a whole, and this bureau is the Nation's logical agent for this work." [45]

The Bureau reported the year 1916 had seen a greater tendency toward cooperation in the movement of Americanization through education. It pointed optimistically to the fact that much progress had been made toward the Americanization of the immigrant, and that healthy tendencies toward the centralization of the work were well underway. " Private agencies especially have shown more desire to unite with governmental authorities in dealing with the problem of immigrant education. Chambers of commerce, industrial establishments, patriotic societies, philanthropic organizations, newspapers, women's clubs, labor unions, and public-spirited citizens, alike, have put sincere endeavor into the Americanization movement. In many instances privately maintained schools have been transferred to the supervision of the constituted school authorities. This indicates a healthy tendency toward centralizing work for immigrants." [46]

Indicative of the progress in Americanization work during the year 1916 was the inauguration of many local activities in support of the movement, particularly in certain centers where the immigrants had settled in large numbers. Thus a survey of the evening schools maintained by the city of Chicago made by the Immigrants' Protective League in the spring resulted in the formation of a Joint Committee on the Education of the Foreigner of delegates from the Chicago Association of Commerce, the Union League Club, the City Club, the various Women's Clubs, and the League itself. The Committee agitated actively for a bigger and better immigrant education program in Chicago.[47] In the same city, the Chicago Hebrew

45 *Report of the Commissioner of Education for the Year Ended June 30, 1916,,* I, p. xxiv.

46 H. E. Wheaton, " Education of Immigrants ", *ibid.*, pp. 350-351.

47 Immigrants' Protective League, *Seventh Annual Report for the Year Ending, January 1, 1916*, pp. 10-11 ; *ibid.*, 1917, pp. 10-12.

Institute inaugurated classes in English for foreigners, and carried on effective Americanization work. A special Bureau of Citizenship and Civics was established on an open-every-day basis to act as an information bureau for immigrants. Special surveys were made of the Jewish immigrant population of the city in an effort to increase the citizenship status of that ethnic group.[48]

In Pittsburgh, a special bureau was opened to deal with all immigrant questions by the Civic Club of Allegheny County. The Bureau assumed the duties of a clearing house for immigrants and had as one of its chief objects, the bringing of the city to a realization of its responsibility to the immigrant.[49] Cincinnati issued a special mimeographed *Course of Study in History and Government for Petitioners for Naturalization in the Citizenship Schools* of that city as an aid to the Americanization of its foreign-born,[50] while Detroit held a special institute for its evening school teachers in June which dealt with the immigrant problem, teaching for citizenship, and general Americanization problems.[51] In Cleveland, the Survey Committee of the Cleveland Foundation issued its section of the survey dealing with the school and the immigrant, and criticized the arrangement of the adult immigrant education program. As a result, a more intensive effort was made to interest the immigrant in the evening schools and to make the classes more attractive.[52]

In Buffalo, a number of citizens formed the Civic Educational Association in the spring of 1916 for the express purpose of making Buffalo an English-speaking city and opening

48 "Work of the Chicago Hebrew Institute", *Immigrants in America Review*, II, No. 2 (July 1916), p. 25.

49 *Bulletin of the Public Affairs Information Service*, 1916, p. 123.

50 Cincinnati, Ohio, *Course in Study in History and Government for Petitioners for Naturalization in the Citizenship Schools*, Jan. 1916.

51 *Bulletin of the Public Affairs Information Service, op. cit.*, p. 124.

52 "Immigrant Education in Cleveland", *Immigrants in America Review*, II, No. 2 (July 1916), p. 25.

the way for a better understanding between both the native and foreign-born residents. The Association sponsored a vigorous Americanization campaign throughout the rest of the year, and formed one of the most influential of the local Americanizing groups during the next three years.[53] In the neighboring city of Syracuse, the Chamber of Commerce appointed a special Americanization committee to carry on an educational program for the immigrant on a city-wide scale.[54] The city of Rochester, N. Y., did likewise during the spring of the year.[55]

In Detroit, the Americanization committee of the Board of Commerce agitated for the appointment of a special commission on immigration for the state of Michigan,[56] and maintained a free information bureau for immigrants. The Committee published also a special pamphlet, entitled *Preparing to Be American Citizens,* which contained a well of information of use to those desirous of preparing for citizenship.[57] These were but a few of the activities engaged in by local groups on behalf of the movement.

The year 1916 thus witnessed an acceleration of the Americanization crusade very much along the lines pursued the previous year. Progress had been made, particularly in the field of industrial Americanization, and in the realm of local group activities. The interest of the public had been sustained, and thanks to the efforts of the Americanizers, Americanization had been made an important part of the preparedness program. With the coming of 1917 and America's entry into the War,

53 Civic Educational Association of Buffalo, *Participating Americans: the Story of One Year's Work for the Americanization of Buffalo,* 1918, pp. 3-4.

54 Americanization League of Syracuse and Onondaga County, Inc., *Americanization in Syracuse and Onondaga County,* 1920, p. 7.

55 Chamber of Commerce of Rochester, N. Y., *Report of the Americanization Committee of Rochester Chamber of Commerce,* Rochester, 1916, pp. 1-3.

56 Public Affairs Information Service, *Annual Bulletin, 1917,* p. 185.

57 Detroit Board of Commerce, *Information for Immigrants in Detroit, Michigan, Preparing to Be American Citizens,* Detroit, 1916.

came also a heightening of the national spirit to meet the new crisis. With it went hand and glove a new emphasis upon Americanization. Henceforth, the cry went forth for a 'War Americanization' crusade as a part of the war effort to line up the alien behind the national program.

# CHAPTER VII

## AMERICANIZATION AND AMERICA'S ENTRY INTO WAR

THE entry of America into World War I found interest in the problem of the Americanization of the foreign-born fairly general throughout the nation, but especially strong in those areas containing a substantial foreign-born population. For two years, the various Americanization groups had been carrying on a campaign of propaganda and agitation. Not only had individuals and private groups joined the crusade, but federal, state, and municipal bodies had taken action of one sort or another in support of the movement. A broad foundation had been laid upon which the advocates of Americanization could hope to build, thanks to the new crisis that had arisen. Now, the Americanizers realized, as the result of America's entering the European controversy and the heightening of patriotic and nationalistic feeling, was the golden opportunity for pushing their crusade to the limit. This they accomplished by having their movement accepted by the various governmental war agencies as a definite part of the national war program. It was to be expected that as a result of this acknowledgement and the support given later by these agencies that the Americanization movement should wax increasingly stronger as the war-years wore on, until practically every hamlet in the United States which contained an immigrant populace felt the full impact of the crusade.

Americanization activities were relegated temporarily to a comparatively minor place in national interest during the first part of the year 1917 due to the general interest in the ' War ' itself which tended to dwarf all other interests of the American public. Nevertheless, the various groups and agencies heretofore at work continued their efforts very much along the lines established in the preceding years, yet always on the alert to seize any opportunity to keep their program before the eyes of the public.

Ever in the forefront of the Americanization drive was the Committee for Immigrants in America. Realizing the danger to the nation's safety which might result from any disruption of America's industrial output now that the new crisis had arisen, the Committee hammered away at its ' industrial Americanization' drive as a means of bringing home to the employers of foreign-born labor the need for a better understanding of and an improvement in the conditions of the immigrants. Because of its widely publicized pleas for such a program, the Committee found itself beset with numerous requests for information and aid along this line. The need for research and expert counsel to meet this growing need, especially from engineers and others scientifically trained, led the Committee to organize a special sub-committee on Industrial Engineering in March 1917. The new Committee was set up to handle the problem of the adult alien laborer and to formulate methods of what it choose to call 'human engineering work'.[1]

To publicize its findings, the Committee on Industrial Engineering issued a *Bulletin on Industrial Engineering* during the year 1917. The periodical contained brief summaries of leading articles, editorials, and books on industrial management, engineering, bettering of working conditions, and other subjects of interest from an industrial engineering standpoint,

[1] Committee for Immigrants in America, *Memorandum to the Advisory Commission of the Council of National Defense, op. cit.*, p. 9. Members of the Committee were: Frank Trumbull, chairman, Frederick L. Bishop, dean of the School of Engineering, University of Pittsburgh, Harold S. Buthenheim, Hugo Diemer, industrial engineer and professor of industrial engineering, Pennsylvania State College, Gano Dunn, well-known electrical engineer and director of Guaranty Trust Co. of New York City, Philip W. Henry, consulting engineer and vice-president of American International Co., Professor C. R. Mann, E. J. Mehren, editor of the *Engineering Record*, John E. Otterson, president of the Winchester Repeating Arms Co., Calvin W. Rice, consulting engineer of General Electric Co., and secretary of the New York Museum of Science and Industry, and Herman Schneider, Dean of the College of Engineering, University of Cincinnati.

selected to aid in the program of bettering the working conditions for immigrants and for labor generally in the factories of the nation. The new Committee, through Miss Frances Kellor and others of prominence, publicized its industrial Americanization in the periodical press, and had special reprint pamphlets made of several of these for general distribution. It served the very useful purpose of reminding American industry of the importance of carrying on Americanization activities.[2]

The Committee for Immigrants in America credited itself with much of the success of the War Americanization activities which took place during the year 1917. Summarizing its efforts in this respect in a report presented to the Advisory Commission of the Council of National Defense on October 31, 1917, the Committee listed as its special contributions to the cause: the planning of the work connected with the organization of the foreign-language section of the Federal Committee on Public Information and the furnishing of a special assistant to this division, the furnishing of similar services to the Vernacular Press Division of the United States Food Administration in order to reach the foreign-born, and the drafting and submission of a bill for the registration of enemy aliens in assistance to the Attorney-General's office. The Committee also made analyses of plants having government contracts which were troubled by delays in the production of equipment in an effort to ascertain the causes of the delay and to facilitate the delivery of goods. Because of its efforts along these lines,

---

2 *Bulletins on Industrial Engineering Prepared by the National Americanization Committee*, New York, vols. I and II (Apr. 3, 1917–Jan. 4, 1918). Among the articles reprinted were: Miss Kellor's " Engineering Methods Must Replace Paternalism in the Handling of Labor ", from *Engineering News-Record* (Apr. 12, 1917), her " Industrial Americanization and National Americanization" from the *North American Review* (May 1917), her " Industrial Americanization " from the *National Efficiency Quarterly* (Nov. 1918), an editorial entitled " The Engineer and Social Change " from *Engineering News-Record* (Apr. 12, 1917), and an address by John M. Williams before the National Employment Managers' Conference, Apr. 2-3, 1917.

the Committee believed that it had not only aided the national war effort but had done much to forestall I.W.W. " subversive " activities and labor misunderstanding.[3]

Turning its attention to the increasing demands for patriotic literature of good quality at a low cost, and realizing the great value of this material as an Americanization medium, the group appointed a National Committee of Patriotic Literature in April 1917 to help meet this need. The latter took under consideration ways by which the ideals, traditions, and sentiment of America, could be translated readily to the alien in a very simple fashion. As a result of the Committee's efforts, approximately 1,500,000 copies of a patriotic booklet entitled, *Songs of Our Country,* and 500,000 copies of another entitled, *Your Flag and Mine,* as well as 50,000 art flag posters, were published and distributed in immigrant communities. In this endeavor, the Committee was aided by the Metropolitan Life Insurance Company, which cooperated in distributing the literature.[4] The Committee hoped this new published material would meet satisfactorily the patriotic needs of the immigrant and would engender a beneficial psychological effect.

In New York State, the Committee organized and largely finanaced and directed the work of the Division of Aliens in the Resource Mobilization Bureau of the Adjutant-General's Office, using its experience with the immigrant to good stead in demonstrating state military methods of handling aliens in war time. It also compiled war proclamations, orders, and state laws for ready reference in handling alien matters. In Pennsylvania, it submitted a state plan for handling aliens to the

3 Committee for Immigrants in America, *Memorandum to the Advisory Commission, op. cit.,* p. 11.

4 *Ibid.,* p. 10. Members of the Committee were: Frank Trumbull, chairman, Frances A. Kellor, asst. to the chairman, William Fellowes Morgan, John H. Eggers, Clarence H. Mackey, Raymond B. Price, Rodman Wanamaker, Mary Harriman Rumsey, Mrs Vincent Astor, Mrs. Daniel Guggenheim, and Mrs. Cornelius Vanderbilt. *Cf.* National Committee on Patriotic Literature, *Your Flag and Mine,* c. 1917; *ibid., Songs of Our Country,* c. 1917, New York, N. Y.

Committee on Public Safety, and a similar one to the Governor and Commissioner of Labor in New Jersey.[5] Suggestions were prepared by the group for the inclusion of Americanization activities by home defense leagues, which were adopted by the National Committee on Patriotic and Defense Societies and distributed widely.[6]

In New York City, the Committee secured the appointment of a committee on aliens in the Mayor's Committee on National Defense in May 1917. This new agency thereupon started a campaign to increase the night school attendance of the foreign-born, organized community Americanization centers, sponsored a training course for workers among the immigrants, and rendered general advice and information on the problem of the Americanization of the foreign-born. In Cleveland, the Committee for Immigrants cooperated with the Mayor's War Committee in organizing the city's Americanization work in June 1917. It secured also a director to carry on the campaign, and furnished an assistant to organize the work among the foreign-born women.[7]

Continuing its own efforts, the Committee for Immigrants' affiliate, the National Americanization Committee, published and distributed a new pamphlet in October 1917, in an attempt to link up Americanization with the war effort. Entitled, *War Americanization for States*, the pamphlet consisted of an analysis of fifty pages on immigrant conditions then existent in each state. Statistical information of value concerning the

5 *Ibid.*, p. 15.

6 *Ibid.*, pp. 11-12.

7 *Ibid.*, pp. 17-18. The Committee for Immigrants in America also organized the Yorkville Neighborhood Association in New York City in the spring of 1917 in cooperation with Mrs. Vincent Astor and other interested residents of New York City as an experiment and as a means of determining the best ways of reaching alien women, and foreign-born groups and communities in regard to Americanization. The Committee used the results of the experiment to establish principles, standards, and methods of work which it eventually made available to the communities of the nation as a whole. *Cf. ibid.*, p. 10.

immigrant was included. The pamphlet contained helpful information as to proper state action and recommendations, which included the appointing of sub-committees on aliens or Americanization under the state councils of defense or committees of public safety, the setting up of alien information centers, the elimination of plant conditions favoring unrest, agitation, and disloyalty, the improvement of working conditions for all workers, the enforcement of sanitary and labor laws, and the abolition of discriminatory laws which set aliens apart in unjust ways. The inauguration of Americanization campaigns throughout the schools of each state in order to promote a better understanding between citizens and aliens, the bringing about of changes in the education laws of the states to compel the attendance of all non-English-speaking residents between the ages of 14 and 21, and the enactment of laws to provide facilities for instruction in English and civics in all immigrant communities, were also recommended.[8] Although helpful in many cases and utilized by certain municipal groups, definite action as suggested by the respective state councils did not take place until the following year, 1918.

Seeking ardently to get official recognition of Americanization as a part of the official war program, the two Committees, the Committe for Immigrants in America and the National Americanization Committees, after proper analysis and deliberation, presented a joint *Memorandum* to the Advisory Commission of the Council of National Defense concerning a war policy for aliens on October 12, 1917. The Committees gave as their reasons for such a policy the following ten point preamble:

1. The presence of 13,000,000 foreign-born in America, of whom 3,000,000 do not speak English and which America has permitted to live apart from its national institutions and life in colonies, camps, and quarters isolated from American control.

8 National Americanization Committee, *War Americanization for States,* Oct. 1917, New York, *passim.*

2. The ' go-where-you-will-do-as-you-please ' policy pursued by America for the past 50 years towards arriving immigrants resulting in ignorance of where they are, what they are doing and of their attitude toward America.

3. The inheritance of industrial injustices and unfavorable living conditions which decrease manpower and enable pacifists, agitators, and other anti-American groups to ferment unrest, dissatisfaction and disloyalty.

4. The knowledge of activity of agents of the German government retarding production, damaging property, endangering life and otherwise impeding America's effective participation in the war.

5. The certainty that the I. W. W. are making active propaganda and headway among aliens friendly to America.

6. The prevalence of industrial unrest, sabotage, strikes, riots, and other labor disturbances, not only in war industries but throughout the country.

7. The increase in fires, accidents, explosions and other damage to property in industries vital to the production of war materials.

8. The delays in executing war contracts due to the control of industries by aliens and anti-American influences in industries holding war contracts.

9. The influence of some of the foreign-language press among people who do not speak or read the English language.

10. The absence of adequate government agencies to anticipate the inevitable results of these conditions and of coordinated government organizations to deal effectively with these many complex influences and activities.[9]

The Committees then recommended the immediate inauguration of a four-point war policy in respect to the alien problem which should consist of first, the prevention of anti-American propaganda activities and schemes through the surveillance of all aliens, thus assuring the safety of America within its own borders and affording an opportunity to work

9 Committee for Immigrants in America, *Memorandum to the Advisory Commission of the Council of National Defense Concerning a War Policy for Aliens*, Oct. 31, 1917, p. 5.

the alien into a useful role in respect to the war effort. Second, the elimination of incentives of unrest, disorder, and disloyalty, and the removal of conditions which tended to reduce manpower, limit production, and render men and women susceptible to anti-American influences. It hoped thereby to assure America's effectiveness in the war. Third, the mobilization of alien enemies in internment camps on probation, or in non-war industries, and of friendly aliens in the military lines of America or of their own country according to the best advantage of the country. This the Committees felt would assure military efficiency and the stability of industry and of communities upon an American basis. Fourth, the provision of opportunities for all aliens who desired loyally to become Americanized in respect to language, citizenship, and cooperation.[10]

Declaring that the object of this policy was to safeguard the country, assure America's efficiency, make certain American control of communities and industries, and to Americanize aliens so that America would stand forth a united and effective nation, the two Committees recommended that practical steps be taken immediately to set up the necessary machinery for carrying them out. The Committees felt that the federal government alone had the power and prestige to initiate such a program and to carry it out to a successful conclusion, asking states, municipalities, and citizens everywhere to cooperate by rendering service at such times and places as the government might direct.[11]

The following specific steps were suggested to the Advisory Council by the two Committees. First, administrative action to include the appointment by the Council of National Defense of a committee on aliens or on Americanization, the appointment of alien officers in the various federal departments to cooperate with the new committee, the creation of sub-committees on aliens in the various state councils of defense, and

10 *Ibid.*, p. 15.

11 *Ibid.*, p. 38.

the designation of plant and community correspondents. Second, legislative action to include the semi-annual registration of the inhabitants by real estate owners, the passage of an amendment to the immigration law to require declarations of intention upon entrance and an obligation to learn English, the passage of another amendment to the naturalization law which would remove obstacles to citizenship, raise the standards for such, and lessen technical difficulties and delays, the establishment of a federal bureau of employment with authority to regulate private employment agencies, and the passage of proper legislation which would render federal aid to the education and Americanization of aliens. Third, regulative action to include the creation of a priority board on labor, the prohibition of the soliciting of labor by employers from war industries, the setting up of rules for standard safety measures and for the presence and location of aliens in industrial plants as well as uniform rules of health protection, welfare and housing of workers, and the granting of governmental appropriations for housing. Finally, the setting up of an Americanization program to consist of the study of citizenship laws and their operation as a basis for legislation and Americanization, the granting of support of the 'America-First' campaign by federal agencies, the announcement of a war policy for aliens and the securing of the cooperation for it from the foreign-born leaders and societies, and the making of provisions for teaching to aliens in cantonments.[12]

This was a very ambitious program, but one aimed at correcting the existing abuses in the immigrant situation while in

12 *Ibid.*, p 38. Other recommendations included the consideration of human elements as a basis for awarding war contracts, provision for automatic methods for the enforcement of pre-contract agreements, the appointment of government representatives to safe-guard women workers entering new and unusual employments, government regulation of housing and lodging places, the entering into of international agreements by which aliens would be included in the next draft or made subject to conscription by their home countries, and the connection of the federal employment system with the draft to enable families of enlisted men to find employment.

the members of the two Committees striving to
nation. The Advisory Commission of the Coun-
nal Defense took the *Memorandum* under consid-
Those features of the program which it could provide
elf it proceeded to do, especially those concerned with the
Americanization of the foreign-born. It was not until 1918,
however, that the Council found it possible to lend its full
support to the movement.[13]

Following up on their own recommendations, the two Committees tackled the Congress of the United States in an attempt
to get some of their proposals made law. They sponsored and
had three bills introduced successfully. The first, S. 621, would
have appropriated $50,000 to the Federal Bureau of Education
for the promotion of Americanization " through education,
a common language, American ideals, and an understanding
of American citizenship." The second, H. R. 1999, called for
the creation of a commission on illiteracy to investigate the
conditions and causes of illiteracy, to ascertain methods of instructing native and foreign-born illiterate adults, and to
cooperate with state and local educational authorities in eliminating illiteracy. The bill would have appropriated $100,000
for carrying out this program. The third, H. R. 4043, called
for the creation of a division of civic training in the Bureau
of Education to increase the efficiency of American citizenship
by giving information and personal assistance for the introduction and use of American democracy in schools, institutions, and associations. The Committees also approved H. R.
21,103, which would have provided federal aid to Americanization in the various states. To the regret of the Americanizers, the proposed measures were snowed under by the
avalanche of priority ' war ' legislation, so that no action was
taken. The initial attempt of the Americanizers to convince
Congress of the necessity of taking steps to aid their cause had
been made and lost. A precedent had been set, however, and

13 For action taken by the Council of National Defense, *cf.* Chapter VIII.

attempts would be made again in 1918 and the immediate post-war years.[14]

The two Committees continued to find their most useful ally in the Americanization drive in the Federal Bureau of Education. As we have seen, these groups had been financing the Bureau's Division of Immigrant Education as well as furnishing personnel to work for the agency in carrying on its work. The Bureau cooperated wholeheartedly with the Americanizers and through its prestige as a federal agency did much to give an official air to the plans and publicity of the two Committees. For all practical purposes, the work done by the Federal Bureau of Education in regard to Americanization can be credited to the two Americanization groups, since they were the motivating spirits behind the Bureau, and furnished the necessary wherewithal to make its program of action a possibility.[15]

The Federal Bureau of Education carried on an active campaign on behalf of Americanization of the immigrant during the first of the war years. Pamphlets, news letters, syllabi, and posters were circulated widely. Hundreds of letters were answered and all types of advice given on every aspect of the Americanization of the immigrants. A special *Schedule of Standards and Methods in the Education of Immigrants* for the benefit of educators was published by the Bureau in February 1917. As a result of its publication, several hundred superintendents, principals, and teachers were made acquainted with a standardized form of procedure in regard to immigrant education, and established it in their own communities. Numerous conferences and institutes were held in many places to consider the Bureau's plans for Americanization, and in certain instances, the Bureau's specialists instructed large numbers of teachers in the most approved methods of teaching the immigrants. To gain greater cooperation in support of the edu-

14 *Ibid.*, p. 19.

15 See above, Chapter IV.

cation of the immigrant, officials of the Bureau attended and addressed thirty-three conferences and visited over fifty cities. A plan worked out by the Bureau in conjunction with the New York State Department of Education resulted in the appointment by the latter of a special supervisor to plan standards of immigrant education in every city of the state.[16]

The Bureau's Commissioner, P. P. Claxton, had appointed a National Committee of One Hundred on December 21, 1916[17] to act as an advisory council to assist the Bureau in carrying out its 'America-First' campaign, and to represent and to mobilize all forces interested in Americanization. On February 3, 1917, the National Committee held an ' America First' conference, at which industrial leaders and officials were present, to lay plans for carrying out the Americanization campaign for the coming year. As a result of the meeting, the executive committe opened headquarters in Washington so that it might promote the Bureau's progress more effectively. The Committee marshaled several national organizations located in Washington and a number of federal departments behind the Bureau's undertaking. The new committee attempted to make all state and local groups coordinate their programs so that they could work effectively with the Bureau, and propagandized ardently on behalf of Americanization for the remainder of the war.[18]

The Federal Bureau spent the better part of the year devoting its attention to a ' War Americanization Plan ', which included the organization of a section in the new National

16 *Report of the Commissioner of Education for the Year Ended June 30, 1917*, I, pp. 62-63.

17 Public Affairs Information Service, *Annual Bulletin*, 1917, p. 186. J. P. Jackson, Commissioner of Labor and Industry of Pennsylvania, was appointed chairman of the Committee. H. H. Wheaton, specialist in immigrant education work of the Bureau, was appointed to direct the campaign as chairman of the executive committee. *Cf. Report of the Commissioner of Education for the Year Ended June 30, 1917*, I, p. 63.

18 *Ibid.*, p. 63.

Safety Council with the chief of the Division of Immigrant Education as its chairman. The plan, however, was not put into effect until 1918. It also cooperated with many chambers of commerce in holding 'America First' dinners, helped arrange Americanization programs for various organizations, and made two sample surveys of immigrant education conditions, one in Elyria, Ohio, and the other in San Francisco. Two very useful pamphlets in support of the movement entitled, *Public Facilities for Educating the Alien*, and *Adult Illiteracy*, were published by the Bureau during the year 1917.[19]

Another affiliate of the two Americanization Committees, the Immigration Committee of the Chamber of Commerce of the United States, continued its publicity for the Americanization of the immigrant during the first of the 'war' years. The Committee reported that great civic enthusiasm had greeted its efforts, and that as a result of its publicity, eighty-eight chambers of commerce in as many American cities were engaged in active programs for Americanization as of June 15, 1917.[20] By the end of the year, this number had increased to 104.[21] In practically every instance, regular Americanization Committees were appointed or special sub-committees named to carry on the work. The various committees carried on campaigns to inaugurate classes in English and citizenship for the immigrant residents of their communities, supported the efforts of the local school authorities where such classes had been established already, and stimulated interest in the whole problem of the immigrant through publicity campaigns, meetings, and programs in industrial plants.[22] In certain larger immi-

19 *Ibid.*, p. 63. *Cf.* U. S. Bureau of Education, "Public Facilities for Educating the Alien", *Bulletin*, 1916, No. 18; *ibid.*, "Adult Illiteracy", *Bulletin*, 1916, No. 35.

20 Chamber of Commerce of the United States, Committee on Immigration, *Bulletin*, No. 13 (June 15, 1917).

21 *Ibid.*, *Bulletins*, No. 14 (Aug. 25, 1917), No. 15 (Nov. 15, 1917), No. 16 (Dec. 1, 1917), and No. 17 (Dec. 15, 1917).

22 *Ibid.*, *Bulletins*, Numbers 14, 15, 16, and 17, *op. cit.* Chambers of commerce having active Americanization programs during 1917 were: Los

grant centers, namely, Youngstown, Ohio, Syracuse, N. Y., and Buffalo, N. Y., the chambers actually became the nucleus around which the Americanizers rallied to carry on active city-wide Americanization campaigns.[23]

The Immigration Committee of the Chamber reported that an increasing interest had been shown throughout the year 1917 in factory Americanization activities. These were in many cases the direct result of the industrial Americanization drive of the Committee for Immigrants in America and its affiliated groups including the Immigation Committee of the Chamber. Actual classes in English were started in at least twenty-seven industries, while many more gave their full support to the local authorities in behalf of their Americanization activities.[24] The

---

Angeles, Oakland, Sacramento, and San Francisco, Cal., Pueblo and Denver, Col., Bridgeport, Bristol, Hartford, Manchester, New Britain, New Haven, and Norwich, Conn., Washington, D. C., Wilmington, Del., Chicago, Granite City, Maline, and Streator, Ill., DesMoines and Mason City, Ia., Baltimore, Md., Boston, Brockton, Fall River, Framington, Lowell, and Taunton, Mass., Ann Arbor, Detroit, Grand Rapids, Kalamazoo, and Monroe, Mich., Hibbing, St. Paul, and Minneapolis, Minn., St. Louis, Granite City, and Kansas City, Mo., Omaha, Neb., Berlin and Manchester, N. H., Elizabeth, Hoboken, Jersey City, Newark, New Brunswick, Passaic, Paterson, and Perth Amboy, N. J., Auburn, Buffalo, Geneva, Jamestown, Lockport, Niagara Falls, Olean, Rochester, Syracuse, White Plains, and Yonkers, N. Y., Akron, Canton, Cincinnati, Cleveland, Dayton, Elyria, Newark, and Youngstown, Ohio, Altoona, Easton, Hazleton, Monessen, Philadelphia, Pittsburgh, Scranton, Sharon, Washington, and Wilkes-Barre, Pa., Providence, R. I., Nashville, Tenn., Austin and El Paso, Tex., Spokane, Wash., Wheeling, W. Va., and LaCrosse and Kenosha, Wis. Cf. Bulletin, Number 13 (June 15, 1917). Later, such were established in Manistee, Mich., South Bend, Ind., Poughkeepsie, N. Y., Watertown,, S. D., Waterbury, Conn., Holyoke, Mass., Battle Creek, Mich., New York City, Flint, Mich., Pasadena, Cal., Portland, Ore., Sault Ste. Marie, Mich., Bisbee, Ariz., Lincoln, Neb., Norwich, Conn., South Bend, Ind., and New Orleans, La. Cf. Bulletins, Nos. 14, 15, 16, and 17, op. cit.

23 Ibid., Bulletins, 1917, passim.

24 Such industries carrying on Americanization activities during 1917 were: D. E. Sicher Co., New York City, Ford Motor Co., Detroit, Bethlehem Steel Co., Bethlehem, Pa., DuPont Power Co., Hopinhill, Va., General Chemical Co., Ellsworth Collieries, Pa., Johnson and Johnson, New Brunswick, N. J., A. B. Kirschbaum Co., W. H. McElwain Co., Cleveland-

Committee felt that its campaign for 'industrial Americanization' had been more than successful during the first of the war years. It believed that its efforts to arouse the industrialists of the nation to the menace of an illiterate and un-Americanized industrial populace had been realized by most of the leaders of industry, and had been largely successful.[25]

The first of the war years also saw the enactment of state legislation in two quarters on behalf of the Americanization movement. Massachusetts finally took action to create a special Bureau of Immigration in conformance with the recommendations of the Immigration Commission of 1913.[26] The new Bureau was created to employ " such methods, subject to existing laws, as, in its judgment, will tend to bring into sympathetic and mutually helpful relations the commonwealth and its residents of foreign origin, to protect immigrants from exploitation and abuse, to stimulate their acquisition and mastery of the English language, to develop their understanding of American government, institutions and ideals, and generally to promote their assimilation and naturalization." [27] The Bureau received an appropriation of $10,000 for the first year, and similar financial support yearly thereafter. It carried on work very similar to the New York Bureau of Industries and

---

Cliffs Iron Co., Sidney Blumenthal Co., Krower-Tynberg Co., Carnegie Steel of Youngstown, American Hard Rubber Co., Maryland Casualty Co., Hartford Rubber Works, Republic Iron and Steel Co., Youngstown, O., Joseph Campbell Co., Camden, N. J., American Rolling Mill Co., Aluminum Company of America, Cooper Underwood Co., Eastman Kodak Co., Rochester, N. Y., Rome Brass and Copper Co., Westinghouse Air Brake Co., Youman and Erb Manufacturing Co., Scoville Manufacturing Co., and the J. L. Candee Co. Cf. ibid., Bulletins, No. 7 (Feb. 15, 1917), No. 11 (Apr. 15, 1917), No. 12 (June 15, 1917), No. 17 (Dec. 15, 1917), and No. 18 (Jan. 2, 1918).

25 Ibid., Bulletins, passim.

26 Commonwealth of Massachusetts, General Acts of 1917, Chapter 321, section 2.

27 Commonwealth of Massachusetts, First Annual Report of the Bureau of Immigration, 1917-1918, Boston, 1919.

Immigration in helping to prevent exploitation and fraud, checking on notaries public, giving advice to the immigrant in the state courts, and aiding and stimulating the education of the foreign-born in cooperation with the educational authorities. The Bureau planned and sponsored patriotic meetings for the foreign-born, and arranged for special classes in the industries of the state. It cooperated with the Department of University Extension of the Massachusetts Board of Education in its activities on behalf of immigrant education. For the next five years, it was the chief force behind the Americanization movement in the Commonwealth of Massachusetts.[28]

New York State also took action on behalf of the Americanization movement by passing the Lockwood Act of 1917. This act provided that boards of education or the trustees of each district or city could conduct forums and community centers in their respective communities, and provided funds for that purpose upon petition of twenty-five citizens. The passage of the Lockwood Act made permanent the series of Americanization forums which the New York *Evening World* had inaugurated in New York City in the spring of 1917, and which had attracted an attendance of approximately 270,000 people in a three-month period. The forums had been held in public school buildings in the immigrant sections of the city and had been addressed by city officials and others of prominence.[29]

Both the New York Bureau of Industries and Immigration and the Pennsylvania Division of Labor and Industry continued to render their support to the Americanization movement, while the California Commission of Immigration and Housing also took an active part in the campaign. The latter made special effort to determine the reasons for the irregularity of attendance in the immigrant education classes of that state. As a result of its findings in the Los Angeles district, the Com-

28 *Ibid., passim.*

29 Chamber of Commerce of the United States, Committee on Immigration, *Bulletin*, No. 14 (Aug. 25, 1917), p. 3.

mission issued a special pamphlet entitled, *A Discussion of Methods of Teaching English to Adult Foreigners with a Report on Los Angeles County*. The pamphlet was circulated widely and used by many teachers to improve their teaching methods.[30] The California agency also sponsored special work for teachers of immigrants in the Los Angeles Normal School. An experiment with the foreign-born women was made by the Commission in cooperation with the Los Angeles School Board, the International Institute of the Y.W.C.A., and the Normal School. Twenty-four classes in citizenship were conducted for the women of the various nationalities. The experiment was so successful that the Commission published the results in a pamphlet entitled, *Report on Experiment Made in Los Angeles in the Summer of 1917 for the Americanization of the Foreign-Born Women*.[31]

The accelerated progress of the Americanization drive during the year 1917 was noted well by the Federal Bureau of Naturalization, which continued to push its citizenship training campaign in cooperation with the public schools of the nation. In a special bulletin entitled, *The Work of the Public Schools with the Bureau of Naturalization*, the Bureau published the results of its first two years of activity along this line. The results showed remarkable progress in the spread of the movement to virtually every section of the country which had an immigrant population.[32]

Stimulated by the actions and propaganda of the Committee for Immigrants in America, the National Americanization Committee, the Federal Bureau of Education, the Immigration Committee of the Chamber of Commerce of the United States, and other Americanization groups both large and small, the

30 California Commission of Immigration and Housing, *Annual Report*, Jan. 1919, pp. 43-44.

31 *Ibid.*, p. 45. *Cf. ibid.*, *Americanization of Foreign-Born Women*, 1917 [also carries title used in text].

32 U. S. Bureau of Naturalization, *Report of the Commissioner of Naturalization*, 1917, p. 508.

Bureau of Naturalization reported an 'astonishing' advance of its program during the year 1917. Whereas 613 centers had inaugurated the cooperative scheme of the Bureau prior to that year, 1,141 new localities joined the movement by the end of July 1917, and advanced to 1,754 by the end of the year. In all these centers, the work had gone on " rejuvenating, rebuilding, and placing within reach of the adult immigrant candidate for citizenship those opportunities which exist on every hand but from which he is shut off by the barrier of a foreign tongue and foreign traditions." In these centers, the Bureau reported, the greatest attention had been given to the declarant and that great emphasis had been placed upon the importance of his attendance upon one of the public night schools that were opening their doors by the thousands all over the country in direct response to the appeals of the Bureau.[33]

Although admitting that the general stimulated interest in Americanization greatly aided its program, the Bureau felt that its unique approach to the problem was the best, and fitted in most timely in view of the national crisis besetting the country. It expressed the belief that the readiness for cooperation on the part of the public schools was traceable undoubtedly directly to the realization felt locally of the need for more compactness, more thoroughness of organization, and a greater unity and efficiency of action between local, state, and federal agencies. The Federal Bureau felt that this closer cooperation would mean the elimination of the hostile alien from among the body politic for it believed that " the spirit of 'alienage ' could not hope to survive in the presence of this intense Americanizing force that was being built up in the public schoolhouses of the land ". In all large cities and many of the small ones, the Bureau reported, those in supervision of the school work had urged the continuance and strengthening of the ties

33 *Ibid.*, p. 508.

of relationship which had been created through the Bureau's program.[34]

The Bureau realized that until acknowledgement was felt locally of the need for Americanization, and until every effort was made by local agencies to cooperate with the federal government on behalf of the movement, there would be a failure to utilize all the forces available for the Americanization of the immigrant. Accordingly it continued to urge that concerted action of this sort be taken. It extended invitations to 1,759 cities and towns to cooperate in the work, and received assurances of such cooperation from the local authorities in each case. For some, this meant the first time an opportunity had been created for the alien candidate for citizenship and all other resident aliens to attend night classes organized especially for their instruction by the public school authorities. It meant also the opening of a new activity on the part of the public schools in over a thousand cities, towns, and villages, and the breaking away from the old idea that the public schools were for use only from the hours of nine to three, five days per week. The Bureau felt that this meant the embracing within the American atmosphere and environment of millions of foreign-born who had previously been disbarred as distinctly from that sphere as though they lived in communities located in "mountain fastnesses". 1,754 communities had cast their lot already with the program of the Bureau. 1,828 other communities had given favorable responses to the Bureau's inquiries but took no steps during the year to organize citizenship

34 *Ibid.*, pp. 509-510. The Bureau continued to send out the cards containing the names of candidates for citizenship to the respective school districts concerned. It felt they had proven their value by the high favor with which they had been received and acted upon. In most cases, the cards became the means by which the schools recruited their night classes in many communities. The Bureau reported that the large cities had praised the card system in particular as an aid in securing the attendance of those not ordinarily reached.

classes. The Federal Bureau hoped to expand its work into these communities during the succeeding year.[35]

Verifying the optimistic reports of the Committee on Immigration of the Chamber of Commerce of the United States, the Bureau reported extensive interest in Americanization on the part of commercial and industrial groups. Extensive cooperation from commercial organizations of all kinds, in all sections of the country, in initiating and supporting local activities on behalf of the foreign-born was received by the Bureau. These organizations counted greatly in supporting movements initiated by the school authorities to obtain financial provisions for the inauguration of night school classes for immigrants. In 117 cities and towns, mass meetings were held which resulted in better cooperation in respect to Americanization. New ideas were injected into the local activities, and plans aiming at far-reaching and practical effects were evolved.[36]

As a result of the mass meetings, a greater interest in naturalization proceedings was achieved than ever before. Hearings became more formal, with the proceedings of the renunciation of allegiance and the investing of the new allegiance surrounded by an atmosphere of dignity and solemnity—a radical departure from the old informality. In all these places, practical results were uniformly achieved, with citizenship classes almost invariably organized as a direct result of the mass meetings. Enrollments were made ranging from ten or fifteen to over one hundred. Increases invariably resulted in large percentages over the preceding attendance, and in a greater awakening in the opinion of the Bureau, of the civic conscience throughout the entire country in all matters relating to the immigrant.[37]

35 *Ibid.*, pp. 510-511. For list of places cooperating with the Bureau arranged according to states, *cf. pp.* 511-530.

36 *Ibid.*, pp. 531 and 533.

37 *Ibid*, pp. 533-534. Places where these mass meetings were held: Birmingham, Ala., Los Angeles, Oakland, Pasadena, San Diego, and San Jose, Cal., Aurora, Belleville, Benton, Bucknow, Chicago, Chicago Heights, Christopher, Geneva, Johnston City, Joliet, LaSalle, Marion, Moline, Pana,

An active interest in Americanization on the part of the employers of foreign-born labor was also noted by the Bureau as having occurred during the year 1917. Supporting the campaign for 'Industrial Americanization' being conducted by the National Americanization Committee and the Chamber of Commerce of the United States, the Bureau sent its personnel to interview industrial leaders and employers of alien labor to urge that they prevail upon their workers to attend classes in the public schools. Excellent results were achieved thereby, it reported. Through this activity, the organization of citizenship classes had been achieved in hundreds of communities. In all such places, the association of local organizations with the federal government stimulated a new interest and led to the setting up of many public schools as Americanization centers.[88]

In four states of the Union, laws were in existence which prohibited the use of public funds for the education of adults. To assure the success of its program in those states, therefore, the Bureau wrote letters to the governors of North Dakota, Minnesota, Iowa, and New Mexico, calling their attention to the work of the Bureau and recommending that legislation be enacted to supersede these laws so that the Bureau could

---

Peru, Rock Island, Spring Valley, Streator, Taylorville, Waukegan, and West Frankfort, Ill., East Chicago, Gary, Hammond, Indianapolis, Mishawaka, South Bend, Vincennes, and Whiting, Ind., Albia, Cedar Falls, Pella, Rock Rapids, and Sioux City, Ia., Louisville, Ky., Amite, Hammond, and Independence, La., Cambridge, Fitchburg, and Westfield, Mass., Ann Arbor, Bay City, Benton Harbor, Detroit, Flint, Grand Rapids, Kalamazoo, Lansing, Muskegon, Saganaw, and Stambaugh, Mich., Duluth, Minneapolis, New Duluth, St. Paul, Virginia, and West Duluth, Minn., Kansas City, Mo., David City, Elyria, Lincoln, Norfolk, Omaha, Wahoo, Wilber, and Wymore, Neb., Newark, N. J., Albany, Auburn, Carthage, Cohoe, Ithaca, Jamestown, Mt. Vernon, Rochester, Schenectady, Troy, and Yonkers, N. Y., Washburn, N. D., Ashtabula, Massilon, and Steubenville, O., Coalgate, Muskogee, and Wilburton, Okla., Astoria and Portland, Ore., Braddock, Erie, McKee's Rocks, Pittsburgh, Presston, Scranton, Vandergrift, Williamsport, and Wilmerding, Pa., Aberdeen, S. D., Park City and Salt Lake City, Utah, Seattle, Wash., and Aubrey, Kenosha, La Crosse, Madison, Milwaukee, Oshkosh, Racine, and Sheboygan, Wis.

38 *Ibid.*, pp. 535-536.

engage in its programs in those commonwealths. In each case, the Bureau reported, the executives urged the passage of the desired legislation. North Dakota passed an act in the early part of 1917 authorizing the establishment of night schools for adult foreigners, and provided a specific appropriation of $7,000 to meet the expenses incurred. Minnesota passed an act for the same purpose on April 10, 1917 with an appropriation of $25,000. On March 24, 1917, Iowa enacted a law to provide the compulsory installation of courses of instruction in night schools upon a petition of 10 or more adults, while New Mexico passed a similar act on March 13, 1917. The Bureau looked upon these acts as great forward steps toward a uniform movement throughout the United States to provide means of furnishing citizenship training for the foreign-born.[39]

Indicating further the intense interest in the Americanization movement, the Bureau of Naturalization reported having received numerous requests from all over the United States for advice and information. Insistent, too, were requests that the Bureau issue a standard textbook on citizenship. The latter was finally authorized for publication as an appendix to its *Proceedings of the First Citizenship Convention.* The federal agency also cited the aid furnished it by patriotic, social, and religious bodies, and praised their interest and participation in the Americanization drive. From all parts of the country, it received encouraging reports indicative of the enthusiasm of the cities and communities in support of its program, and the

---

[39] *Ibid.,* p. 534. The Bureau summarized the situation as follows: "Throughout the United States there is a greater demand in evidence for the inauguration of this work than can be met with the funds available. In nearly every community with which the Bureau had communicated there has been the uniform response of immediate cooperation. Volunteer workers are solicited by the school authorities from among the ranks of the school-teachers and from among the patriotic citizens. In some places classes have been organized where only one candidate has presented himself. Such commencements have steadfastly persisted and such interest has followed that the membership of the classes has steadily increased." *Cf.* pp. 534-535.

eagerness of the adult aliens to satisfy their ambitions to become citizens. As a result of all these encouraging factors, the Bureau felt rightly optimistic about carrying on its program to even greater success in 1918.[40]

The first of the ' War ' years thus witnessed a steadily widening interest in the Americanization of the immigrant. Continued progress had been made along the lines previously followed as the authorities of city after city inaugurated special programs on behalf of their immigrant residents. Interest had been whipped up as the result of America's entry into war and the consequent heightening of patriotism. So far, the Americanization drive had not been made a definite official part of the war program. Recommendations that this be done had been offered and favorably received in high governmental quarters. It was not until the succeeding year, however, that the nation had time to take stock, note the progress of the war drive, and then begin to devote its united attention to this very important supplement to its all-out effort for victory.

40 *Ibid.*, pp. 535-536.

# CHAPTER VIII

## THE MOVEMENT BLENDED INTO
## THE WAR EFFORT

THE year 1918 saw the continuation of the Americanization movement and its expansion under the auspices of two new federal agencies, the Council of National Defense and the Committee on Public Information. The preceding year had been one of experimentation in all ways as the nation attempted to work out a program of united support of its war effort. The new year was to witness the maturation of the steps taken the preceding year and the more or less stabilized functioning of those agencies which had been set up to meet the war crisis. Americanization, soon to be one of the fundamental parts of the war program, was to benefit from this stabilization, and to obtain the full benefit of the prestige and publicity of the new federal agencies which were to push the movement to the fullest during the nation's second year of war.

Of great significance in arousing the nation to the seriousness of the immigrant situation and to the necessity of even greater Americanization efforts was the revelation that 700,000 out of 10,000,000 registrants for the Draft, most of whom were immigrants, could not sign their names let alone read or write English. Even those who had heretofore been apathetic to the question of immigrant education now realized just how serious an impairment to the nation's military efficiency and productive capacity these figures represented. " With one out of thirteen unable to respond intelligently to military or industrial orders on the one hand, and moral or spiritual appeals on the other, all because of the lack of a common medium, the necessity for immediate action on the part of the schools became a matter of national importance. Additional facilities for Americanization were speedily provided and the teaching of English to the immigrant as the first step in Americanization engaged the serious attention of school authorities all over the country ".[1] Unfortunately, the common tendency was to blame the immigrant for his failure to learn the language of America. Actually, his failure to do so could be attributed less to his lack of desire rather than to unfortunate circumstances that prevented him from so doing as well as to lack of opportunity.[2]

The Federal Bureau of Education took the lead in publicizing the Americanization movement during the year 1918. Through its Division of Immigrant Education, the Bureau made its principal work the placing of Americanization before the country as a fundamental part of the war effort. To achieve this end, it took steps to secure through the National Committee of One Hundred, its advisory council, a resolution from the Council of National Defense indorsing the federal program of Americanization as it was then being worked out by the Bureau. This was done, and the resolution passed and approved as early as December 13 of the preceding year.[3] Later, on February 12, 1918, the Council of National Defense joined with the bureau in putting forth a national plan of Americanization.[4] The action of the council of National Defense was a distinct compliment to the Committee for Immigrants in America and the National Americanization Committee as sponsors and financiers of the Americanization work of the Federal Bureau of Education. With the official approval of this powerful body, the Americanizers felt encouraged to push on with ever greater vigor than before.

In a special Bulletin issued by the Council of National Defense to the various state councils, the former agency urged

1 J. H. Van Sickle and John Whyte, " Public Education in the Cities of the United States ", U. S. Bureau of Education, *Bulletin*, 1919, No. 88. *Cf. Biennial Survey of Education, 1916-1918*, I, pp. 117-120.

2 *Ibid.*, p. 117.

3 U. S. Bureau of Education, *Report of the Commissioner of Education for the Year Ended, June 30, 1918*, I, p. 132.

4 Council of National Defense, *Bulletin*, No. 86, *Americanization of Aliens*, Feb. 12, 1918.

support of the Bureau's program, and requested the several state councils of defense to lend their assistance in carrying out the Bureau's program in the several states. It asked that where such committees did not exist already, that each form a committee on Americanization of aliens. Such committees were to assist the Bureau in carrying out its national Americanization program according to the plans outlined by the Bureau of Education. It recommended also that the work be undertaken in close cooperation with the woman's divisions of the state councils. Attached to the *Bulletin* was an outline of national and state programs of the state councils and the state divisions of the Woman's Committee on Defense in regard to the Americanization movement.[5]

Under this plan, twenty states were organized by June 30, 1918, a number that rose to thirty-five by the end of the war, including every state that had any significant immigrant population. The work of the state and local agencies was correlated and coordinated under the Americanization committees of the state and local councils of defense as suggested by the Bureau. The object was to avoid duplication of work and to effect the greatest unity of action possible. The Bureau supplied every state council of defense and a large number of local and community councils with its national plan for Americanization, and all the special schedules of operation and circulars of information published by the Bureau.[6]

The Federal Bureau went one step further to assist in placing Americanization before the country as a war measure. At the suggestion of the National Committee of One Hundred, Secretary of the Interior Lane called a conference on April 3, 1918 of all the state governors, the chairman of the state defense councils, and the presidents of industrial corporations and chambers of commerce. About three hundred persons attended. Every aspect of the Americanization movement was

5 *Ibid.*

6 *Report of the Commissioner of Education, 1918, op. cit.,* p. 132.

discussed and methods suggested for furthering the work. Resolutions were adopted calling upon Congress to appropriate adequate funds to the respective federal departments doing Americanization work, endorsing the principle of federal aid in Americanization to states and communities, urging industrial and commercial organizations to cooperate with the federal and state authorities in a nation-wide plan, and recommending that all elementary instruction in all schools be conducted in the English language.[7] Secretary Lane presided. H. H. Wheaton, of the Bureau of Education, acted as secretary.[8] Addresses were given by Secretary Lane, Elliott Smith of the Federal Bureau of Education, Levi Mayer of Chicago, Arthur S. Somers, chairman of the Board of Education of New York City, George Creel of the Committee on Public Information, Senator Young of Iowa, Simon J. Lubin of the California Commission on Immigration and Housing, Gus Ohlinger of the Toledo Commerce Club, and by each of the governors.[9]

A resolution was adopted requesting the Secretary of the Interior to appoint a committee of nine members, representing the various groups in attendance, to request a hearing before a joint session of the Senate and House Committees on Education. The purpose of the hearing was the furthering of legislation that would give federal direction and leadership to the movement for teaching English to the illiterate and non-English-speaking persons of foreign origin residing in the United States, and the promoting of systematic instruction of such persons in American ideals, standards, and citizenship. The resolution was accepted by Secretary Lane, who appointed Governor Samuel F. Stewart of Montana, Governor Richard Manning of South Carolina, Levi Mayer of Chicago, and

7 *Ibid.*, p. 132.

8 U. S. Bureau of Education, "Americanization As a War Measure", *Bulletin*, 1918, No. 18, p. 5.

9 *Ibid.*, p. 43.

Messrs. Clark, Somers, Gompers, Lynch, and Holden to serve on the Committee.[10]

One result of the conference and the stimulated interest in Americanization that followed was the announcement by the Carnegie Corporation of New York that it would undertake to finance a study of the methods by which the immigrant population of the country was being Americanized. Work began at once on the project, under the direction of Allen T. Burns, the survey director of the Cleveland Foundation, assisted by an advisory council consisting of former President Theodore Roosevelt, Professor John Graham Brooks of Harvard University, and Dr. John Glenn, director of the Russell Sage Foundation. The project was calculated to take at least a year and a half in time.[11]

The Bureau's National Committee of One Hundred expanded its representation in time to include a greater number of industrialists and foreign-born leaders, and made its principal activity during the year the formulation of two bills, one working out the principle of federal aid to the states for Americanization work, and the other calling for funds to carry out the war Americanization plan. It was not until the end of hostilities, however that the legislation could be brought to the attention of Congress. The Committee was also instrumental in drafting and securing the passage of three bills in New York State providing for compulsory attendance of non-English-speaking persons between the ages of 16 and 21, for the compulsory maintenance of educational facilities for their instruction, and for the training of teachers to teach the newcomers English and citizenship. A model bill for compulsory attendance was also drafted and furnished to several state educational authorities and legislatures.[12]

10 *Ibid.*, p. 44; for complete list of those who attended, *cf.* pp. 5-12.

11 *New York Times* (Apr. 16, 1918); see below, Chapter IX, p. 260.

12 *Report of the Commissioner of Education, 1918, op. cit.*, p. 133. The National Committee of One Hundred made its headquarters in New York City in 1918, having previously had its headquarters in Washington.

The Bureau of Education extended its clearing-house service during the year with a variety of publications covering a greater range than previously. Over 100,000 circulars, news letters, schedules of operation, and schedules of standards and methods were sent out. Over 100,000 individual enrollment blanks were disseminated for the signatures of those desiring to enroll in the Americanization campaign. 25,000 other bulletins, pamphlets, and 'America First' and flag posters, were also distributed.[13] Fifteen new circulars of information and schedules of operation for official and unofficial agencies were drawn up, while special research into the activities of industrial corporations and chambers of commerce was undertaken during the year.[14]

In an attempt to secure better coordination and correlation of the varied activities of unofficial agencies, the Bureau contacted patriotic organizations, women's clubs, civic organizations, fraternal orders, councils of defense, and Americanization committees, and offered advice and suggestions as to how to carry on the work. Special cooperative plans were worked out with the American Bankers' Association, the Pennsylvania Department of Labor and Industry, the National Committee of Patriotic Societies, the Philadelphia Chamber of Commerce, and many local chambers, and with the New York State Department of Education. It reported having cooperated, too, with a large number of local superintendents of education, industrial corporations, and patriotic and civic associations in support of Americanization activities. Many of these were correlated with the national plan of Americanization as sponsored by the Council of National Defense.[15]

In the meantime, the National Americanization Committee had presented a proposition to Secretary Lane for the extension of the work of the Bureau of Education in Americanization

13 *Ibid.*, pp. 132-133.

14 *Ibid.*, p. 133.

15 See below, pp. 201-205.

with a special view to promoting the work of education among the foreign-born "in order to give them a knowledge of the resources of the country, of American manners and customs, of American social, civic, economic, and political ideals, and through cooperation with loyal leaders of 'racial' groups to win the full loyalty of these people for the United States and their hearty cooperation in the war for freedom and democracy." [16] Under the plan of cooperation adopted, the National Americanization Committee agreed to bear the additional expense for salaries and travel of specialists, assistants, clerks, and other employees, as well as the necessary expenses for office equipment. All employees were selected by the Commissioner of Education and appointed by the Secretary of the Interior. On May 2, 1918, Secretary Lane announced the acceptance of this plan.[17]

In presenting the new plan, the Bureau sought to afford the immigrant better opportunities and facilities to learn about America and to understand his duties. It also sought to unite in service for America the different factions among the several

[16] *Report of the Commissioner of Education, 1918, op. cit.*, pp. 133-134.

[17] The National Americanization Committee explained the reasons for the new arrangements as follows: Demands throughout the country for war Americanization work among the foreign-born were so great that the Secretary of the Interior asked the Committee to cooperate in the extension of this work until an appropriation could be secured from Congress. This War Work Extension was organized in May of 1918 and combined a few months later with the immigrant education work as the Department's Americanization Division. The latter's work was that of getting various racial groups in the United States intelligently behind American war policy and active participants in the war program, preparing them for a fundamental understanding of citizenship, familiarizing them with the Government's war activities, provisions, and needs, through war information centers, industrial plants, racial societies, and the foreign-language press, bringing them together with the native-born, employers, and employees, and securing the active cooperation of other governmental agencies reaching the foreign-born. *Cf.* letter from Frank Trumbull, chairman of the National Americanization Committee to P. P. Claxton, dated New York City, Apr. 1, 1919, Independent Agencies Archives, Federal Security Agency, Office of Education, *Binder 106*, "Americanization War Work, 1917-1918".

nationality groups, and to minimize in each group the antagonisms due to old-country conditions, hoping thereby to cement friendships and to discourage the enmities then existing. Turning to the native Americans, the Bureau hoped to bring these into a more intimate and friendly relationship with the foreign-born by giving them a better understanding of the newcomers so that joint cooperation might result. It also sought to develop among employers a more kindly and patriotic feeling toward foreign-born workmen. Special effort was made to encourage the foreign-born to assist in the work of Americanization and to develop a more patriotic feeling toward the work in which they were then engaged. A final goal of the Bureau's was to have the school made the center of Americanization activities of all sorts.[18]

As a result of the new arrangements, the Bureau of Education was able to enlarge its division of immigrant education by the addition of a war extension service station with offices both in Washington and in New York City. The offices were under the direction of Joseph Mayper and Miss Frances A. Kellor, respectively, and served the useful purpose of information bureaus and coordinating centers for all activities concerning Americanization.[19]

The National Americanization Committee took full credit for making possible the work which the Bureau of Education undertook during this period. In addition to furnishing the Bureau with a New York headquarters with full equipment for 'racial' and other types of publicity work, it also staffed the two offices with thirty-six workers, including field officers, translators, writers, speakers, and specialists on immigrant groups. It arranged for a conference group of twelve men who represented each of the twelve important immigrant groups in America to advise and assist the government. Over 100

18 *Report of the Commissioner of Education, 1918, op. cit.,* p. 133-134.

19 *Ibid.,* p. 134.

others were employed by the Committee in various capacities in support of the Bureau's Americanization activities.[20]

The Committee also supplied the funds necessary to carry on the work done during the year in connection with the plant Americanization committees appointed in 1,000 industrial organizations at the request of the Department of the Interior. It continued to bear the burden of furnishing the financial means whereby the work of the Bureau of Education could be carried on in regard to Americanization until March 4, 1919, when the relationship was severed due to the passage of legislation prohibiting the federal government or any of its agencies from accepting financial aid from private groups or organizations. The Committee also continued to support the activities of the Immigration Committee of the Chamber of Commerce of the United States, which carried on its campaign of sustaining interest in 'industrial Americanization' during the year 1918. The latter succeeded in securing the appointment of many more local Americanization committees among the chambers of commerce until the number reached 150. It also made surveys of 165 industrial towns, and distributed approximately 300,000 sets of the Americanization leaflets for insertion in pay envelopes.[21]

The National Americanization Committee promoted through the foreign-language newspapers the publication of American

20 The National Americanization Committee claimed it was largely responsible for the Department of the Interior's maintaining its Americanization program through the utilization of its racial advisors who helped to work out "a sound policy and program of racial relations and to carry the message back to their own people through conferences, lectures, articles, and active participation in local activities." The Committee also claimed to have aided the Department through reaching the employers of the foreign-born workers through trade periodicals, house organs, the foreign-language press, and Americanization committees in some 800 industrial plants. Seven numbers of the Bureau's publication, *Americanization*, were made possible by the Committee and carried the progress of the work being accomplished to some 20,000 interested agencies and individuals. Letter from Trumbull to Claxton, *op. cit.*.

21 *Ibid.*

almanacs containing citizenship information, and the publication of civic lessons. It secured, prepared, and distributed to thousands of plants employing the foreign-born operating schedules on " How to Safeguard Industries from Enemies Within ", " How to Reach the Alien with War Information ", " War Information for Local Chambers of Commerce ", " Americanization of Foreign-Born Labor in Controlled Districts", " How to Make Shop Talks Help with the War ", and " Developing Local Latent Labor Resources ". The Committee continued its neighborhood association activities in Americanization in order to deal with homes and individuals, housing, protection, personal service through home visiting, and breaking down barriers between classes and ' races '. The experience gained thereby it evaluated and distributed for possible use elsewhere.[22]

From February until June 1918, the National Americanization Committee's staff directed and supervised for the Committee on Public Information a survey of the activities of some 50,000 national, state, and local agencies working for or reaching foreign-born groups, such as mayors' councils of defense, chambers of commerce, boards of trade, trade organizations, and foreign, racial, religious, philanthropic, immigrant, patriotic, social, and civic societies. The result " was a compilation for the government of invaluable lists of agencies reaching the foreign-born and the presentation of an excellent index of existing war conditions among the foreign-born and the agencies working with them. It served to stimulate hundreds of agencies to organize work for the sympathetic and intelligent Americanization of the foreign-born." [23]

22 *Ibid.* Until the passage of appropriate legislation by New York State in 1918, the Committee supported Dr. John H. Finley, the Commissioner of Education for that state, in his immigrant education work by employing an assistant to act with him in the development of this work.

23 *Ibid.* Cf. Howard C. Hill, " The Americanization Movement ", *American Journal of Sociology*, XXIV, No. 6 (May 1919), pp. 613-614.

In order to secure accurate and complete information, letters of inquiry were sent to approximately 2,376 mayors of cities, 1,108 chambers of commerce, 2,353 trade organizations, 48 state councils of defense and their woman's divisions, 295 national, ' racial ', patriotic, immigrant, and philanthropic societies, 50 national religious societies and organizations, 1,071 foreign newspapers, 5,274 superintendents of schools, and 269 railroads. As a result, the names of approximately 50,000 agencies, foreign, native, industrial, and educational, were obtained. To each of these a registration card was sent asking for information on the principal foreign-language spoken, the kind of service and work being done among persons of foreign-birth and origin, or requesting suggestions or plans for the promotion of Americanization. About 15,000 of the cards were filled out and returned. Replies were often unsatisfactory owing to errors in filling them out. Nevertheless, the head of the survey, Joseph Mayper, felt that the results obtained could be of valuable use in aiding the Americanization work of the Committee.[24]

Mayper found that the foreign-born agencies and societies were divided among themselves and were not getting, as he expressed it, " the American point of view ". He also found that the native-born agencies were not reaching the foreign-born. Moreover, they had the utmost diversity of standards, methods, and material in their approach to the immigrant, and distributed information without a proper knowledge of the needs of the immigrant or of what would best fit the existing conditions. Investigation revealed that industrial plants in various parts of the country were devoting their attention especially to the foreign-language workmen, and were, for the most part willing to be used in the Americanization campaign, but did

24 Hill, " The Americanization Movement ", op. cit., pp. 613-614. A number of important cities were not heard from at all. Labor unions, steamship ticket agencies, hotel employers, churches, and educational institutions were valuable sources of information either not investigated or from which inadequate returns were obtained.

not know just how to do the work themselves. Educational agencies, particularly the public schools, were alive to the situation, but needed the propaganda itself to vitalize the work.[25]

These and other facts of significance were revealed as the result of the survey. On the basis of the results thus obtained, the Committee on Public Information was able to plan its strategy in support of the Americanization movement and in organizing the immigrant elements behind the war effort. Other Americanization agencies used the information to strengthen their methods and eliminate many of the weaknesses revealed by the survey.

The National Americanization Committee also helped other organizations in starting Americanization bureaus by releasing members of its staff for initial work with these groups. Particularly close relations were maintained along these lines with the Americanization Division of the National Security League and the Americanization Committee of the National Women's Suffrage Party.[26]

The Federal Bureau of Education praised the work of the Committee very highly, especially the help rendered its New York and Washington centers. The latter center was charged particularly with the promotion of the education of the foreign-born through classes in schools and industrial plants and in connection with social organizations, thus carrying on the work which the Bureau had been doing for several years under its immigrant education division. The New York center, on the other hand, specialized in preparing material of a nature which would appeal to the immigrant, and included among its personnel editors, research specialists, translators, 'racial advisors', and clerks of various sorts. The Bureau reported considerable satisfaction with the efforts of this division. The 'racial advisors' in particular "were men of such character and having such general knowledge both of America and of

25 *Ibid.*, p. 615.

26 *Ibid.*, p. 616.

their own people in America as to gain for them the confidence
of a large number of their fellows." Advisors of this sort were
appointed for the Armenian, " Assyrian " [*sic.* Syrian], Greek,
Italian, Russian, Polish, French, and English nationality
groups. Through the ' racial advisors ', the Commissioner of
Education was kept aware constantly of the general conditions
and needs of persons of these groups, of their attitude toward
the work of Americanization and the ideals and policies of the
federal government, and of the best ways of reaching them with
instruction.[27]

The ' racial advisors ' also served as messengers for the
Bureau, holding conferences among their people, speaking in
their lodges and in public gatherings, translating material for
publication in their foreign-language papers, and a host of
other duties. The Bureau of Education sought constantly to use
them and the New York center for the purpose of lining up
the various ethnic groups intelligently behind the American
war policies, and inducing them to become active participants
in the war program as well as preparing them for a fundamental understanding of citizenship. Through the center and
its workers, the Bureau also sought to familiarize the immigrants with the government's war activities, provisions, and
needs, utilizing war-information centers, industrial plants,
' racial ' societies, and the foreign-language press in the process.
Special emphasis was placed on attempting to bring together
both foreign and native-born residents and employers and
employees, as well as gaining the active cooperation of other
governmental agencies through which foreign-born residents
could be reached.[28]

General conferences of from 20 to 60 representative men of
the several nationalities were held by the Commissioner of
Education, P. P. Claxton, in New York City. On one occasion

27 *Report of the Commissioner of Education, 1919*, I, pp. 189-190.
28 *Ibid.*, pp. 190-191.

a conference was attended by representatives of more than 30 such groups. Similar conferences on a smaller scale were held from time to time by the director of the New York office. More than 100 men of the different nationalities were organized into small permanent conference groups, each of which held frequent meetings at the New York office to discuss the progress and problems of the campaign. In this fashion, the Bureau of Education helped to shape its Americanization activities and to rally the immigrant in support of the general war program.[29]

In addition to the activities carried on by its two district offices, the Bureau of Education prepared many articles for publication in the English and foreign-language press. The federal agency reported that these articles were accepted by papers having a total circulation of more than 5,000,000. Its policy of working for the appointment of Americanization committees composed of both foreign and native-born citizens in industry, which it had inaugurated the preceding year, was expanded successfully until more than 800 such committees were actively at work. Many of these rendered exceedingly valuable service on behalf of the movement.[30]

The Bureau's most influential effort during the year was the publication of its *Americanization Bulletin,* the first issue of which appeared on September 15, 1918. The *Bulletin* served the purpose of a general information medium for all national, state, and local activities in behalf of the Americanization program. It appeared monthly until its discontinuance in the autumn of 1919. The *Bulletin,* later issued under the title *Americanization,* began with a 16 page issue of 10,000 copies. Circulation was later boosted to 22,000 copies to meet the growing demand for information on Americanization from societies and individuals directly interested in the work. The files of the *Bulletin* contain a practical store-house of informa-

29 *Ibid.,* pp. 190-191.

30 *Ibid.,* p. 191.

tion on Americanization activities being carried on throughout the country during the period.[31]

As we have noted above, the Federal Bureau of Education had received the support of the Council of National Defense in its Americanization campaign. The latter organization not only approved the emphasis which the Bureau was placing upon Americanization but itself engaged in propagandizing on behalf of the movement. The Council sent out various mimeographed circular letters and circulars to the various state and local sections on the subject of Americanization urging that programs of Americanization be put into effect. In addition to its bulletin, *Americanization of Aliens,* in which it announced its support of the Bureau's drive, the Council sent out one of a similar nature, *Americanization, Cooperation with the United States Bureau of Naturalization,* endorsing the Americanization activities of the latter Bureau as well.[32] The bulletin urged the local groups to cooperate with the Bureau of Naturalization in arousing each local community to the war necessity of continuing classes which taught citizenship responsibilities to candidates for naturalization, and arousing each local community which had not so far established such classes as to the necessity for so doing. Local groups were also urged to assist the school authorities in starting and maintaining adequate citizenship classes, and to take steps to assure that such classes were continued throughout the entire year. The bulletin recommended strongly that the local groups provide speakers equipped to tell the reasons for the war, the advantages of citizenship, how to conduct oneself as a good citizen, and other things of interest to the immigrant in connection with the citizenship-training program. Efforts to induce all adult aliens to attend citizenship classes under the slogan, 'An All-American Community', were urged, while every effort to

31 *Ibid.,* p. 181; The last issue of the periodical appeared Nov. 1, 1919. Cf. *Americanization Bulletin,* II, No. 3.

32 Council of National Defense, *Bulletin* No. 91, *Americanization Cooperation with the United States Bureau of Naturalization,* Apr. 18, 1918.

prevail upon all aliens the necessity of preparing themselves for citizenship was recommended by means of publicity in foreign newspapers, speeches in foreign languages, and house to house canvasses.[33]

In response to the appeals of the Council of National Defense, thirty-five state councils formed special Americanization committees or designated some special agency to formulate and to carry out constructive Americanization programs adapted to the conditions of their state. In several states, special war information bureaus were established for the benefit of the immigrants.[34]

The Americanization activities of the state councils of defense were varied in character. A number cooperated with educational authorities to secure additional classes for the teaching of English to the foreigners. Nearly all issued press releases to bring the aims of the United States in the war before the foreign-born of the country through the foreign-language press. A number of councils encouraged actively and facilitated naturalization as well as disseminated information on how to set about becoming a citizen. Whereas early action by the state councils in regard to the foreign-born consisted primarily of registration and surveillance to prevent sedition, with the development of the campaign by the State Councils Section of the Council of National Defense and the Bureaus of Education and Naturalization, constructive activities looking toward ultimate Americanization predominated. The range of the work being done by the state councils continued to be broad for the duration of the war, and included the coordination of the work of voluntary agencies interested in Americanization, the development of general policies for these agencies to follow, the encouragement and facilitation of naturalization in cooperation with the public schools, and the maintaining of

33 *Ibid., cf. Second Annual Report of the Council of National Defense for the Fiscal Year Ended June 30, 1918*, Washington, 1918, p. 19.

34 Council of National Defense, *ibid.*, pp. 19-20. For list of states, *cf.* p. 19.

publicity both through the foreign-language press and through
contact with foreign-born workers in industrial plants to bring
them into fuller accord with the national war policies.[35]

The Council prepared a nation-wide program for community
Fourth of July celebrations in conjunction with the Committee
on Public Information and sent this out to all state councils.
It met with a patriotic response in all parts of the country. The
program was drafted in accordance with the desire of the President that the foreign-born of the country be given an opportunity to express their loyalty to the United States on the
nation's birthday. The Council felt it had a direct influence on
the Americanization work of the various state councils in
stimulating greater effort along those lines.[36] The States
Council Section of the Council of National Defense sent out
bulletins periodically during the remainder of the war period
urging action along lines of Americanization and stimulating
interest in the movement. The Council's Woman's Division did
likewise. In each instance, the special bulletins and circulars
urged a more active interest in Americanization and outlined
or suggested proper steps which might be taken to insure the
success of the movement.[37]

The Woman's Division of the Council, recognizing the importance of bringing the foreign-born into a fuller understanding of American thought and ideals, joined with the States
Councils Section in doing everything possible to promote uniform activity in regard to the federal plan of Americanization
as proposed by the Bureau of Education and endorsed by the
Council of National Defense. In addition to sending out special
bulletins of a general nature, the Woman's Division suggested
ways of working in industrial plants and discussed ways of
reaching German-speaking people and others in an effort

35 Council of National Defense, *Third Annual Report of the United States
Council of National Defense*, Washington, 1919, p. 35.

36 Council of National Defense, *Second Annual Report, op. cit.*, p. 17.

37 For list of such bulletins and circulars, see Bibliography.

to further in every way the work of "making the foreign peoples a united body of Americans". The Division reported that the women of America responded eagerly to the opportunity to engage in this work. It reported having received nearly 30,000 'America First' pledges to help in the work. Nearly that many more were sent out daily and returned, signed and designating the kind of work the signer could do.[38]

Through its Educational Propaganda Department, the Woman's Committee made Americanization its principal work for the rest of the year 1918. Joint committees with the state councils were formed (thirty-seven such state committees were reported so engaged). In some instances, all agencies interested in Americanization were brought together and a plan for the coordination of activities secured. A campaign to secure the attendance of the foreign-born at night schools was carried out generally. In many instances, the Department reported, new classes were established through the efforts of the Americanization committees. The Department found that the best approach to foreign-born women was through the Red Cross, or through child welfare or food conservation work.[39]

Both Committees reported little uniformity in the methods by which Americanization was conducted in the various states owing to the widely differing conditions existing among the foreign-born throughout the nation. Several states held Americanization conferences with demonstrations of methods of teaching English. Others published pamphlets and articles in the foreign-language press. One committee concentrated on teaching Americans the actual and potential value of the immigrant with demonstrations given to arouse interest in foreign customs and to show the contributions which had been made to the United States by its foreign population. Another com-

38 Council of National Defense, *Second Annual Report, op. cit.,* page 48; Council of National Defense, *The Woman's Committee, United States Council of National Defense, an Interpretative Report, April 21, 1917, to February 27, 1919,* pp. 85-86.

39 Council of National Defense, *Third Annual Report,* op. cit., pp. 56-57.

mittee received pledges from employers that only English would be spoken at their plants. Still another conducted investigations to discover to what extent, German, the "enemy language", was being taught, and how far patriotic education had been introduced. A committee from a state having a large German population secured the cooperation of the leading foreign-language newspapers and in a single county held 109 Americanization meetings and established 33 classes for the foreign-born.[40]

With the ending of hostilities, the Field Division urged that the Americanization work conducted by the state councils and the state divisions of the Woman's Committee be continued or else transferred to a permanent agency. At various times after the signing of the Armistice, fourteen state councils and seventeen state divisions reported that their Americanization committees were going on with their work, while in four states plans were being made for permanent disposition of this activity under a state department of Americanization.[41]

While the Council of National Defense and its women's affiliate were aiding the Americanization movement through their influence with local groups, another federal agency, the Committee on Public Information, took an active role in the movement as one of the means by which it hoped to bring home to the immigrant residents of the country "the truths about the war, and the tremendous idealism of America". As has been pointed out already, the Committee utilized the services of the National Americanization Committee to make a survey of the Americanization activities and to make recommendations. In view of the findings, the Committee on Public Information realized that the best way of approaching the foreign-born would not be through the usual medium of the native-born stock. Instead, it sought to find group leaders able and

40 *Ibid.*, pp. 56-57. For accounts of individual state actions, *cf. Americanization Bulletin, passim.*

41 *Ibid.*, p. 75.

willing to undertake this type of evangelism in order to develop 'loyalty leagues' within the ethnic groups themselves that would discharge the task.[42]

The Committee's first success along this line was the formation of the Friends of German Democracy, with Franz Siegel as president, and others of prominence in German-American circles active members. The Friends carried the message of the war to the German-American groups for the duration of the conflict and encouraged actively an interest in American ideals, the English language, and citizenship. Similar work was accomplished by the Hungarian-American Loyalty League, founded by Alexander Konta and supported by the Committee on Public Information.[43]

As the war continued, the Committee expanded its work with the foreign-born by establishing in 1918 a Division of Work among the Foreign-Born, under the direction of Miss Josephine Roche. Under her guidance, direct and continuous contact was made with fourteen nationality groups by means of special bureaus set up for that purpose.[44] Representatives were appointed from the nationalities to act as managers of the foreign-language bureaus, and were given the responsibility of developing the work among their people. The various bureaus acted as information centers, and sent out official releases in their own languages concerning the work of the Committee, the need for unity, the duties of the foreign-born, and other types of information of value to the development of the war program. The Bureaus also attempted to rectify un-

42 Committee on Public Information, *Complete Report of the Chairman of the Committee on Public Information, 1917:1918:1919*, Washington, 1920, p. 79.

43 *Ibid.*, p. 79; others of importance included Rudolph Blankenburg, Dr. Abraham Jacobi, Dr. Karl Mathie, and Frederick Hoffman.

44 *Ibid.*, p. 80. The Bureaus were: Italian, Hungarian, Lithuanian, Russian, Czecho-Slovak, Polish, German, Ukrainian, Danish, Swedish, Norwegian, Finnish, Dutch, and the Foreign-Language Information Service Bureau.

fortunate conditions affecting the foreign-born, and to furnish them with important facts concerning their own groups.[45]

The Committee's bureaus were largely responsible for the petition which was presented to President Wilson on May 21, 1918, asking that July 4, 1918 be especially recognized as a day for the foreign-born to demonstrate their loyalty to their adopted country. Representatives of all the foreign-language groups presented the petition, and were received sympathetically by the President. As a result, the latter issued a proclamation calling upon the Committee on Public Information to cooperate with the various nationality groups in observing July 4 in such fashion.[46]

The Committee set to work at once to plan an enthusiastic celebration of the day by the various immigrant groups. Under the direction of Will Irwin, arrangements were made for demonstrations in practically every town containing foreign-born residents. For weeks prior to the day, the national and local organizations of the immigrant groups worked on the plans that would assure their peoples' complete participation in the Fourth of July celebrations. Probably never were there such gigantic preparations throughout the entire country for Independence Day, the Committee reported, and "certainly never was there such an outpouring of the nation's millions of new citizens and citizens to be, as on July 4, 1918." The Committee received reports of parades, pageants, mass meetings, resolutions, declarations, and inscriptions from all over the country indicating the enthusiasm and devotion of all immigrant groups. The Committee felt the demonstration was significant proof of the loyalty of the foreign-born groups to their adopted country.[47]

45 *Ibid.*, p. 81.

46 *Ibid.*, pp. 81-82. Following Wilson's reply, the governors of the various states and mayors of cities issued similar proclamations regarding the celebration of July 4.

47 *Ibid.*, p. 83.

While the groups were celebrating the nation's birthday, each of the thirty-three nationalities sent representatives on a pilgrimage to the tomb of Washington as the guests of President Wilson. In response to the President's speech of welcome, the representative of the Belgians delivered a message bearing the signatures of all the representatives expressing their appreciation of their new homeland and their desire to serve it to the best of their ability.[48]

The work of the Committee on Public Information in regard to Americanization fell under four heads: foreign-language press work, foreign-language organizational work, general field work, and the issuance of pamphlets. In regard to the first, approximately 745 out of 865 foreign-language newspapers cooperated with the fourteen foreign-language bureaus, although news service was not started by all the bureaus until November 1918. The total releases given out by the Committee from the inauguration of the program in the spring of 1918 amounted to 2,318. In nearly every case, the news releases were based upon the information received from governmental bureaus. For the benefit of the foreign-language organizations, information on governmental activities was prepared in the form of bulletins or circular letters and sent to these organizations. Field service consisted for the most part of personal conferences between bureau managers and the leaders of the various nationality groups throughout the nation. Approximately 124 trips were made by agents of the bureaus to 53 different towns. The Committee issued twenty-five pamphlets in all. It felt there was little need for this type of approach in any large quantity because of the facilities offered by the foreign-language press.[49]

---

48 *Ibid.*, pp. 83-84. For text of message, *cf.* p. 84. The nationalities represented were: Albanian, "Assyrian", Belgian, Chinese, Czecho-Slovak, Costa-Rican, Danish, Dutch, Ecuadorian, Finnish, French, French-Canadian, German, Greek, Hungarian, Italian, Japanese, Lithuanian, Mexican, Norwegian, Polish, Filipino, Russian, Venezuelan, Roumanian, Spanish, Yugo-Slav, Swedish, Swiss, Syrian, and Ukrainian.

49 *Ibid.*, pp. 96-97; for list of pamphlets, *cf.* pp. 90, 96-97.

The Committee's Division of Work among the Foreign-Born was responsible for the creation of an agency which was to serve the foreign-born residents of the United States in an informative capacity for the next five years. In August 1918, it started a Foreign-Language Information Bureau under the direction of Donald Breed, and later Barett Clark. The Bureau had as its policy the encouragement of the foreign groups to participate in the nation's affairs through releasing stories telling of their cooperation with the government, the Red Cross, local bodies, and in other ways. It also sought to assist the foreign-language press in securing prompt and efficient cooperation from the various government departments as well as to inform the American people through the English-language press of the good work being done by the foreign-language newspapers in helping the foreigners to become better Americans. Over fifty such stories were released to 3,300 American newspapers, while fourteen news bulletins giving brief accounts of the activities of the foreign-born were sent out. The Foreign Language Information Service Bureau acted as the chief liaison between the foreign-language Bureaus and the government departments in getting the former the official information for their releases and for the individual cases appealing to them.[50]

Upon the abolition of the Committee on Public Information in the spring of 1919, the Foreign-Language Information Bureau assumed the full duties of the Division of Work among the Foreign-Born, and continued the work which the Division had been undertaking privately under a special emergency fund given by the Carnegie Corporation until August 1, 1918. It then passed to the joint management of the War Camp Community Service and Community Service, Incorporated. The work of the Bureau was continued under their auspices until December 1919, when these organizations terminated their services and left the Bureau dependent largely upon voluntary

50 *Ibid.*, pp. 98-99.

effort without practically any finances. Both the foreign-language groups and the personnel of the Bureau felt the work should continue. This they succeeded in doing until February 1920, when the entire organization was taken over by the American Red Cross. It became a national bureau in the latter's Department of Civilian Relief under the name of Bureau of Foreign-Language Information Service, with headquarters in New York City.[51] The affiliation with the Red Cross was severed in 1921, and thereafter the Bureau maintained itself as an independent non-partisan agency. It continued the work inaugurated in the summer of 1918 along the same lines through the early twenties.[52]

One other agency actively at work in behalf of Americanization during the second of the war years was the Federal Bureau of Naturalization, which continued its activities very much along the lines of the preceding years. The Bureau reported great satisfaction with the growth of interest and action in support of the movement and the steady increase in the number of classes organized for the purpose of teaching the immigrants who were candidates for citizenship. Commenting upon the spread of the movement, the Bureau revealed that the daily and periodical press had devoted many columns to the stimulation of Americanization, and that committees had been organized in virtually every community of the United States including state and county organizations. All of these were directly or indirectly aiding the Bureau and the public schools in the accomplishment of this purpose.[53]

Continuing its summary of the progress of the Americanization movement, the Bureau stated that educators were in-

51 American Red Cross, *Work of Foreign Language Information Service of the American Red Cross* (June 20, 1920), p. 5.

52 Foreign Language Information Service, *Five Years Work with the Foreign Born*, New York (Oct. 12, 1922), p. 5.

53 U. S. Department of Labor, "Report of the Commissioner of Naturalization", *Reports of the Department of Labor, 1918*, pp. 606-607.

tently striving to meet the responsibilities which the Americanization plans of the Bureau had thrown upon them, while chambers of commerce had organized Americanization committees extensively which cooperated with the federal agency. Scarcely a commercial or business organization of the nation was not represented in some way in support of the Bureau's efforts. In most cases, the Bureau stated, these organizations no longer retained a formal character, but had assumed a potential, active forcefulness in increasing numbers which was indicative of the realization of the vital nature of Americanization and of the original purposes of the movement. Desire for accomplishment gripped the members of these organizations whereas heretofore the ideal had been the sole influence which had brought them together.[54]

The federal agency reported that churches in many areas had organized definite programs for personal Americanization work by both the ministry and the laity regardless of denominational lines, while the public schools of the nation received complete recognition of the valuable work that they were doing in support of the Americanization drive. In this latter connection, the Bureau praised the Americanization features of the National Educational Association's convention at Portland, Ore., in 1917. This it pronounced most fruitful in effective demonstration and later results. The Bureau felt, too, that the N.E.A.'s convention in Pittsburgh held in 1918 had been a boon to Americanization activities in that all subjects had been subordinated to that of the movement, so much so, that the convention had been characterized as an Americanization Convention of school people.[55]

The Bureau sponsored classes in industrial plants, and called a special conference in Chicago to stimulate interest in this type of program. The conference resulted in the city's agreeing

54 *Ibid.*, p. 607.
55 *Ibid.*, p. 607.

to furnish 1,000 teachers for the organization of such work through the director of foreign-classes. Special films were planned at a nominal cost for projection in citizenship classes. The Bureau presented a textbook to each foreigner when he filed his declaration of intention, and effected a still closer union with the public school authorities by presenting certificates of graduation from the federal government through the public school authorities of each community. In many communities, the presentation of the certificates of graduation were presented concurrently with the certificates of naturalization. The Bureau urged each state to prepare a textbook treating of state, municipal, and county forms of government as a companion to the Bureau's textbook on the federal government.[56]

The federal agency reported that mass meetings continued to be held in various parts of the country, in most cases where none had been held before. The meetings reflected the fact that the communities had advanced beyond the mere " talking stage " and had developed to the point of concerted action looking to the increase in the enrollment of night classes and the need for securing a maximum of attendance. An increase was noted in the number of cities and towns cooperating either directly or indirectly with it in its citizenship plans.[57]

The Federal Bureau of Naturalization considered itself to be the authorized agency to carry on citizenship training activities. It believed such was the case, because no other governmental agency could have the contact with the alien population of the entire nation in the same way that it had due to its peculiar relationship to the candidates for citizenship. It viewed with annoyance the encroachments upon its activities by the Federal Bureau of Education. Evidences of bad feeling between the two Bureaus over their respective immigrant programs became apparent upon occasion during the year 1918. The

56 *Ibid.*, p. 607. *Cf.* National Educational Association, *Journal of Proceedings and Addresses, 1917; 1918, passim.*

57 *Ibid.*, p. 622; *cf.* Table 22, p. 621.

whole question of conflict of authority embittered the personnel of the two Bureaus for quite some time.[58]

Apparently jealous of its prerogative in this respect, the Bureau of Naturalization succeeded in having a law passed by Congress specifically recognizing its national undertaking and patriotic endeavor, and authorizing the Bureau of Naturalization to continue its work of cooperation with the public schools in sponsoring citizenship training activities. The same act, passed May 9, 1918, authorized the publication and distribution of the course in naturalization and in preparation for citizenship, a step recommended for years by scores of educators. The act authorized the Bureau to meet the expense involved in producing the course from the naturalization fees paid into the Treasury of the United States by aliens seeking citizenship.[59]

Taking cognizance of the feeling expressed by many of the leading articles in the press that there should be a central bureau of the federal government whose function and province should be the assimilation of the entire foreign-born population through duly authorized state and municipal agencies, the Bureau of Naturalization induced Senator William H. King of Utah to introduce a bill in the Senate which would have provided such a bureau in the Department of Labor. Bill S. 4792 was introduced on July 2, 1918. It would not only have created such a Bureau to assure the assimilation of foreigners who had established permanent residence in America, but would also serve to arouse a higher regard for the privileges and responsibilities of American citizenship in the minds of all citizens and permanent residents. The creation of a bureau of citizenship and Americanization, the Bureau of Naturaliza-

---

58 *Ibid.*, p. 608. *Cf.* Hill, " The Americanization Movement ", *op cit.*, p. 624; also, P. P. Claxton, " Reply to Memorandum of Elliot Dunlap Smith in Regard to Conflict Between Federal Agencies for Americanization ", *op. cit.*, Chapter IV.

59 *Ibid.*, p. 609.

tion felt, could not only be effected at a minimum expense but could also prevent that "bane of all governmental organizations, the overlapping of functions, the duplication of features of work and the consequent perpetuation in a new organization of features of the governmental organizations heretofore created—a situation every administrative officer strives to his utmost to avoid." In a special letter to Senator King, Secretary of Labor William B. Wilson expressed his approval of the bill.[60] S. 4792 was referred to the Committee on Immigration, but was never reported out of committee. Evidently, the pressing importance of more important war legislation stood in the way of consideration of the bill at the time.[61]

The Bureau of Naturalization endeavored to do all within its power, consistent with its federal position, to arouse as it expressed it, "the local mind of each community to the point of a full, red-blooded American campaign for bringing together the public schools and the adult foreigners to the end that under the best presentation possible they may make the choice between their present allegiance and allegiance to the United States government."[62] It felt that each community should have its best citizens go forward among the foreign colonized groups and carry to them "the gospel of American citizenship increasingly until foreign colonization groups are only of historical interest—until they are a thing of the past." The Bureau believed this endeavor to be a responsibility belonging to each community and to each state. It allied itself, accordingly, with

60 *Ibid.*, p. 609. For text of letter from Wilson to King, dated Washington, Sept. 12, 1918, *cf.* pp. 609-610.

61 United States Council of Defense, *Readjustment and Reconstruction Information, Bills Introduced in the Sixth-Fifth Congress*, Washington (May 15, 1919), p. 7. Senator King later introduced a similar bill S. 5001, Oct. 21, 1918. It also was referred to the Committee on Immigration and never reported out of committee. *Cf. ibid.*, p. 9. The bill's provisions were exactly the same as those of S. 4792.

62 "Report of the Commissioner of Naturalization", *Reports of the Department of Labor, 1918, op. cit.*, p. 609.

the state councils of defense, and with the Americanization committees of every community where they had been organized whether these were affiliated with chambers of commerce, churches, industrial enterprises, or other organizations. In all cases it presented them with the necessity of carrying out the Bureau's program of Americanization.[63]

Thus the second of the war years saw the Americanization movement made a vital part of the war effort. In addition to the groups and agencies that had been engaged in the work during the previous years, two new federal organs, the Council of National Defense and the Committee on Public Information, used their power and prestige to back the efforts of the Americanizers and to carry on in their own right. The interest of the American public in the movement had been sustained and in many cases strengthened, while the reaction of the immigrants themselves had been gratifying. The fond hopes of the Americanizers had been realized to a satisfactory degree. They now bent their efforts to carry on with the program into the post-war period.

63 *Ibid.*, pp. 618-619.

# CHAPTER IX

# THE POST-WAR AMERICANIZATION DRIVE

WITH the cessation of hostilities in November 1918, the movement to Americanize the immigrant entered its final phase. The latter was characterized at first by a continuation of the interest in the Americanization of the immigrant on the part of the American public as a carryover of the general war spirit. Then a heightened spurt of activity set in during the autumn of 1919 and the spring and summer of 1920, as an immediate effect of the steps taken to rid America of the malevolent influence of the so-called 'alien radical'. Finally, a return to a state of indifference to the problem almost akin to that of the first decade of the century occurred,—another indication that the American people had recovered from the psychology of wartime and had returned to a state of 'normalacy'.

The Federal Department of Justice under the leadership of Attorney-General Mitchell Palmer was unquestionably influential in arousing American public opinion once again on the subject of the necessity for Americanizing the nation's foreign-born at a time when that interest had begun to subside. The deportations of the notorious agitators, Emma Goldman and Alex Berkman, by orders of the Department in November 1919, the similar action taken on behalf of 249 Russian aliens aboard the transport, Buford (the so-called 'Soviet Ark'), on December 22, 1919, the trial the same month of 33 members of the I.W.W. in the Kansas City Court on the charge of attempting to overthrow the government of the United States, and the raids by federal agents in Detroit, Toledo, and other cities which resulted in the arrest of from 100 to 150 aliens,— all did their part in arousing America to an awareness of the possibility of nascent tendencies toward radical action on the part of the immigrant population then resident in the United States. As a result, fear and suspicion of the alien was engendered which in many cases expressed itself in mob action and highhanded tactics on the part of the superpatriotic elements of the population. By the end of the year 1919, nearly 5,000 persons had been arrested by agents of the Department, and 2,635 aliens had been judged sufficiently guilty of actions against the government to warrant deportation.[1] The raids and arrests were continued well into the spring of 1920, when an additional 2,700 aliens, most of whom were Russian in extraction, were arrested in thirty cities of the United States.[2]

As a result of this sensational campaign, enough support was obtained in Congress to pass the Sterling-Johnson Act of June 5, 1920, which authorized the proper federal authorities to exclude all alien anarchists and others advocating the overthrow of the government of the United States by force, and the deportation of all such aliens living in the country. Similar action was to be taken concerning all aliens who assaulted or killed officers of the United States, unlawfully destroyed property or resorted to sabotage, or who wrote and circulated written or printed matter advocating such actions. The law was aimed at the I.W.W., the Communist Party, and the Communist-Labor Party.[2]

The 'anti-Red crusade' gradually slackened in the late spring of 1920, due in part to the quarrel which broke out between the Department of Justice and the Department of Labor over the activities of the latter's Bureau of Naturalization. Accusations and recriminations were bandied about which tended to discredit the recent actions of the Department of Justice, with the result that a saner attitude was assumed by the agents of the latter, and the radical hysteria gradually ran itself out. Not, however, before leaving a definite mark upon

1 For a brief account of the 'alien raids', see Irwin S. Guerncey, "United States", *New International Year Book, a Compendium of the World's Progress for the Year 1919*, p. 707.

2 *Ibid.*, *1920*, p. 697.

the Americanization movement as such. In practically every case, the old agencies and groups that had sponsored Americanization activities redoubled their efforts.

Two groups in particular led the new crusade to Americanize the immigrant and forestall the indoctrination of this important part of the populace with Bolshevistic principles. The first, the National Security League, had come into existence during the immediate pre-war years and had played an important part in agitating for preparedness and in arousing the American national spirit to new patriotic heights. The other, the Inter-Racial Council, was a lineal descendant of the Committee for Immigrants in America and the National Americanization Committee, which had disbanded with the ending of the war.

The National Security League had shown its awareness of the importance of the immigrant as a likely source of possible infection by foreign doctrines and by Bolshevism in particular. In a pamphlet issued in February 1919, the League stressed the utter necessity of Americanizing the immigrant, and urged support of all activities along that line. As a " disinterested and patriotic organization ", the League offered itself as a means of working for the general good of the nation by teaching Americanism, which it defined as " the fighting of Bolshevism and other un-American tendencies by the creation of well-defined National Ideals, and the marshalling of all our people in the determination to achieve them." [3] It then outlined its program of action, which consisted of a two-point roster: the Americanization of those of school age, and the Americanization of those beyond or outside the influence of the schools. In regard to the first, the League embarked upon a project of training teachers through means of study groups and eventually had as many as 1,000 of these groups functioning. In addition, it organized students for the study of national and international problems and for the " scientific " propaganda of " an intelligent faith in and support of American institutions and ideals ". It also

3 National Security League, *Future Work* (Feb. 1919), p. 3.

set up " scientific experimental stations " for the development and perfection of methods of the teaching of Americanization in the schools. Two such stations were established, one in Lowell, Mass., and the other in Los Angeles, Cal.[4]

In regard to the second point of its roster, the League embarked upon a patriotic publicity campaign among the foreign-born which included the celebration of the birthday of the American Constitution on September 17, 1919, the circulation of patriotic pamphlets, and the holding of patriotic meetings in conjunction with the D.A.R., the S.A.R., the League for Constitutional Government, and other patriotic groups. It urged the teaching of English to the foreign-born, the prohibiting of foreign-languages as the basic languages of the country's schools, the steadily decreasing use of foreign-languages by the country's populace, the restricting of the exercise of the franchise to citizens of the United States through the repeal of state laws which allowed aliens to vote, and the spreading of propaganda for the domination of American-born politicians and national sentiment over those of foreign origin.[5]

In addition, the League continued the program which it had inaugurated during the war and which it now felt would help engender Americanization, namely, agitating for universal military training to " guard against militarism ", keeping a special Congressional committee active which sponsored a national educational program of insistence upon the nomination of candidates for Congress who were representative and patriotic (and which published the records of Congressmen on vital questions), and finally maintaining its ' Flying Squadrons ' (hundreds of speakers sent out by the League to teach patriotism and Americanization). The spirit of the League in regard to Americanization was well illustrated in the concluding paragraph which appeared in the pamphlet : " Thousands of patriotic citizens must be educated ' to take the stump ' for

4 *Ibid.*, p. 4.

5 *Ibid.*, p. 5.

America. They must tell the immigrant population our living faith in American doctrines of law, liberty, progress and justice, as explained by the Constitution and our representative form of government. They must preach Americanism and instill the wisdom of America's Wars and that American spirit of service which believes in giving as well as getting. Before the war, Americanization work was a philanthropy. Now it is a plain business of citizenship. The immigrant to whom Government has been a synonym for despotism and who hears without contradiction through the mouthing of agitators that Government here is a tyranny is easily misled. The propaganda against the spirit of Bolshevism must be met by a stronger propaganda by American Americans. NATIONAL SECURITY IS THE DUTY OF EVERY GOOD AMERICAN!" [6]

The Inter-Racial Council, the second of the two most active post-war Americanization groups, was organized in March 1919 " by industrial and racial leaders to carry on the racial adjustments and educational work begun by the government but which would soon cease through the failure of proper legislation." [7] Listing as its aim not only the usual ones of im-

---

[6] *Ibid.*, pp. 5-6.

[7] Inter-Racial Council, *The Inter-Racial Council, Aims and Purposes*, c. 1920. For list of officers, *cf.* Inter-Racial Council, *Proceedings, National Council on Immigration Held Under Auspices of Inter-Racial Council*, New York, April 7, 1920, p. 3. Included were: Officers: T. Coleman DuPont, chairman of the Board, William H. Barr, president, Frances A. Kellor, vice-chairman, Mrs. David Rumsey, vice-president, A. J. Hemphill, chairman of the board of Directors of the Guaranty Trust Co., New York City, treasurer, Dr. Antonio Stella, well-known Italian immigrant physician, vice-president, and M. I. Pupin, physicist, and immigrant from Yugo-Slavia, secretary. Others: W. Redman Crosse, Philip T. Dodge, president of Mergenthaler Linotype Co., Gano Dunn, James A. Emery, general counsul for the National Association of Manufacturers, Lindley M. Garrison, former Secretary of War under Wilson, Charles Evans Hughes, Marcel Knight, William Loeb, Jr., vice-president of the American Smelting and Refining Co., Herbert F. Perkins, president of the International Harvester Co., Guy E. Tripp of Westinghouse Electric, Felix M. Warburg, Albert Shiels, Mrs. Vincent Astor, Earl D. Babst, president, American Sugar Refining Co., Walter C. Baylie, Boston banker, A. C. Bedford, Gutzon

proving Americanism and the betterment of racial relations in the United States, the Council added the following as one of the results hoped to be obtained through supporting its efforts: " To stabilize industrial conditions. To apply American business methods to the foreign-born press by building up an American advertising base under it. To reduce unrest and disorder through plant analyses which point out conditions that create industrial unrest. To decrease radicalism through the issuance of information and counter education in the foreign language press dealing with attacks upon American institutions, law and order, and industry." [8]

Once again, Miss Frances A. Kellor assumed the active leadership in the Americanization movement as chief executive officer of this newly organized council. The new agency at-

---

Borglum, prominent sculptor, Charles W. Bouring, Irving T. Bush, president of Bush Terminal Co., New York City, William Butterworth, president of Deere and Co., of Illinois, C. Carusos, B. Preston Clark, president Plymouth Cordage Co., R. Floyd Clinch, president, Chicago, North Shore, and Milwaukee Railroad, Howard Coonley, president, Walworth Co., New York City, Joseph M. Cudahy, well known meat packer, Dominik d'Alessandro, Cleveland H. Dodge, vice-president and director of Philip Dodge Corp., Forrest F. Dryden, president of Prudential Life Insurance Co., Pierre S. DuPont, manager and director of DuPont & Co., John H. Fahey, James Cardinal Gibbons, E. G. Grace, president of Bethlehem Steel Corp., A. R. Hamilton, W. Averell Harriman, chairman of Board of Directors, W. Harriman & Co., Inc., Arthur E. Holden, Fred C. Hood, E. D. Hulbert, Lucien Jouvaud, Thomas W. Lamont, banker and director of the U. S. Steel Corp., Henry M. Leland, president of Cadillac Motor Car Co., Victor A. Leraner, J W. Lieb, Alfred M. Marling, Edward J. Mehren, editor, *Engineering Record*, Adalbert Moat, Charles A. Munroe, vice-president of Peoples' Gas Light and Coke Co. of Ill., Frank C. B. Page, secretary, American Relief Administration of NYC., Joseph Parks, John H. Patterson, president of National Cash Register Co., Alex Petrunkevitch, prominent zoologist, A. Portfolio, E. W. Rice, Jr., president, Thompson, Houston Electric Co., Julius Rosenwald, president, Sears, Roebuck & Co., Homer E. Sawyer, Jacob H. Schiff, Herman Schneider, Dean of the College of Engineering, University of Cincinnati, and Philip Stockton, president, First National Bank of Boston.

8 The Inter-Racial Council, *Aims and Purposes, op. cit.* The members of the Council included many who had been members of the National Americanization Committee and the Committee for Immigrants in America.

tempted a new emphasis in approach to the Americanization problem through the use of the foreign-language press. In an address on May 21, 1919, to the National Association of Manufacturers at their 24th Annual Convention, Miss Kellor outlined the program of the Council then in progress. After stressing the fact that Bolshevism was gaining a foothold among the foreign-born because Americans were devoting their efforts at that time to forestalling it among the American born and neglecting to do so among the foreign-born, Miss Kellor cited figures to show the importance of the foreign-language press (1,257 foreign-language newspapers with a circulation of over 10,000,000) and hence the need to use it as a most practical approach to the foreign-born. " The intelligent thing to do is to use that foreign-language press and we can make it pro-American if we go about it the right way." [9]

What was needed, said Miss Kellor, was industrial Americanization which she interpreted as the stabilization of labor conditions among the foreign-born, the need for forestalling Bolshevistic and I.W.W. activities among the immigrants by getting the " right " ideas about American business, American life, and American opportunities before the newcomers and not leave the whole problem to the agitators as was the situation at that particular moment. The Inter-Racial Council attempted to do this through the foreign-language press and

9 Kellor, "Address of Miss Frances A. Kellor before the National Association of Manufacturers of the United States, May 21, 1919 ", *Proceedings of the 24th Annual Convention of the National Association of Manufacturers of the United States* (New York City, May 19, 20, and 21, 1919), New York, 1919, pp. 361-368. The National Association at its next annual meeting unanimously endorsed the work of the Inter-Racial Council in the following resolution: " Whereas, the Inter-Racial Council is engaged in a notable effort to investigate the general subject of immigration, both to secure the adoption of a constructive national policy of selective immigration and to systematically aid in the practical distribution, assimilation, and Americanization of the immigrant, Be it Resolved, that we endorse the purpose of the Organization and recommend cooperation with it by all manufacturers." *Proceedings of the 25th Convention of the N.A.M., op. cit.,* p. 297.

through the leaders of the foreign-born. Unfortunately, Miss Kellor stated, the Council found so many obstacles in its path that it saw the necessity of obtaining a pro-American control of the foreign-language press "so the papers would be for America!" The Council did this through obtaining control of the Association of Foreign-Language Newspapers, an agency which furnished advertising to the foreign-language newspapers. Miss Kellor appealed to the members of the National Association of Manufacturers to use the facilities of this subsidiary of the Council for advertising purposes and in this way help to "make this a means of controlling the foreign-language press and shaping its influence along the lines of better Americanism and in opposition to Bolshevism." [10]

The Council rapidly expanded its work along the lines outlined by Miss Kellor until it was composed eventually of more than 1,100 leading industrial establishments in the United States. It organized conference groups among thirty-two of the ethnic groups then resident in the nation. According to William H. Barr, president of the Council, the two groups worked together in "the interests of good wholesome Americanism", and they were directed in their efforts through the foreign-language press with news and advertisements relating the impracticability of Bolshevist theories, and the real meaning of American democracy, and through the English-language press for the purpose of eliminating racial antagonisms which he claimed were the "fertile soil for the seeds of Bolshevism." [11]

10 Enlarging upon the merits of the foreign-language press as an aid to Americanization, Miss Kellor stated in the same speech before the N.A.M. "...it is essential to develop in the foreign-language press a friendly interest in American affairs, an attitude that is pro-American. I believe it to be one of the best antidotes to Bolshevism, that when anything good is being done in industry, the story of it should be told in the foreign-language press, so that these men get something besides attacks on capital...We think it is one of the most practical ways of reaching these people and getting them interested in Americanism." *Ibid.*, pp. 367-368.

11 Statement of William H. Barr, president of the Inter-Racial Council, as quoted by Edward Hale Bierstadt in "Pseudo-Americanization", *New*

The Council called a national conference on immigration in New York City on April 7, 1920, which was attended by 639 individuals. Addresses were made on all aspects of the immigrant problem. Resolutions were passed condemning Bolshevism and those seeking to overthrow the American government, advocating the creating of a federal board of assimilation to work toward that end and federal responsibility for the assimilation of the foreign-born, and condemning the literacy test as without merit and a direct injury to the integrity of commerce.[12] Indicative of the gradual decline of interest in the subject of Americanization on the part of the general public was the fact that out of the sixteen recommendations made, only one, that condemning the literacy test, aroused public discussion. Although the findings of the conference on this subject did not necessarily reflect the opinions or actions of the Council itself, "the assumption immediately was made that the repeal of the literacy test was the sole object of the meeting, and, because of this false impression, two of the labor members of the Council resigned." [13]

The Inter-Racial Council sought to maintain an attitude of understanding toward the immigrant throughout its existence, and constantly deplored the alien baiting and repressive

*Republic*, XXVII (June 1, 1920), p. 20. Indicative of the fear of Bolshevistic influences among the foreign-born felt by the Council was Barr's further statement: "We have seen the ultra-radicals spreading their doctrines of violence and revolution, while American business men have been going placidly about their business not realizing that they are sitting on top of a volcano. Revolutionary agitators have been boring from within the labor organizations; they have been running magazines and papers in English and in foreign languages. It is conservatively estimated that the I.W.W. sells $300,000 worth of literature a year. What has the business man been doing besides giving inspirational addresses and besides playing with amateurish experiments in Americanization?" The Council recognized the nature of the problem hence its organizaton according to Mr. Barr. *Cf.* Bierstadt, *ibid.*, p. 20.

12 Inter-Racial Council, *Proceedings, National Conference on Immigration under Auspices of the Inter-Racial Council*, New York, Apr. 7, 1920.

13 Kellor, *Immigration and the Future, op. cit.*, p. 26.

measures which swept the country as the result of the Bolshevist scare. It preferred to use the means of education and what it thought to be pro-American propaganda in the foreign-language press instead of the use of force urged by many of the professional patriots. Indicative of its leanings along this line was its opposition to the bill introduced into the Senate at the height of the hysteria which would have excluded foreign-language newspapers from the second-class mail unless they conformed with rules and regulations set up by the Post Office Department, and would have required the use of the English language in a portion of the paper as well as other provisions which would have made the further publication of many of the newspapers an impossibility. The Council and its affiliate, the American Association of Foreign-Language Newspapers, Incorporated, sent an attorney, Louis Marshall, to Washington to oppose the bill. Marshall stressed the unconstitutionality of the measure and its unsoundness as a part of public policy. The Council defended the loyalty of the foreign-language press and was unquestionably influential in preventing the passage of the bill.[14]

While the Inter-Racial Council and the National Security League were working for Americanization and actively combating the supposedly 'red' influences at work among the immigrant groups, the Federal Bureau of Education continued its activities along the lines of Americanization during the first part of the year 1919. It was soon forced to withdraw from the field as prime mover however because of the failure of Congress to appropriate the necessary funds to carry on its program. We have seen in Chapter VIII that the National Americanization Committee and its affiliated groups were forced to discontinue the financial aid which they had been giving to the Bureau since 1914 due to the passage of legislation

14 Inter-Racial Council, *Brief in Opposition to the Exclusion of Foreign-Language Newspapers from Second Class Mailing Privileges*, 1921 [in regard to Senate Bill 3718, entitled "A Bill to Exclude Certain Foreign Publications from 2nd Class Mailing Privileges", 66:3rd Sess.].

in 1917. Accordingly, the National Americanization Committee and the Committee for Immigrants in America ceased rendering such assistance on March 4, 1919, leaving the Bureau with slim funds to carry on the work of Americanization.[15] Anticipating the inevitable, the Bureau obtained an allotment of $50,-000 from the President's special fund for the purpose of maintaining a division of educational extension,[16] and diverted $18,000 of this fund for its Americanization program. From January to July 1919, it managed to continue to carry on its campaign with the aid of the fund.[17]

A special director of Americanization work was appointed with four regional directors stationed at strategic centers throughout the nation to assist him. In all these areas, the regional directors made contact with state officials, heads of state organizations, men and women of influence and other individuals, to discuss and make plans for the Americanization of the foreign-born. In every state, the Bureau's agents urged legislative action and rendered help in drawing up suitable bills. They appeared before legislative committees, state gatherings, local meetings, and presented the problem of Americanization to the various State chief executives.[18]

15 Letter from Frank Trumbull, chairman of the National Americanization Committee to Commissioner of Education, P. P. Claxton, dated New York City, April 1, 1919, National Archives, Independent Agencies Archives: Federal Security Agency; Office of Education, *Binder 106*: "Americanization War Work, 1917-1918".

16 "Report of the Secretary of the Interior in Regard to the Bureau of Education", *Reports of the Department of the Interior for the Fiscal Year Ended June 30, 1919*, I, p. 87.

17 *Report of the Commissioner of Education for the Year Ended June 30, 1919*, I, p. 191.

18 *Ibid.*, p. 191. The centers were Albany, N. Y., for the states of New York and New England; Toledo, Ohio, for the states of Michigan, Ohio, Indiana, and West Virginia; Chicago, Ill., for the states of Minnesota, Wisconsin, Illinois, Iowa, and Missouri; and Philadelphia, Pa., for the states of Pennsylvania, New Jersey, Maryland, Delaware, and the District of Columbia.

In presenting the necessity for state Americanization work at that time, the Bureau recommended that such activity be placed under the guidance of the various state departments of education in as much as education played such an important role in the process of Americanization. It also pointed out very carefully that Americanization in its opinion was a much broader process than merely one of education through books. The Bureau reported that its agents were very successful in securing the sympathetic support of the various governors and other officials on behalf of such legislation. It took credit for being instrumental in aiding the successful passage of Americanization bills through nine state legislatures during the first part of 1919.[19]

In two states, the Department of the Interior named state committees composed of two representatives of state bodies whose duties were to try to secure state legislative action and see that the work of Americanization in those states did not lapse pending the passage of the proper legislation. In four states, it compiled lists for the appointment of similar committees. The Bureau reported its regional directors were instrumental in all the states in aiding the elimination of duplication in Americanization work, and in removing cases of friction which existed among the various agencies taking part in the movement. It felt that it had brought a better understanding of the problem in every state through its making the acquaintance of key men and women. It felt, too, that it had made possible the creation of the machinery of Americanization and had put such to work under a common and definite program. Although its general practice was to avoid entering into community projects until the state programs had been inaugurated, the Bureau did call a number of large community undertakings in various cities. In such cases, the regional directors rendered very helpful advice and suggestions which tended to save the cities from

19 Ibid., p. 192. For specific actions taken by the states, see below, pp. 237-252.

many of the mistakes that had been made elsewhere and which might have been disastrous to the movement.[20]

The Bureau of Education sponsored the third and last of the national conferences on Americanization which was held from May 12 to 15, 1919, in the auditorium of the Department of the Interior in Washington, D. C. More than 400 individuals interested in Americanization from all sections of the country attended, including some of most experienced workers in the field. Fifty-three papers and speeches on all phases of Americanization were read and given by such well known figures as Commissioner Claxton, Secretary Lane, Peter Roberts of the Y.M.C.A., Raymond F. Crist, John H. Finley, Mrs. Vladimir G. Simkhovitch of Greenwich Settlement House, Allen T. Burns, director of the Americanization studies sponsored by the Carnegie Foundation, and many others.[21]

The conference revealed a sharp difference of opinion on just what constituted Americanization. Father John O'Grady, the man largely responsible for the reconstruction progam of the National Catholic War Council, sharply criticized the exclusion of labor representatives from the conference particularly at a time when organized labor was developing an increasingly vital interest in educational problems. The reply of the Bureau, that Samuel Gompers had been invited but that his recent accident had prevented representation on the part of the American Federation of Labor, was viewed by ' liberal ' circles as a rather lame excuse. To Felix Morley, writing in the *Nation*, the conference revealed the sharp difference in attitude held by officialdom and the broader-minded educators and social workers. " The meetings revealed a conviction on

20 *Ibid.*, pp. 192-193. The Bureau of Education accumulated a large amount of material of all kinds on Americanization. It classified and digested this material, and then distributed it in the form of mimeographed brochures. The brochures covered various aspects of Americanization, including bibliographies, selected lists of readings on the subject, and statistics on the progress of the movement.

21 *Ibid.*, p. 193. *Cf.* U. S. Bureau of Education, *Proceedings, Americanization Conference*, Washington, May 12, 13, 14, and 15, 1919, *passim*.

the part of the Department of the Interior and the Bureau of
Education that Americanization is primarily a new bulwark
to maintain the old order inviolate while to a majority of the
two hundred delegates this was obviously unimportant compared with the sincere desire to broaden the avenues of opportunity for our foreign-born." Typical of the difference in
attitudes was the speech of Secretary Lane which stressed the
danger of ' red ' agitation among the immigrants, and that
of John Ihlder of the Philadelphia Housing Association which
held that there would be little progress in Americanization
until the tenement environment of the immigrant had been
eliminated.[22]

The Conference recommended the necessity for a centralized
program of Americanization in order to avoid duplication and
overlapping of effort. The federal government was urged to
establish a central agency with full power and responsibility
for developing a definite Americanization program to be carried out in cooperation with the several states. Most of the
conference's attention was devoted to the education of the
immigrant in a knowledge of the English language rather than
in ways of eliminating impossible labor conditions, bad housing, and the prevention of fraud. From the Bureau's standpoint, the conference was a success. It prepared a textbook on
community work in Americanization as a result of the findings

22 Felix Morley, " Making Americans ", *Nation*, CVIII, p. 878. Said
Secretary Lane: " We have no apologies to make for what it [the United
States] is. This is no land in which to spread any doctrine of revolution,
because we have abolished revolution. When we came here we gave over
the right of revolution. You cannot have revolution in a land unless you
have somebody to revolt against, and whom would you revolt against in
the United States—who is there to revolt against? The people of the United
States. And when we won our revolution one hundred and forty years ago
we said, we give over that inherent right of revolution because there can
be no such thing as revolution against a country where the people govern ".
Said Father O'Grady: " The immigrant has some reason for failing to
recognize the idealism of a country which has often exploited him abomin-
ably, surrounded him with intolerable conditions, and generally refused him
even the fundamentals of industrial democracy." *Ibid.*, p. 878.

of the conference.[23] Others, however, like M. E. Ravage and Felix Morley, felt that the conference had been unsuccessful and confused. To these writers, the conference appeared to consider Americanization as chiefly and exclusively a problem in English instruction.[24]

The Bureau of Education made several vain attempts during the period 1919-1921 to obtain appropriations from Congress which would have allowed it to continue with its Americanization program. The Secretary of the Interior, Franklin K. Lane, exerted his influence in support of the work which the Bureau had undertaken, and spoke extensively on behalf of its program. As early as 1918, the Bureau had made its first bid for federal support of Americanization. We have seen in Chapter VIII that one immediate result of the Conference called by Secretary Lane in the spring of 1918 was the appointment of a committee to draw up an Americanization bill to present to Congress for approval. The committee did so, but it was not until January 28, 1919, that the bill was presented to the Senate by Senator Hoke Smith of Georgia, and to the House by Representative William B. Bankhead on January 30, 1919.[25]

The bill (S. 5464; H.R. 15402) directed the Bureau of Education to cooperate with the various states in the education of illiterates and of non-English-speaking residents and in preparation of teachers of such work. Appropriations from Congress were to be made immediately and were to continue until 1926; such appropriations to be used for training teachers and for salaries. The states on their part were to require the instruction of illiterates and non-English-speaking minors more than 16 years of age for at least 200 hours per year in order to share in the distribution of the appropriations. Un-

23 *Report of the Commissioner of Education, 1919, op. cit.*, p. 193.

24 M. E. Ravage, " Standardizing the Immigrant ", *New Republic*, XIX (May 31, 1919), p. 145; Felix Morley, " Making Americans " *op. cit.*, p. 878.

25 U. S. Council of National Defense, *Bills and Resolutions Introduced in the Sixty-Fifth Congress, op. cit.*, pp. 17, 50-51.

fortunately for the Bureau, the first ' Smith-Bankhead Americanization Bill' died with many other measures in the log-jam at the end of the 65th Congress.[26]

This did not discourage the Bureau, however, for the bill was introduced again at the beginning of the 66th Congress. The measure was soon relegated to the background upon the introduction of a similar bill by Senator William S. Kenyon of Iowa (S. 3315) on October 27, 1919, and by Representative Albert H. Vestel of Indiana (H.R. 10710) in the House on November 19, 1919. The 'Kenyon-Vestel Americanization Bill' fared much better than the ' Smith-Bankhead' measure. The bill provided for the promotion of Americanization by authorizing the Bureau of Education to cooperate with the various states in the education of illiterates and non-English-speaking persons.[27] A graduated sum of money was to be set aside for that purpose. $5,000,000 was to be devoted to this end until the end of the fiscal year, June 1920, while $12,000,-000 was to be expended each year thereafter until the end of the fiscal year, June 1923. $500,000 was to be used annually for studies, reports, and surveys which might help in the Americanization of the foreign-born and the elimination of illiteracy. The remainder was to be distributed among the respective states in the proportion the number of their residents involved in the provisions of the act bore to the number of such persons resident in the nation as a whole. The states on their part were to cooperate with the Bureau, and appoint proper custodians. No state was to receive less than $5,000. The Secretary of the Interior was to be authorized to withhold or deduct any amount to fit the local conditions and was to make rules and regulations to carry out the act.[28]

The Senate Committee on Education and Labor reported the Bill out of committee favorably on October 27, 1919, but it

26 *New York Times* (Feb. 23, 1919), III, p. 6; *ibid.* (Apr. 20, 1919), III, p. 1.

27 *Congressional Record*, LVIII, part 9, p. 8823.

28 *Foreign-Born*, I, No. 3 (Jan.–Feb. 1920), p. 4.

did not come up for debate until January 16, 1920. For the next ten days, Senator Kenyon defended his bill before an economy-minded Senate, which finally reduced the proposed appropriation from $42,500,000 to $6,500,000, and the duration of the act from 1923 to 1921. The measure passed the Senate on January 26, 1920 by a vote of 36 to 14. Opposition centered on the constitutionality of the measure, and in the desire of certain of the Senators to return to a more economical legislative program after the huge spending spree indulged in by the preceding ' war ' Congress.[29]

Unfortunately for the Bureau of Education, the Vestel Bill, its companion measure, failed to be reported out of committee by the House's Committee on Education, and the Kenyon-Vestel Americanization measure died a natural death with the ending of the first session of the 66th Congress in the spring of 1920. A further attempt on the part of Representative Vestel to obtain favorable consideration for the bill was made at the beginning of the second session when he reintroduced it (H.R. 14059) on May 13, 1920. In spite of very favorable editorials supporting it in the newspaper press, the measure was never reported out of committee.[30] The economy-minded Congress had definitely set its mind against even such a modified attack upon the national treasury.[31] The bill was submitted

29 *Congressional Record*, LIX, part 2, p. 2059; for discussion of the bill, *cf.* pp. 1649-1653, 1777, 1833, 2059.

30 *Congressional Record*, LIX, part 3, p. 2428.

31 Commenting on the reasons for the curtailment of the Bureau of Education's Americanization program, the chief clerk of the Bureau wrote as follows: " Secretary Lane's conference of 1918 was at the close of rather than the beginning of the Americanization work. The work of Americanization as conducted by the Bureau of Education was in no sense an emergency war measure. It is possible that Congress looked upon it as a war measure and for that reason did not appropriate funds for its continuance, but I feel that the reason for the failure of the appropriation was rather in a sentiment that arose about that time for retrenchment in Government expenditures." Letter to the Lusk Committee, dated Washington, Nov. 3, 1920 (*sic.* 1919), *Report of Joint Legislative Committee Investigating Seditious Activities Filed April 24, 1920 in the Senate of the State of New York*, Albany, IV, p. 4261.

for Congressional approval again on June 8, 1921 at the beginning of the 68th Congress but suffered a similar fate.[32]

Faced by an unresponsive Congress, the Bureau attempted to carry on its Americanization work for the rest of the year 1919, but was soon forced to discontinue its active program. It issued the last number of *Americanization* on November 1, 1919. The Bureau continued to maintain that federal support of the Americanization program was essential for its success as a movement; hence its ardent agitation for the passage of the above mentioned measures. It felt that such federal aid would result quickly in the initiation of a definite and practical program. " In the twenty Northeastern States, in which are found most of the foreign-born population of the country, a definite and practical program could be quickly initiated and the great State agencies easily mobilized to carry it into effect if sufficient funds were at the command of the bureau for that purpose. Left entirely to their own resources,

---

32 Commissioner of Education, P. P. Claxton, recommended once again the passage of suitable legislation in regard to federal support of Americanization in his annual report for 1919. Commenting on the presence of approximately 5,000,000 persons of foreign-birth in the United States who could not read, write, or speak English, Claxton urged immediate passage of the Smith-Bankhead Americanization bill. " Such a large proportion of our population unassimilated constitutes a constant menace. With a sufficient appropriation to assist in paying the salaries of teachers and State and local supervisors, and funds for a staff of experts under its immediate direction, the Bureau of Education could promote effectively this work of Americanization, so vitally important to the strength and welfare of the Nation. The passage of the bill now pending in both Houses of Congress for the appropriation of $14,250,000 a year for seven years for the purpose of enabling the Federal Government through this bureau to cooperate with the several States in this and in the teaching of native-born illiterate men and women would have results of incalculable value. It is sincerely hoped that this bill may become law." *Report of the Commissioner of Education, 1919, op. cit.,* I, p. xi. *Cf. Hearing Before the Committee on Education, House of Representatives, 65th Congress, 3rd Session on HR 15402* (Feb. 14-15, 1919) [in two parts], Washington, 1919; *Hearing Before the Committee on Education and Labor, United States Senate, 66th Congress, 1st Session, on S. 17* (Sept. 11, 1919), Washington, 1919; *Hearing Before the Committee on Education, House of Representatives, 65th Congress, 2nd Session, on HR 6490* (Mar. 4, 1918), Washington, 1918.

Americanization work by the States and communities will, no doubt, continue in the future as in the past to be sporadic and largely ineffective. The time has come when this work should be undertaken by the Federal Government and the States on a scale comparable to the magnitude of the task and issues at stake." [33]

The Bureau of Education felt it had served the country well through the Americanization work it had inaugurated and carried on by its Americanization Division: " As a result of the work of this division of the Bureau, the country has obtained a broader and clearer conception of what Americanization means, and its importance has been greatly emphasized. Several States have enacted laws, and made appropriations for teaching English and other subjects to foreign-born residents in the public schools and elsewhere. Numerous societies have been organized for the promotion of Americanization work, and many more organized for other purposes have adopted some form of Americanization work as a part of their program." [34] The Bureau closed its Americanization Division in the autumn of 1919. Thereafter, the Bureau of Education was forced to limit its Americanization efforts to creative suggestions in reply to occasional correspondence.[35]

Although the Bureau of Education was forced to abandon the important role which it played in supporting the movement to Americanize the immigrant in 1919, the Federal

33 *Report of the Commissioner of Education for the Year Ended June 30, 1919*, I, *op. cit.*, p. 193.

34 *Ibid.*, p. 193.

35 Letter from the chief clerk of the Bureau of Education to the Lusk Committee: " Congress would appropriate no funds for Americanization work so we were compelled to close our Division a number of months ago and to discontinue the publication of the *Americanization magazine*.", dated Washington, Oct. 28, 1920 [*sic.* 1919], *Report of the Joint Committee ... of the State of New York, op. cit.*, p. 421. *Cf.* also, letter from P. P. Claxton to the author dated Clarksville, Tenn, Mar. 4, 1941, expressing similar opinion that retrenchment in government expenses had led Congress to view the bills unfavorably.

Bureau of Naturalization continued to carry on the work which it had started in 1914, and thus became the sole federal agency actively supporting Americanization. Intimate relations were maintained by the Bureau with practically every community of 2,500 population or over having an immigrant population. The Bureau reported that each of these towns had taken some initial step toward the reorganization of its school system by the end of the fiscal year, July 1, 1919, to take up " the national and local responsibility for the Americanization of the foreign-born." Whereas, the Bureau declared, the school year in 1915 at the beginning of the national campaign in behalf of Americanization opened with a mere 38 communities pledging their school systems to spreading the doctrines of Americanism, the school year 1919 closed with 2,240 communities actively supporting the movement and carrying on classes on behalf of the immigrant. The year 1918-1919 saw a new increase of 438 over the preceding fiscal year." [36]

Many of these municipalities embarked upon elaborate Americanization campaigns in addition to furnishing the usual evening facilities for teaching English and citizenship to their immigrant residents. Chief among these were Akron and Cleveland, Ohio, Cincinnati, Boston, Detroit, Buffalo, Chicago, New York City, Rochester, and Syracuse. Cities like Duluth, Grand Rapids, and Minneapolis published special literature on Americanization, while smaller cities like Butte, Mont., the Shenango Valley towns of Pennsylvania, and Redlands and Watsonville, Cal., conducted special programs of Americanization. A full treatment of the steps taken by each community on behalf of Americanization would fill several volumes. A perusal of the *Americanization Bulletin*, and the Y.W.C.A.'s immigrant periodical, *Foreign-Born*, reveals interest in Americanization on the part of practically every town and municipal-

---

36 " Report of the Commissioner of Naturalization ", *Reports of the Department of Labor, 1919*, p. 784. For table of cities, *cf*. p. 785.

ity in the United States which contained a substantial immigrant population during the years 1919-1920.[37]

The Bureau of Naturalization remained the sole federal agency at work on behalf of Americanization after the decline of interest in the movement after 1921. It continued the program it had worked out in cooperation with the public schools of the nation in support of immigrant education. Slight modifications were made from time to time in regard to procedure, but for the most part the Bureau continued its program very much in accordance with the procedure followed during the war years. It ceased sending letters directly to candidates for naturalization and their wives as it had in the past in which attendance at the local public school classes was urged. Instead, the Bureau entered into an agreement with the National Council of Boy Scouts of America in 1919, whereby the youngsters cooperated with the local superintendents of schools in bringing the message of the Bureau to the attention of the immigrants. The Boy Scouts also served the Bureau's agents as guides and ushers in the citizenship receptions held for the newly naturalized citizens from time to time. A total of 44,489 invitations had been so delivered by the Scouts to the immigrants by the end of June 1920.[38] This figure rose to 103,060 in 1921,[39] fell to 91,168 in 1922,[40] and then declined rapidly thereafter as the drop in immigration set in due to the passage of the quota legislation.[41]

The Bureau continued to distribute its textbook on citizenship and various posters advertising the opening of evening schools for the foreign-born in the several foreign languages. Its representatives cooperated with the school authorities in

37 *Cf.* files of *Americanization Bulletin*, 1918-1919, and *Foreign-Born*, 1920-1921.

38 "Report of the Commissioner of Naturalization", *Reports of the Department of Labor, 1920*, pp. 802-803.

39 *Ibid., 1921*, p. 17.

40 *Ibid., 1922*, p. 21.

41 *Ibid., 1923*, p. 23; *1924*, p. 2.

arranging for citizen receptions in the many cities and municipalities of the country. On occasion, the agency rendered advice and suggestions to industrial concerns which desired to
establish classes for their immigrant workers.[42] As the decade
of the twenties advanced, and the flow of immigration slackened
considerably, the Bureau noted a gradual decline in the number
of enrollees in immigrant education classes. It activities on
behalf of such were reduced accordingly.[43]

The years 1919-1920 witnessed the passage of a good deal
of state legislation in support of Americanization and the education of the adult immigrant. As we have seen, a considerable
amount of influence was exerted by the Bureau of Education's
Americanization Division in support of this legislation. There
can be no doubt, however, that many states passed such legislation as a consequence of the wave of hysteria that swept
the nation during this period resulting from the actions of the
Department of Justice in conducting its crusade against the
alien radical.

Connecticut established a Department of Americanization in
1919, and appropriated the sum of $50,000 to carry out a state-
wide Americanization campaign for a two-year period.[44] Its
publicity program was especially well organized. A special
speakers' bureau with a corps of thirty foreign-language
speakers was set up, and a series of bulletins and circular letters
was issued and spread broadcast throughout the state's educational circles. Approximately 10,000 posters in seven different
languages were also distributed. The Connecticut Department
of Americanization also produced a special moving picture
dealing with Americanization which was widely used and

42 " Reports of the Commissioner of Naturalization ", *1921-1925*, and
thereafter.

43 *Ibid.*

44 State of Connecticut, *Public Acts of Connecticut, 1919*, Chapter 286
(approved May 21, 1919).

adopted by other states in support of their Americanization efforts.[45] The Department remained in existence until 1926 when it merged with the division of adult education of the State Bureau of Education.[46] Interest in immigrant education was expressed by the State's Bureau of Education during the entire decade of the 1920's.[47]

Delaware passed an Americanization Aid Law in 1919, which provided an appropriation of $15,000 for the two-year period beginning January 1, 1919 to assist in the Americanization of foreigners and providing classes for adult immigrants in English.[48] The state thus took over the Americanization work which had been carried on by the Delaware Council of Defense and the Service Citizens of Delaware, a group of prominent industrialists, social workers, and business men, upon the abolition of the Council with the ending of hostilities. For six months in 1919, the Service Citizens had carried on an active Americanization campaign with the chief emphasis upon the city of Wilmington which contained most of the immigrant population of the state. The state's Education Department then continued the work much along the lines laid out by the

45 State of New York, *Report of the Joint Legislative Committee Investigating Seditious Activities ... State of New York*, IV, *op. cit.*, p. 4293. [Hereafter this publication will be referred to as *Revolutionary Radicalism*]. The Department published *Classes for Foreign Adults; Information Regarding Naturalization with Outline of History and Government in the United States*, Hartford, 1920, and *Information for New Americans*, Hartford, 1921. It also distributed circular letters on "Duties of a Local Director of Americanization", "Americanization Work in Urban Communities", "Americanization Work in Rural Communities", "Americanization Work for Women and Women's Organizations", and "Americanization Work for Religious Bodies and through Parochial Schools", Hartford, 1919.

46 *Report of the State Board of Education of the State of Connecticut for 1926-28*, part 2, pp. 186-193.

47 *Ibid., 1922-23* and *1923-24*, pp. 209-215.

48 *Revolutionary Radicalism*, IV, *op. cit.*, pp. 3487-3488.

Service Citizens Committee. Delaware, too, maintained an interest in immigrant education throughout the twenties.[49]

The influence of the Americanization movement was felt in Illinois, which created an Immigrants' Commission in 1919 for the purpose of making a survey of the state's immigrant population. As the result of its findings, the Commission later published two *Bulletins* on the needs of the immigrants in Illinois which tended to stimulate further interest in Americanization.[50] The legislature of Iowa passed legislation making the teaching of Americanization compulsory in the public schools. A special text-book was published by the State Board of Education for the use of immigrant education classes.[51] Kansas, too, passed special legislation in 1919, providing for the establishment of night schools for adults including adult immigrants.[52] North Dakota, which had passed legislation in 1917 for the setting up of evening schools for the purpose of the Americanization of foreigners and to promote the growth of American ideals and good citizenship, passed supplementary legislation in 1919, which provided the sum of $7,000 for one year for the purposes of Americanization.[53] A special conference of county superintendents of schools held in January 1919,

49 For Delaware's Americanization efforts, *cf.* Delaware State Council of Defense, *Americanization in Delaware, a State Policy*, 1919. On the work of the Citizens, *cf.* Service Citizens of Delaware, *Six Months of Americanization in Delaware*, Wilmington, Sept. 1919; Joseph H. Odell, *Report Made to the Annual Meeting of the Service Citizens of Delaware*, May 7, 1920; Service Citizens, *Voices of the New America, 1920-1921, ibid., 1921-1922*, all published by the Citizens. For further state efforts, *cf. Reports of State Superintendents of Education for the Years 1920-1930*.

50 Illinois Immigrants' Commission, *The Educational Needs of Immigrants in Illinois*, Springfield, 1920; also, *The Immigrant and Coal Mining Communities of Illinois*, Springfield, 1920 [both written by Grace Abbott].

51 Clinton, Iowa, *Advertiser*, Oct. 4, 1920.

52 State of Kansas, *Laws Relating to Education, Sessions of 1919*, Chapter 271, paragraph 9396; Chapter 24, Section 604.

53 State of North Dakota, *General Schools with 1917 Enactments, Revolutionary Radicalism*, IV, *op. cit.*, pp. 3949-3951.

agreed to emphasize and push Americanization.[54] Thereafter, the work was pursued vigorously well into the twenties.[55]

The state of Maine made funds available in 1919 for carrying on evening schools and classes in English for adult immigrants, and placed the work of promoting such classes in the division of vocational education of the State Board of Education. Maine carried on work of this kind all through the 1920's.[56] The legislature of Minnesota appropriated $25,000 to aid Americanization through the passage of its "Americanization Aid Law" in 1919. Instruction in English, the essential facts of American history, and American government, were to be given. The state agreed to pay one-half the salaries of the teachers so engaged. Active cooperation was maintained with the University of Minnesota, which set up an Americanization training program under the capable guidance of Professor A. E. Jenks.[57] The same year witnessed the passage of legislation by the state of Montana, providing for the establishment of Americanization schools throughout the school districts of the state. The school boards and the boards of trustees of the several school districts were authorized to establish and maintain such schools for all persons over sixteen years of age for

54 Letter from Miss Minnie J. Nielson, state superintendent of Public Instruction, Oct. 27, 1919, *Revolutionary Radicalism*, IV, *op. cit.*, p. 3951.

55 State of North Dakota, *Sixteenth Biennial Report of the State Superintendent of Public Instruction for the Two Years Ending June 30, 1920*, pp. 119-120.

56 State of Maine, *Report of State Superintendent of Public Schools of State of Maine for the Year Ending June 30, 1920*, p 20. *Cf.* subsequent issues. Fifteen special Americanization schools were organized in the various immigrant centers. A special summer course sponsored by the State Board of Education was held at the Castine Normal School during the summer of 1921. Classes continued to be carried on as late as 1928. *Cf. Reports, 1920, 1921, 1922-28*.

57 *Revolutionary Radicalism*, IV, *op. cit.*, pp. 3728-3729; letter from P. C. Towning, deputy commissioner of education, St. Paul, Oct. 30, 1919, *ibid.*, p. 3729. Also, University of Minnesota, *Bulletins*, 1918-1919, and 1919-1920 re course of study in Americanization training.

instruction in the English language, American history, and citizenship.[58]

Massachusetts, too, joined the parade of states which passed special legislation in 1919 for the promotion of Americanization work among the foreign-born, twenty-one years of age and over. The sum of $10,000 per year was granted to the State Board of Education for that purpose. A special director of Americanization, John J. Maloney, was appointed to supervise the work. Each town and city received one-half the money expended on its Americanization classes from the state.[59] The state carried on one of the most successful of the state Americanization programs. Several conferences were held for educators during 1919 concerning the Americanization question,[60] the most important having been held at the State House on November 13, 1919, which was attended by sixty superintendents and local directors of Americanization. Another, initiated by the Associated Industries of Massachusetts, held at Nantasket in June 1919, drew representatives from industries from all parts of the country. The following year, 1920, an important state conference on immigrant education in Massachusetts industries was held at Plymouth, which stressed the imperative need for such education throughout its entire three-day sitting.[61] The Commonwealth carried on an active immigrant education program throughout the entire decade of the 1920's.[62]

58 State of Montana, *School Laws of the State of Montana*, June, 1919, Chapter V, Section 508, paragraph 4, p. 72 [approved Feb. 21, 1919].

59 Commonwealth of Massachusetts, *Massachusetts Acts of 1919*, Chapter 295, "An Act to Promote Americanization through the Education of Adult Persons Unable to Use the English Language". Cf. *Revolutionary Radicalism*, IV, *op. cit.*, p. 3678.

60 Commonwealth of Massachusetts, *Fifth Annual Report of the Division of University Extension, Bulletin of Department of Education of Massachusetts*, V, No. 2 (Mar. 1920).

61 Massachusetts Department of Education, *Proceedings of the State Conference on Immigrant Education in Massachusetts Industries*, 1920.

62 Commonwealth of Massachusetts, *Annual Reports of the Division of University Extension of the Department of Education of the Common-*

Two other New England states, New Hampshire and Rhode Island, passed Americanization legislation in 1919. The former's legislature approved a measure providing the sum of $162,000 for the instruction of foreign-born adults in the English language, civics, and American history for the year ending August 31, 1920, and an additional sum of $150,000 for the year ending August 31, 1921 for the abolition of illiteracy and for the Americanization of immigrants. Americanization work was placed under the direction of the State Board of Education. A deputy commissioner of education became to all extents and purposes a state director of Americanization.[63] A law prohibiting the employment of anyone between 16 and 21 who could not speak English, unless such attended immigrant education classes, was passed also in 1919.[64] It became effective October 1, 1919.[65] By 1922, classes in immigrant education had begun to lag, however, due to the decline in immigration.[66]

Rhode Island put into effect an act to promote Americanization on July 1, 1919, which provided for the establishment of free public evening schools for the purpose of teaching the English language to the foreign-born. A special compulsory clause made attendance on the part of all those unable to speak or read or write English between the ages of sixteen and twenty-one a necessity. A special supervisor of Americaniza-

---

wealth of Massachusetts, 1919-1930. Cf. J. J. Mahoney, "Americanization in the United States", U. S. Bureau of Education, Bulletin, 1923, No. 31, pp. 7-9.

63 Letter from Maro S. Brooks, deputy commissioner of education of the state of New Hampshire to Lusk Committee, dated Concord, Nov. 26, 1919, Rev. Radicalism, IV, op. cit., pp. 3819-3820. Cf. State of New Hampshire, School Laws of 1919, sections 16, and 30.

64 The New Hampshire Americanization Committee issued a special Americanization pamphlet, cf. Report of the Superintendent of Public Instruction, Being the Sixtieth Report Upon the Public Schools of New Hampshire, Concord, 1918, p. 27.

65 Cf. footnote 63.

66 State of New Hampshire, Report of Superintendent of Public Instruction, 1922, p. 137; ibid., Report, 1924, p. 164.

tion was appointed. Appropriate fines were to be imposed upon those who failed to comply with the provisions of the act.[67] In 1920, an amendment to the Americanization law was enacted which provided $5,000 for the establishment of factory classes. Provision for the employment of truant officers to enforce the law accompanied the amendment. A liberal increase in the amount appropriated for the purpose of Americanization was also voted.[68] Interest in Americanization work continued well into 1923 despite the decrease in immigration due to the inauguration of the quota system.

In the far west, various states showed their interest in the Americanization movement by passing appropriate legislation or by instructing their state departments of education to sponsor and support local Americanization efforts. Arizona organized a special committee on Americanization work, under the direction of the Federal Bureau of Education, composed of representatives of women's clubs, the D.A.R., the American Legion, and other patriotic groups to stimulate interest in the movement. The new agency took over the work of the disbanded state council of defense upon the repeal of the law creating it in 1919. The committee centered its activities chiefly in the mining communities of the state.[69] The same year saw the passage of legislation providing $25,000 for the carrying on of Americanization work through the State Department of Public Instruction. Because of the objections to the compul-

67 *Rev. Radicalism*, IV, *op. cit.*, pp. 4072-4075. *Cf. Bulletin of the Board of Education of the State of Rhode Island, an Act to Promote Americanization, April 25, 1919.*

68 State of Rhode Island and Providence Plantations, *Fifty-First Annual Report of the State Board of Education Together with the Seventh-Sixth Annual Report of the Commissioner of Public Schools of Rhode Island*, Jan. 1921, pp. 12-13.

69 *Foreign-Born*, I, No. 3 (Jan.-Feb. 1920), p. 2. The Arizona legislature had provided in 1918 for the establishment of night schools by the various school districts for those not able to speak, read, or write English and desirous of attending night school. *Cf. Americanization Bulletin*, I, No. 1 (Sept. 1918), p. 8.

sory features of the legislation, however, the succeeding session of the legislature failed to continue the appropriation.[70] Oklahoma passed legislation in 1919 which made it incumbent upon the public school authorities to organize a class in English and citizenship whenever presented with petitions signed by ten residents of foreign-birth over sixteen years of age. The new law also provided an Americanization Commission consisting of the Governor and six others appointed by him to supervise the inauguration of the new provisions.[71] Ardent Idaho Americanizers finally succeeded in having a bill of compulsory educational nature passed in 1921, after having failed upon two previous occasions in 1917 and 1919.[72] The law provided for the compulsory education of foreign-born adults unable to read, write, or speak English, both in that subject and in American history and civics.[73]

Three other western states passed legislation in support of the Americanization movement during the immediate postwar years. Oregon, taking a leaf from California, provided for the appointment of special home teachers by the local school authorities in 1921 to interest parents and children in school attendance, sanitation, the English language, household duties, and the fundamental duties of American citizenship. Illustrative of the current fear of the Bolshevist menace was the wording of the law: " Whereas, owing to the appalling turbulency of the world's chaotic political and social conditions particularly in the bolshevik and soviet countries of eastern Europe and the probability of such contagion extending over and

70 Letter from C. O. Case, state superintendent of public instruction, to Lusk Committee, dated Nov. 26, 1919, *Rev. Radicalism*, IV, *op. cit.*, p. 3408.

71 Oklahoma, *School Laws of Oklahoma, 1919*, Article III, Section 356.

72 Letter from E. A. Brown, commissioner of education to Lusk Committee, dated Sept. 15, 1920, *Rev. Radicalism*, IV, *op. cit.*, pp. 3623, 4339; also letter from governor to U. S. Council of National Defense, July 3, 1919, U. S. Council of National Defense, *Readjustment and Reconstruction Information*, II, p. 72.

73 *Foreign-Born*, II, No. 8 (June–July 1921), p. 248.

permeating our own American government . . . be it enacted
. . . .", etc.[74] The schools of the state cooperated actively in
seeing that teachers gave necessary instruction in regard to
naturalization.[75]

The state of Utah, too, showed its interest in the patriotic
movement by passing a compulsory Americanization act effective September, 1919. The new law provided that every
alien residing in the state (except those physically and mentally
disqualified), between the ages of sixteen and forty-five unable
to speak, read, or write English required by 5th grade standards must attend public evening school classes under pain of
fine. A special director of Americanization was created within
the State Board of Education to supervise and standardize
the Americanization work. The sum of $20,000 was appropri-
ated for the purpose.[76] A very active Americanization effort
was carried on under the terms of the act,[77] although the
appropriation failed to provide enough money to cover the
expense of the work.[78] Supplementary legislation strengthened
the program in 1921, but the same year saw the elimination
of the director of Americanization.[79] Much resentment was

74 *Ibid.*, II, No. 7 (May 1921), p. 215; also, *ibid.*, I, No. 3 (Jan.–Feb.
1920), p. 2.

75 Letter from J. A. Churchill, superintendent of public instruction, to
Lusk Committee, Oct. 28, 1919, *Rev. Radicalism*, IV, *op. cit.*, p. 4059.

76 Utah, *School Laws Reprinted from the Session Laws of Utah*, 1919,
Chapter 93, pp. 19-21. *Cf.* also, *Rev. Radicalism*, IV, *op. cit.*, pp. 4116-4118;
also *Thirteenth Report of the Superintendent of Public Instruction . . . 1920*,
pp. 63-65.

77 Letter of E. J. Norton, assistant superintendent of school instruction
to the Lusk Committee, dated Oct. 28, 1919, *Rev. Radicalism*, IV, *op. cit.*,
p. 4119.

78 *Foreign-Born*, II, No. 9 (Aug.-Sept. 1921), p. 278; also II, No. 6
(Apr. 1921), p. 173; also II, No. 6 (Apr. 1921), p. 169.

79 State of Utah, *Fourteenth Report of the Superintendent of Public Instruction*, 1922, pp. 79-80; *Fifteenth Report of the Superintendent of Public
Instruction*, 1924, p. 109; *School Laws of the State of Utah*, 1939, pp. 66-68.

expressed against the compulsory nature of the legislation as the 1920's advanced, but evidently was not strong enough to bring about the dropping of the compulsory regulations. The latter remain a part of the Utah School Code to date.[80] Wyoming, authorized its State Board of Education in 1921 to organize classes in Americanization in its evening schools and to fix standards concerning the education of the foreign-born. An appropriation of $8,000 was made to carry on the work.[81] The State Board of Education, which had actively supported Americanization work in the local districts, carried on the program all through the 1920's.[82]

New Jersey passed special legislation in support of Americanization during 1920. By means of new measures, the board of education of any school district could establish classes for the instruction of foreign-born residents over fourteen years of age in the English language and the government and laws of the United States and New Jersey, either in day or evening classes. A yearly appropriation of $100 was to be given to each local county unit for each teacher so employed.[83] The financial aid so rendered proved to be a mere " drop in the bucket ". Subsequent attempts to push through bills to create a state department of Americanization under the Department of Public Instruction in 1921 failed to receive a favorable reaction from

---

80 *Foreign-Born*, II, No. 7 (May 1921), p. 215; also, II, No. 6 (Apr. 1921), p. 173; *cf. Biennial Report of the State Department of Wyoming, 1921-1922*, pp. 56-58.

81 The work was still being carried on as late as 1930, *cf. Biennial Report, 1929-1930*; also, *First Report of the State Board of Education of Wyoming* (May 14, 1917–Oct. 1, 1918), 1918, pp. 30-31.

82 Letter from John Enright, assistant commissioner of education, to the Lusk Committee, Sept. 3, 1920, *Rev. Radicalism*, IV, *op. cit.*, p. 4374. For text of the act, ibid., pp. 4373-4375.

83 State of New Jersey, *Annual Report of the State Board of Education and of the Commissioner of Education of New Jersey for the Year Ending, June 30, 1920*, p. 23. *Cf. Foreign-Born*, II, No. 7, p. 217; III, No. 4 (Apr. 1922), p. 116; III, No. 5 (May 1922), p. 143.

an economy-minded legislature.[84] Indicative of the interest of the state in Americanization was the conference called by Governor W. N. Runyon in the fall of 1919. Leading manufacturers, business men and professional men discussed emigration of alien labor and concrete programs for the Americanization of aliens.[85]

The state of Ohio, whose executive and educational departments had shown their interest in Americanization by urging vigorous programs of Americanization of the immigrant during the years 1917 and 1918, embarked upon definite legislative steps in support of the movement in 1919 by authorizing the creation of a special standing committee on Americanization with the state superintendent of education as its head. The new committee took over the work of the former state council of defense, and used its best efforts to work for the eradication of illiteracy and for the promotion of Americanization and better standards of living among the state's immigrant population. The new Americanization Committee of Ohio, as it was called, carried on the battle for the Americanization of the immigrant.[86] Subsequent legislation in the spring of 1921 strengthened the Committee.[87] Ohio's State Department of Public Instruction sponsored special training courses for Americanization teachers during the summer of 1920 at the Cleveland School of Education and at Akron.[88] In cooperation with the Department, the Ohio Americanization Committee held teachers' training institutes at Toledo, East Youngstown, Can-

84 *New York Evening Post*, Dec. 27, 1919; also, *Foreign-Born*, I, No. 3 (Jan.-Feb. 1920), p. 13.

85 Memo from Americanization Division of U. S. Bureau of Naturalization to U. S. Council of National Defense, July 23, 1919, *Readjustment and Reconstruction Information*, II, *op. cit.*, pp. 251-253.

86 *Foreign-Born*, II, No. 6 (Apr. 1921), pp. 171-172; II, No. 9 (Aug.-Sept. 1921), p. 278.

87 State of Ohio, *Sixty-Seventh Annual Report of the Superintendent of Public Instruction to the Governor of Ohio for the Year Ending June 30, 1920*, p. 23.

ton, and Martin's Ferry during the fall of 1920, and also published two pamphlets on Americanization in addition to three others dealing with the Americanization crusade. One of these, *A Manual for Teachers,* gained general recognition as one of the very best in regard to the teaching of immigrants.[88]

Others of the states, although not passing specific legislation in regard to Americanization, rendered valuable aid to the movement through the active support of their respective state departments of education during the immediate post-war years. Such was true of Louisiana, whose state Department of Education took an active part in furthering the work started by the Americanization Committee of the state council of defense in the parishes during the summer of 1919.[89] Wisconsin, also, through its State Board of Education, carried on an active campaign in sponsoring Americanization classes throughout the state.[90] A strong bid was made to secure appropriate Americanization legislation during the 1919 session of the legislature, but the proposals were defeated because of the great opposition to the compulsory nature of the bills.[91] Indicative, however, of the interest of the State Board of Education in Americanization was the need for such expressed by Cecile White Flemming, the state superintendent of education, in her

88 *Foreign-Born,* II, No. 2 (Dec. 1920), p. 47. The pamphlets: *Americanization in Ohio, a Constructive Program,* Columbus, 1920; *A Handbook of American Citizenship,* 1920; *Fundamental Facts for New Citizens,* 1922; *Manual for Teachers,* 1922; and *Adult Education in Ohio,* 1922.

89 Letter from Secretary of Louisiana State Council of Defense to U. S. Council of National Defense, May 16, 1919, *Readjustment and Reconstruction Information,* II, pp. 111-112; also, letter from T. H. Harris to Lusk Committee, dated Oct. 27, 1919, *Rev. Radicalism,* IV, *op. cit.,* p. 3662. *Cf. Christian Science Monitor,* Nov. 23, 1919.

90 Letter from C. P. Cory, state superintendent of public instruction of Wisconsin, to Lusk Committee, dated Oct. 27, 1919, *Rev. Radicalism,* IV, *op. cit.,* p. 4160; also, letter from John Callahan, secretary of Board of Vocational Education, Dec. 4, 1919, *ibid.,* p. 4161. See also, letter from Dan D. Lescohier, asso. prof. of University of Wisconsin, dated Nov. 3, 1919, to Lusk Committee, *ibid.,* pp. 4160-4161.

*Report* for 1916-1918.[91] Nevada,[92] West Virginia,[93] Maryland,[94] Indiana,[95] and Washington,[96] all took advantage of their respective night school legislative acts to sponsor Americanization locally. The latter state attempted in 1921 to pass an act authorizing travelling teachers to carry on Americanization activities, but the measure failed to pass the legislature.[97]

The Department of Public Instruction of Michigan pushed an active program of Americanization in rural communities in cooperation with the Federal Bureau of Education.[98] An attempt to adopt specific Americanization legislation in 1921 by providing for Americanization through the education of all persons over eighteen years of age unable to read, write, or speak English, and the appointment of a director of Americani-

91 Cecile White Flemming, *The State and the Public Schools, Two Years Progress in Education in Wisconsin,* Madison, 1919, pp. 138-150.

92 *Rev. Radicalism,* IV, *op. cit.,* p. 3809. *Cf. Nevada Educational Bulletin* published in same, p. 3815, for description of certain phases of Americanization work in Nevada.

93 State of West Virginia, *Biennial Report of State Superintendent of Free Schools of West Virginia for the Two Years Ending June 30, 1922,* p. 8. West Virginia State University provided Americanization courses for teachers in response to the great interest in Americanization and the education of the immigrant. *Ibid.*

94 Maryland State Board of Education called a special conference of thirty representative men and women of the state on November 12, 1919 in regard to Americanization. *Cf.* letters from M. Bates Stephens, state superintendent of schools, dated Nov. 19, 1919 and Oct. 30, 1919, to Lusk Committee, *Rev. Radicalism, op. cit.,* IV, 3670-3671.

95 Letter from L. N. Hines, state superintendent of public instruction dated Oct. 27, 1919, to Lusk Committee, *Rev. Radicalism,* IV, *op. cit.,* pp. 3636-3638.

96 State of Washington, *Twenty-Fifth Biennial Report of the Superintendent of Public Instruction for the Period Ending June 30, 1920,* pp. 181-188; *cf. Twenty-Sixth Biennial Report,* 1922, pp. 172-176; also, *Foreign-Born,* II (Apr. 1921), p. 173, *re* traveling teachers.

97 *Ibid.*

98 Letter from Thomas E. Johnson, superintendent of the Department of Public Instruction of Michigan, to Lusk Committee, dated Oct. 27, 1919, *Rev. Radicalism,* IV, *op. cit.,* pp. 3713-3714,

zation as assistant to the superintendent of public instruction failed, although the bill did succeed in passing the Senate.[99] Colorado's State Department of Education actively sponsored Americanization in the schools and followed the example of Minnesota by using its state university as its chief sponsor of Americanization activities. A special Americanization commission of twelve members attempted in 1919 to have a compulsory education law similar to that of Utah's passed by the legislature, but failed to muster enough strength in support of it. The commission held two conferences on Americanization with the result that a considerable interest in the movement was aroused. The State University's Extension Division took up the work of active encouragement of Americanization upon the dissolution of the state council of defense. It organized classes in English and citizenship in cooperation with the Federal Bureau of Naturalization. The Division sponsored the formation of community Americanization committees for the purpose of securing closer cooperation between native and foreign-born.[100] This action carried on the Americanization program inaugurated early in April 1918 by ' America First ' societies to awaken a new spirit of patriotism and to pave the way for further steps in the education of immigrants and their future Americanization.[101]

Four other states inaugurated Americanization legislation during the period. California, carrying on the good work accomplished during the previous four-year period, passed an act in 1921 providing for the establishment of classes in instruction in citizenship for applicants who had filed their declar-

99 *Foreign-Born*, II, No. 8 (June–July 1921), p. 252.

100 Letter from Henry R. Spangler, secretary, Bureau of Americanization of the University of Colorado, to Lusk Committee, dated Nov. 24, 1919, *Rev. Radicalism*, IV, *op. cit.*, pp. 3456-3457; also, letter from Mary C. Bradford, state superintendent of public instruction, to Lusk Committee, dated Oct. 27, 1919, *ibid.*, p. 3455.

101 *Readjustment and Reconstruction Information*, II, *op. cit.*, pp. 40-41.

ations of intention.[102] South Dakota embarked upon an ambitious Americanization program in 1919 by passing an act to promote the movement. All immigrants between the ages of sixteen and twenty-one (not physically or mentally disqualified), not possessing a knowledge of English equal to that of a 5th grade youngster were forced to attend public school classes subject to fine for failing to do so. $15,000 was provided for the purposes of holding special classes to meet this need. A special state director of Americanization was appointed on July 1, 1919.[103] The State carried on a vigorous campaign for Americanization and education of the foreign-born, particularly in the rural areas, well into the twenties.[104]

The Commonwealth of Pennsylvania passed an act in 1919 providing public instruction in citizenship and the principles of American and state government for the foreign-born.[105] The following year the State Department of Public Instruction took over the Americanization work that had been carried on by the State General Welfare Commission during the war years. An Americanization bureau was established in the Department, which undertook to sponsor Americanization classes in the local communities throughout the state.[106] The Bureau issued releases and formational data from time to time, and otherwise stimulated interest in Americanization work until

102 *Foreign-Born*, II, No. 6 (Apr. 1921), p. 172; II, No 10, (Oct. 1921), p. 309.

103 *Ibid.*

104 South Dakota, *Session Laws of 1919*, Chapter 169, section 1; *cf. Rev. Radicalism*, IV, *op. cit.*, pp. 4090-4093; also, South Dakota State Department of Publication, *Americanization of South Dakota*, Aug. 1919. See, also, *Fifteenth Biennial Report*, 1918-1920, pp. 14-20; and, subsequent *Reports* including that of 1924. *Cf.* Department of Public Instruction, *Patriotic and Civic Instruction*, 1921.

105 Commonwealth of Pennsylvania, *School Laws of Pennsylvania, 1917*, Act No. 311; *cf. Rev. Radicalism*, IV, *op. cit.*, pp. 4063-4064.

106 Letter from Thomas E. Finnegan to Lusk Committee, dated Sept. 9, 1920, *Rev. Radicalism*, IV, *op. cit.*, p. 4385.

the decline in immigration of the early 1920's led to its abolition.[107] Finally, New York passed Americanization legislation
during this period. One law authorized the Commissioner of
Education to provide for the maintenance and conduct of a
course of study and training in the state normal institutions
and colleges, universities, and other educational institutions
for the purpose of training teachers to instruct the foreign-
born in evening, factory, home, and community classes. $40,-
000 was appropriated to carry the program into effect.[108]
Another law authorized the Commissioner of Education to
divide the state into zones and to appoint directors of each in
order to promote and extend the educational facilities for the
education of illiterates and the non-English-speaking foreign-
born,[109] and appropriated $100,000 for the use of local munici-
palities for the carrying on of Americanization classes. Both
went into effect in 1919.[110]

Success had marked the efforts of the Americanizers to obtain the passage of legislation by the several states which would
make it possible for the immigrant to study the English
language and other aspects of American culture in night schools
and other places. They had been successful, too, in arousing
the interest of many who held positions of importance in civic
and municipal affairs in the education of the immigrants.
Although in most cases the Americanizers were people of in-
telligence and of civic and social conscience, there were unquestionably many of a super-patriotic nature, who threw
themselves into the movement enthusiastically, and by so doing
did not hesitate to conduct themselves in a manner of superiority and self-importance which deeply hurt the feelings of
the immigrants and which many times resulted in a feeling of

---

107 *Foreign-Born*, II, No. 2 (Dec. 1920), p. 48.

108 State of New York, *Laws of 1920*, Chapter 851, Article 4, Section
11a; also *Foreign-Born*, I, No. 6 (May 1920), p. 3.

109 State of New York, *Laws of 1920, op. cit.*, Article 4, Sect. 11b.

110 *Ibid.*, Article 4, Section 11c.

resentment on the part of the latter. Then, too, the 'red bait-ing' campaign carried on by the Department of Justice, and the consequent reaction on the part of the people of the United States, did not help matters. Heretofore, the immigrants had reacted to the movement in a friendly manner to a remarkable degree. Immigrant leaders and organizations had volunteered their services and had cooperated closely with the various agencies carrying on Americanization activities. Editorials in favor of the goals of the Americanizers and praising the efforts of the Bureaus of Education and Naturalization, in particular, had appeared in many of the foreign-language periodicals and newspapers.[111] The intelligent immigrant seemed only too eager to take advantage of the opportunities offered to learn English and gain knowledge of his newly adopted country.

As the result of the hysteria engendered by the Bolshevist bogey, however, a change in the approach to Americanization was taken by many in the movement. A definite emphasis was assumed which sought to stamp out the remnants of foreign culture still in existence in America.[112] The passage of the various state laws prohibiting the teaching of the common

[111] This spirit was exemplified at a luncheon given to the editors of for-eign-language newspapers and leaders of opinion among the immigrant groups of Detroit by the Detroit Board of Commerce. They expressed their approval of night school classes for immigrants and their disapproval of hyphenism. *Cf.* "Foreign Editors Endorse Night School Classes", *Ameri-can Leader*, IX (Jan. 13, 1916), pp. 10-11.

[112] According to Miss Kellor: "Many Americans saw a positive menace in the growing power of immigrants' organizations and of the foreign lan-guage press and they began to favor the suppression of all languages but English; the elimination of the foreign language press; the restriction of immigration for a period of years, and the enactment of a compulsory citizenship law." She added, however, "Others ... both native and foreign born found in the revelations brought about by the strains of the conflict [the war] a great faith in the assimilation of the immigrant and a better way to undertake it, and pointed to the fact that the new friendships es-tablished by the war, and the remarkable steadiness shown by the immigrants under great pressure from abroad revealed an unexpected strength in our racial relations." Kellor, *Immigration and the Future*, pp. 57-58.

branches of study in foreign languages,[113] the efforts made to enact legislation prohibiting the use of the mails to foreign-language publications, and other high-handed schemes brought forth on behalf of ' 100% Americanism ', all deeply offended the more sensitive of the immigrants and led to a growth of hostility and suspicion on their part to the activities and aims of the various Americanization groups. The creation by the Department of Justice of a Citizens' Protective Association which " became in effect a voluntary spy organization, did much to destroy the confidence which had been developing before the war between the native and foreign-born in America ".[114]

Typical of the reactions of certain elements among the American immigrant population was the following comment of Carol Aronovici, of the California State Commission of Immigration and Housing, which appeared in the *Annals* of the American Academy of Political and Social Science:

> To one who knows the soul and spirit of the immigrant, who has passed through the painful experience of analyzing, sorting and accepting American life, the spectacle of the rabid and ignorant Americanization efforts was disheartening. It did not represent America as the foreigner has pictured it in his dreams before landing upon these shores. It flavored more of Hungary where the magyarization of several millions of

113 Such legislation was passed in 1919 by Alabama, Arkansas, Colorado, Delaware, Illinois, Idaho, Iowa, Kansas, Michigan, Minnesota, Nebraska, Nevada, New Hampshire, Oklahoma, and Oregon.

114 To quote Miss Kellor on this change of attitude: " Many of them [the immigrants] came out of the war with a sense of resentment and in some cases of bitterness. They have lost most of their faith in American justice and fair play because they have been dealt with in a summary way, with little expressed comprehension of their own peculiar difficulties. They have acquired a supercilious and critical attitude toward Americanization because its pretensions have not coincided with their experience. They have remembered their humiliation by self-constituted bodies who took the law into their own hands; and they are less sure than they were before the war that the guarantees of the American Constitution will protect them." *Cf.* Kellor, *Immigration and the Future*, p. 58.

people was attempted by means not consistent with American tradition, or of Russia of the Tsarish days with the persecution of the Jew and the denationalization of the Poles. For these reasons the Americanization movement could not survive during normal times. It was a negative movement; one that demanded sacrifice and which did not stop with the expressions of the mob, but dragged into the struggle some of the high officials of the United States Government. Should we be surprised or sorry that it is now denied by many of the spontaneous organizations of the war period and that it is allowed to pass away of autointoxication and will remain unmourned by its once staunch friends? [115]

Similar sentiments were expressed by such immigrant leaders as Elbert Aidline of the Yiddish Press,[116] Morris Debower of the *American Hebrew*,[117] Walter Hart Blumenthal,[118] and Barbara E. Pollak, feature story writers,[119] Professor Sarka B. Hrbkova, the Czech-American intellectual,[120] Gino Speranza, the Italian-American writer,[121] Julian Korski Grove, Polish writer and Polish Consul-General of New York,[122]

115 Carol Aronovici, "Americanization", American Academy of Political and Social Science, *Annals*, XCIII (Jan. 1921), p. 134.

116 Elbert Aidline, "The Yiddish Press and Americanization", *American-Hebrew*, CIV, No. 21 (Apr. 4, 1919), pp. 488 and 498.

117 Morris Debower, "Americans without Fireworks", *American Hebrew*, CV, No 7 (June 27, 1919), pp. 158 and 165.

118 Walter Hart Blumenthal, "Cavier Americanism, a Reply to the 'Comedy of Americanization'—in the *Saturday Evening Post*, October 29", *American Hebrew*, CX, No. 2, pp. 30, 42 and 46.

119 Barbara E. Pollak, "Americanism That Works Both Ways", *American Hebrew*, CVI, No. 22 (Apr. 16, 1920), pp. 726-727.

120 Professor Sarka B. Hrbkoya, "'Bunk' in Americanization", *Forum*, LXIII (April–May 1920), pp. 263-269.

121 Gino Speranza, "Does Americanization Americanize?", *Atlantic Monthly*, CXXV (Feb. 1920), pp. 263-269.

122 Julian Korski Grove, "The Polish Group in the United States", American Academy of Political and Social Science, *Annals*, XCIII (Jan. 1921), pp. 149-153.

Jaroslav F. Smetanka, the Czech Consul-General in Chicago,[123] and many others.

The foreign-language press, too, expressed its disapproval of the methods of the more ardent of the super-patriots and its suspicions of the motives of many connected with the Americanization drive. Typical of the reaction on the part of this medium of expression among the foreign-born was the editorial which appeared in *Dziennik dla Wszystkich,* a Polish-language newspaper of Buffalo, on August 29, 1919:

> All foreigners dislike the imposition of mass naturalization methods which they consider bad. Americanization is a natural process and has nothing to do with first and second papers; yet the cultured foreigner who has long been a resident of the United States and yet has no citizenship papers is not considered more desirable than the ignorant immigrant street sweeper who has become naturalized. Under the present conditions foreigners are likely to take out naturalization papers simply in order to be left unmolested. This is a foolish movement which creates hypocrisy.[124]

Another from the same paper stated:

> Poles! do not deny your mother tongue and use English only. It is deplorable that so many Americans object so much to foreign customs. It smacks decidedly of Prussianism, and it is not at all in accordance with American ideals of freedom.[125]

Typical, too, of this disapproval of the methods of the more ardent of the Americanizers was the editorial which appeared in *Szabadzag,* the Hungarian language newspaper of Cleveland on February 28, 1920:

---

123 Jaroslav F. Smetanka, "Bohemians and Slovaks—Now Czechoslovaks", American Academy of Political and Social Science, *Annals*, XCIII (Jan. 1921), pp. 149-153.

124 As cited in *Foreign-Born,* I, No. 1 (Nov. 1919).

125 *Ibid.,* I, No. 6 (May 1920).

The first generation of immigrants may serve America without speaking English. *Americanization* does not mean the suppression of foreign languages. As Governor Smith said in his Washington Day address: " If the immigrant performs his task, establishes a home, educates his children, whether he knows English or not, he is as good an American as he who has a right to claim New England ancestry.[126]

Editorials stressing the same beliefs appeared in the Russian, Italian, and Slovak foreign-language newspapers:

From *Russkoye Slovo,* Russian newspaper, New York City, December 20, 1919:

The future of the United States belongs not to Americanization but to Americanism. Franklin K. Lane denies the principle of compulsory assimilation. " We should take the best the immigrant has to give us and give him in return our best cultural customs, if we want to enrich the civilization of our country." This is true Americanism. Americanization expects no contribution from those who are to be assimilated. It is based on the certitude that America is rich in everything and is in need of nothing new.[127]

From *L'Aurora,* Italian newspaper, Reading Pa., June 12, 1920:

Americanization is an ugly word. Today it means to proselytize by making the foreign-born forget his mother country and mother tongue.[128]

From *Czeskoslovensky Legionar,* Slovak periodical, Pittsburgh, May 1920:

There is a mistaken notion among some well-meaning people that the foreign-born would be better Americans if they understood the Constitution of the United States. " We do not agree with this because the average American native does

126 *Ibid.,* I, No. 6 (May 1920).

127 *Ibid.,* I, No. 4 (Mar. 1920).

128 *Ibid.,* I, No. 9 (Sept.–Oct. 1920).

not know it either, and yet he has some very clear conceptions of right and wrong. The very same applies to our foreign brethren." Another mistaken notion is that a person cannot be loyal unless he is able to speak English. Are we going to annoy those who cannot yet do so or are we going to try and retain their friendship in spite of their broken English? [129]

From *Pravda,* Russian newspaper, Olyphant, Pa., September 30, 1919:

> Many Americanization Committees only exist on paper. They make much noise, get themselves into the newspapers, but do not do much good. They mostly laugh at the poor foreigners. If Americans want to help the immigrants, they must meet them with love. The immigrant is by no means stupid. He feels the patronizing attitude the American adopts towards him, and therefore never opens his soul.[130]

Similar editorials appeared in many foreign-language newspapers during the years 1919-1920, all expressing their disapproval of various aspects of the Americanization drive; some mildly almost self-consciously, others frankly and belligerently. It would be, of course, impossible to estimate accurately the reaction of the immigrant population as a whole to the Americanization drive. Most of the populace were far too self-conscious and afflicted with the traditional inferiority complex associated with migration to a new strange land to come out openly and place themselves on record. Such as did, while recognizing the necessity for learning English and a knowledge of American ways of life and American ideals and attitudes as was only befitting if one wished to play a useful role in the new environment, resented very much the attitude of superiority of the more extreme types of Americanizers.[131]

The more progressive advocates of Americanization were not unaware of the impression which the super-patriots and

129 *Ibid.*, I, No. 9 (Sept.–Oct 1920).

130 *Ibid.*, I, No. 2 (Dec. 1919).

131 *Cf.* files of *Foreign-Born,* 1921-1922.

red-baiters were making upon the immigrant and deplored such tactics in their writings on the subject. Miss Frances Kellor, who had perhaps more than any one person given her time and talents to the movement, bitterly condemned in her speeches and writings the alien baiting and repressive measures that swept the country during the years 1919-1920. In an address before the New York Credit Men's Association given in New York City on January 27, 1920, Miss Kellor, while acknowledging the belief that the immigrant was the weakest point in the American economic program which the Bolshevik could attack because of the strategic position occupied by the immigrant workmen in the production of raw materials, nevertheless emphasized the fact that ' alien baiting ' and ' repressive measures ' would not help matters very much. What was needed, said Miss Kellor, was to counteract the influence of Bolshevik propaganda by adopting a selective immigration policy and an active program to acquaint the immigrants fully with American life and its institutions as well as to give them what she chose to call " a full opportunity " in America. In her opinion, it was absolutely essential to have a federal law which would provide a system of receiving, distributing, and assimilating immigrants.[132] She later summarized the situation pessimistically as follows:

> Now that the war is over we are discovering that while it has cemented new friendships among races, and has promoted cooperation between some native and foreign-born Americans, it has just as definitely created new racial antagonisms and brought about new misunderstandings between individuals. The American, influenced as he is by the spread of Bolshevism and by the prevalence of unrest, as well as by some spectacular evidences of disloyalty among some aliens during the war, leans more and more toward repression and intolerance of differences. The immigrant is sensitive to this change and, as

132 Frances A. Kellor, *The Inside of Bolshevism*, an address before the New York Credit Men's Association, New York City, Jan. 27, 1920 [pamphlet; no paging].

he is constantly receiving messages from abroad urging him to return home, he is becoming less friendly toward America. For this reason, assimilation measures, which might have been undertaken with ease and success before the war, now yield but little result, even with greater effort.[133]

Others concerned with the Americanization movement wrote and spoke on behalf of caution and friendliness in approaching the foreign-born. A whole series of sociological works dealing with the ' process of Americanization ' and what might be considered proper procedure to aid this process made their appearance. Among these was the series sponsored by the Carnegie Foundation of New York and edited by Allen Burns. The series dealt with all aspects of the immigrants' contacts with their new invironment, and attempted to outline sympathetically the difficulties involved in the procedure and what might be a satisfactory approach for social workers and others in their attempts to iron out some of these problems.[134]

Aware, too, of the need for a better approach in winning over the foreign-born to the program of Americanization and deploring the attitude and methods of certain of the Americanizers were the several colleges and universities of America whose sociology and educational departments were only too cognizant of the intricate nature of the problem and of the necessity for caution in procedure in approach to the question of Americanization. Special courses in " Americanization ", were offered by many of these during the years, 1918-1921,

---

133 Kellor, *Immigration and the Future, op. cit.,* p. 23.

134 List of *Carnegie Studies in Americanization*: S. P. Breckinridge, *New Homes for Old,* New York, 1921; K. H. Claghorn, *The Immigrant's Day in Court,* New York, 1923; John Daniels, *America via the Neighborhood,* New York, 1920; M. M. Davis, *Immigrant Health and the Community,* New York 1921; J. P. Gavit, *Americans by Choice,* New York, 1922; W. M. Leiserson, *Adjusting the Immigrant and Industry,* New York, 1924; R. E. Park, *The Immigrant Press and Its Control,* New York, 1922; R. E. Park, *Old World Traits Transplanted,* New York, 1921; P. A. Speek, *A Stake in the Land,* New York, 1921; and F. V. Thompson, *Schooling of the Immigrant,* New York, 1920.

which consisted chiefly of instruction on how to teach English to the newcomers, and how to improve their environmental conditions through better standards of sanitation and housing. The University of Minnesota in particular under the guidance of Professor A. E. Jenks, inaugurated an elaborate program of education for teachers and social workers in Americanization activities. The program of the University received the high praise of Americanizers throughout the country because of its excellent analysis of the problem and sensible approach to to the immigrant. Other colleges and universities held classes in "Americanization" during their summer sessions and in their evening extension divisions.[135]

Individauls educated under the programs presented by these institutions of higher learning reflected more of a sociological approach to the problem of Americanization than that of the super-patriots and those more fanatically infected with nationalistic fervor; and since these people were for the most part educators by profession, their influence came in time to bear an ever increasingly important part in the movement. While the un-professional elements in the drive soon tired in their efforts for reasons which will be outlined below, the professional educators and social workers continued to carry on the work of educating the immigrants in the evening schools and in the settlement houses long after the Americanization drive had worn itself out in so far as the public was concerned. Americanization classes then became merely one part of the new emphasis in education, namely—adult instruction.

One other element intimately concerned with the Americanization of the foreign-born, organized labor, remains to be considered in respect to the last phases of the crusade. We have

135 Included among these institutions were: the Universities of Wisconsin, Utah, Colorado, Minnesota, West Virginia, California, North Carolina, Pittsburgh, Indiana, Wyoming, Columbia, Harvard, City College of New York, Cleveland School of Education, and a host of teachers' colleges and normal schools throughout the nation. *Cf. Reports of the Commissioner of Education for the Year 1918-1921*; *Rev. Radicalism*, IV, *passim*, and the annual bulletins of the respective institutions.

seen in Chapter VII that organized labor looked askance at the efforts of the Americanizers at the beginning of the drive. Gradually, however, the attitude taken by the *United Mine Workers' Journal,* namely that through the Americanization movement nothing but possible advantage could accrue to the cause of labor, seems to have become the dominant attitude of labor in regard to the movement, particularly when the federal and state governments began to champion the drive. Samuel Gompers praised the efforts of Secretary of the Interior Lane along this line, and consented to sit on the latter's Committee for Americanization appointed in April 1918.[136] The Committee on Education of the American Federation of Labor endorsed the Americanization Bill sponsored by Senator Smith in 1918.[137] Various of the constituent unions of the Federation embarked on programs in support of the movement, and received this complementary citation from the Bureau of Education's *Americanization Bulletin* of October 15, 1918: " The gratifying extent to which labor and the organizations affiliated with the American Federation of Labor are supporting the program of Americanization which the Bureau of Education is working out is fully revealed in the replies received in answer to its letter sent out to labor unions and read at the various Labor Day celebrations throughout the country. All the answers pledged the most cordial support to the Americanization campaign." Included among these organizations were the National Window Glass Workers' Union, the Granite Cutters' International Association of America, the Amalgamated Lithographers of America, the International Association of Machinists, the Printing Pressmen and Assistants Union, the Railway Mail Association, the United Association of Plumbers and Steamfitters of the United States and Canada, the Boston

---

136 Samuel Gompers, " Educate—Americanize ", *American Federationist,* XXV (May 1918), pp. 390-391.

137 American Federation of Labor, "Attitude Toward Adult Education ", *Report of Proceedings,* 38th Annual Convention, St. Paul, June 10 to 20, 1918, p. 317.

Central Labor Union, the Mansfield, Ohio, Trades Council, the Roanoke, Va., Central Trade and Labor Council, the Huntington, W. Va., Trade and Labor Assembly, the Virginia Federation of Labor, and others.[138]

Later in 1919, a United Labor Educational Committee was formed in New York City, composed of representatives of the Furriers Union, the Headgear Workers' Institute, the Amalgamated Clothing Workers' Union, the Jewelry Workers' Union, the Workmen's Circle, the Women's Trade Union League, and a few local unions of different organizations to carry on all phases of Americanization through education.[139] The same year saw the American Federation of Teachers place itself on record in hearty support of the movement.[140] The United Mine Workers, sharp critics of the Americanization movement in its beginning stages, now went all out in pledging support to the movement. It drew up a resolution calling for the speedy Americanization of all foreign-born at its convention in Cleveland in October 1919,[141] and issued strong editorials in support of the drive in its official *Journal*.[142]

Apparently, with the entry of the federal and state agencies into the Americanization drive, much of the suspicion which labor had held toward the original Americanizers now disap-

138 " Trade Unions ", *Americanization Bulletin*, I, No. 2 (Oct. 15, 1918), p. 2.

139 " Headgear Workers' Institute New Committee ", *Americanization Bulletin*, I, No. 9 (May 1, 1919), p. 8.

140 American Federation of Labor, " Report of the Committee on Education ", *Report of Proceedings*, 39th Annual Convention, Atlantic City, June 9-23, 1919, p. 316.

141 " Resolutions Adopted by the Cleveland Convention ", *United Mine Workers' Journal*, XXX, No. 19 (Oct. 1, 1919), p. 13.

142 *Cf.* editorials, " Night Schools for Foreign Born Should Be Encouraged ", *United Mine Workers' Journal*, XXX, No. 4 (Feb. 15, 1919), p. 7; " Educate the Foreign-Born ", *ibid.*, XXX, No. 12 (June 15, 1919), p. 9; " Labor Takes Steps for Americanization ", *ibid.*, XXX, No. 6 (Mar. 15, 1919), p. 11; and Mary E. McDowell, " Americanization ", *ibid.*, XXIX, No. 7 (June 20, 1918), pp 6 and 11.

peared, and the various bodies were more than willing to do their part in support of the program. To what extent this attitude reflected the fear on the part of the more conservative unions of the growing menace of the I.W.W. with their cry for an all inclusive ' one big union ' and other ' radical ' trends, it would be difficult to estimate. As for the I.W.W., itself, unfortunately, examination of the respective periodicals and journals of that organization by the author revealed nothing in regard to the Americanization movement.

The whole burst of anti-alienism that spread through America during the years, 1919-1920, undoubtedly hastened the passage of restrictive immigration legislation, which in turn tended to quiet the fears of the American public in regard to the possible menace of the immigrant. The result had a profound effect upon the Americanization drive, and undoubtedly aided in diminishing its momentum.

The suspicion of the hyphenated American had resulted in the passage of the so-called Literacy Test Act of February 5, 1917. Passed over President's Wilson's veto by a vote of 287 to 106 in the House and by a vote of 62 to 11 in the Senate, the bill was a harbinger of even stronger restrictive action against the entry of the immigrant once the war was over. The Palmer raids and the resulting controversy over ' red ' agitation in America aroused popular support of stronger measures in support of closing the bars against the growing post-war flood of immigration from Europe. The result was the drafting of the so-called Quota Act of May 19, 1921, and its eventual passage. Although only of a temporary emergency nature, it effectively stemmed the tide for the time being, until extended by the act of May 11, 1922, which definitely outlined a permanent policy of quota arrangements for immigration into America.

The passage of these legislative acts did much to quiet the fears of the American public *vis à vis* the immigrant within its midst, and although patriotic groups like the American Legion, the D.A.R., the Society of Colonial Dames, and others continued to maintain a vigilant alertness for possible continuance of ' red ' agitation among the immigrant groups, most Americans soon forgot the controversy of 1919-1920 in their quest for economic security in the midst of the many post-war problems which beset America in the early 1920's. Many of those who had so eagerly supported the Americanization drive during the war and the immediate post-war years felt content that all was well when the proper state action concerning the education of the immigrants had been taken, and promptly turned their attention to other matters. With the cessation of the flow of immigration as a result of the passage of the quota acts, the question of the immigrant and his Americanization rapidly passed from the public view as a front page issue. The little groups that had campaigned so ardently on behalf of the movement liquidated themselves and turned over the role of educator of the immigrant to the proper constituted educational authorities. Then, too, the depression of 1921 did much to put a crimp to the activities of many of the private groups carrying on the Americanization drive. The cessation of financial contributions to such groups meant the cessation of activity on behalf of Americanization efforts as well. Nothing more is heard of the Inter-Racial Council after 1921.[143]

Thus a combination of the four factors—the passage of the quota legislation, the passage of suitable legislation by the several state governments having a significant immigrant population insuring facilities for the education of the same, the effects of the depression of 1921 upon the financial backing of the groups at work on behalf of Americanization, and finally the return of the American people to a state of ' normalcy ' after the war fever and hysteria of the immediate post-war

143 The author's conclusions in regard to the four factors are agreed to by Mr. Joseph Mayper who headed the Federal Bureau of Education's Americanization Bureau from 1919 until its abolition, and by P. P. Claxton, former Commissioner of Education during the Wilson administration. [Conversation between Mayper and the author, Jan. 18, 1942; letter from Claxton to the author, Mar. 4, 1941.]

period—all contributed not a little in eliminating the problem of the immigrant and the need for his Americanization from the public eye and interest. Henceforth, interest in Americanization as such tended to be confined for the most part to professional educators, sociologists, and social workers. The Americanization drive or movement to educate the immigrant and inculcate him with American ideals and the American language definitely came to an end with the year 1921. The process of Americanization, on the other hand, that peculiar force, ever at work in transforming migrants from other lands into average Americans in thought, word, and deed, continued on throughout the years, a process which is still at work today.

# CHAPTER X

# THE MOVEMENT EVALUATED

In the preceding chapters, the author has attempted to trace the rise and growth of one of those phenomena so typical of American social history—a movement or drive to solve some particular problem or to bring about some particular goal. In the case of the Americanization Movement, the pattern followed was the usual one. First, individuals became interested and active. Then, organization into groups followed which propagandized and exerted pressure on behalf of their desired goal. Finally, government agencies, both state and federal, were induced to join the lists and to aid in the movement.

Fear and suspicion of the large influx of immigrants from eastern and southern Europe, of the influence that these people might exert upon America, and of what might happen to the nation should these immigrants not have some intelligent guidance in American ways and some inculcation in American idealogy, was the dominating stimulus which started the movement on its way. At first, action was confined to the social worker and to social groups generally. These sought to alleviate the exceedingly bad living conditions of the newcomers and to free them from the exploitation of their ' padrones ' and unscrupulous ' racial ' leaders. Idealism of the highest type characterized this early stage of the drive.

Toward the end of the first decade of the twentieth century, however, because of the growth of I.W.W. activity and the increasing activity of ' new ' immigrant individuals in the labor disputes and unrest which developed in the New England industrial area and elsewhere, a fear of the spread of so-called ' radical ' ideals among the great laboring mass of immigrants brought about the formation of special groups. These saw in a program of inculcation and education of the immigrants a means of keeping down unrest and influencing these people along behavior patterns more in keeping with what they believed to be the 'real' American way of life. Idealism was thus wedded to the economic motive, although the latter in itself bore an idealistic tone for the Americanizers of this stripe really believed the so called *laissez-faire* formula to be one of America's foremost ideals and the foundation stone of American economic life.

Idealists and 'economic idealists' joined forces, enlisted the aid of philanthropists, and embarked on a first class crusade of education and inculcation of the immigrant groups in an effort to transform these people, at least idealistically, into 'old line' Americans. What would have happened to their drive had not fortuitous circumstances favored their crusade will never be known, but fortuitous circumstances in the form of the outbreak of European hostilities occurred in 1914, and the resulting increase in national consciousness, of suspicion of the hyphenated immigrant, and of the necessity for national preparedness, gave them the opportunity to push their program to the fullest and to enlist the aid of powerful governmental agencies on behalf of the Americanization crusade.

The movement thus completed the normal cycle. Individuals had been merged into groups, groups had influenced government, and from this point onward, government sponsored the drive using prestige and agencies to carry on the campaign. Although a let-down in activities might have been expected at the close of World War I due to the natural death of war-pitch patriotism, such did not occur in 1919 for across the ocean in Russia a new economic regime had been established which did not find acceptance with a goodly majority of the American people. The fact that the new 'Red Goliath' had certain vociferous champions on this side of the Atlantic, particularly among the I.W.W. and certain immigrant groups, did not help matters either. Thus a second set of fortuitous circumstances kept the Americanization drive at full steam at a time when one would normally have expected it to suffer a decline. The result was the passage by government, in this case state action, of numerous acts on behalf of and in support of the Americanization of the immigrant.

The let-down in the movement occurred in 1920-1921. The return of 'normalcy', the passage of the restrictionist legislation, and the action of the states in regard to Americanization, tended to reassure the fearful and to bring back the indifference of the many. Henceforth, Americanization as a drive or crusade was over. As a process, however it still interested the social worker, sociologist, and teacher. Even here, however, emphasis had changed from the old days when even the most idealistic social worker still felt a bit of the American superiority complex. Recognition of the cultural contributions which the various nationality groups could make to America, and recognition, too, of the fact that the American cultural pattern was not or could never hope to be restricted to a bonafide purely Anglo-Saxon pattern, led to a new approach and study of the immigrant and to a better appreciation of his worth to the American community.

In their choice of terminology, the Americanizers were apt to be vague. Such words and phrases as " good patriotic American ", " Americanism ", " civic loyalty ", " old fashioned American ideals ", " patriotism ", etc., were all used very freely by the advocates of Americanization, yet seldom did they define these terms. Their aim, of course, was to win over the immigrant from his foreign ways, speech, and ideals, through education and inculcation as well as by good example, and thereby transform him into an individual holding the same ideals, speaking the same language, and living the same sort of life as that of his native American contemporary. Beyond this explanation they seldom went, taking for granted that the native American population to whom their literature and propaganda was chiefly addressed would fully understand what constituted " good Americanism ", " American ideals ", and " the American way of life ". What they had in mind by these terms was what was generally believed at that time to

constitute a proper " American " orientation, namely, a staunch
belief in and support of the ideals expressed by the founding
fathers in the great American documents, the Declaration of
Independence and the Constitution, and further revealed by
the writings of such American statesmen as Washington,
Franklin, Jefferson, and Lincoln: democracy, representative
government, respect for law and order, and equality of opportunity both in the political and economic spheres. To these
they added, the belief in the great role played by the public
schools as an educational medium, the great merits of the
capitalistic economy and the blessings of *laissez-faire,* the advantages of thrift, the feeling that the American people had
the highest standard of living and lived under the best sanitary
and hygienic conditions, and the conviction that here in
America and only here were there possibilities for all to become
successful and even rich if they would only exert themselves
sufficiently. A well-grounded knowledge of the English language was deemed essential if one wished to share to the fullest
the blessings of the American environment. That the Americanizers never felt the need to define these vague terms referred
to over a period of time seems to the author to be sufficient
proof that both the terms and the mission presented by the
Americanizers were accepted at face value and so understood
by the native Americans to whom they were addressed. With
passing years, criticism of the movement did arise in time as
noted in the preceding chapter, but such criticism did not hit
at the ' ideals ' stressed by the Americanizers in their propaganda, but rather at their methods or at their integrity. In
time, from the immigrants themselves, as expressed by their
leaders, came a strong challenge as to what constituted a ' good
American '. Here again there was no criticism of the idealism
expressed in the movement but rather at the over-emphasis
placed by certain of the Americanizers on the necessity for
learning English and likewise the necessity for giving up as
rapidly as possible cherished ' foreign ' customs. It was this

rather than the 'idealism' of the movement that aroused a strong protest on the part of the representatives of the 'new' Americans.

That the Americanizers were successful in arousing the American public sufficiently to take steps to bring about the Americanization of the foreign-born in line with their suggestions has been indicated above, namely, through federal, state, and municipal action. That they were successful in bringing about the Americanization of the foreign-born is another matter. Unquestionably, many of the immigrants who were enticed into evening schools as the result of propaganda undoubtedly became more familiar with American ideals and the American way of life, and probably became better Americans thereby. Undoubtedly, many immigrants acquired enough education through the special immigrant educational program to become citizens. But mere acquiring of education and citizenship by an individual did not necessarily mean that he would be a 'good American' then anymore than it does today. Actually, the number of immigrants who became Americanized along the formal lines advocated by the Americanization groups must have been small, indeed, when compared with the great bulk of their fellows who never saw the inside of an American schoolroom or settlement house. The great majority of the latter became Americanized in time through the gradual process of assimilating American customs, attitudes, speech, and ideals from their native American neighbors and from their American-born children. This assimilative process is still actively at work, and is likely to continue as long as immigrants continue to come to America or to be present in the American environment.

Viewed objectively, the results of the movement to Americanize the immigrant were of both a negative and a positive nature. To the first should be credited the growth of a bitterness on the part of the immigrant groups toward the Americanizers which resulted in outbursts of editorial spleen as illustrated in Chapter IX, and the undoubted deepening of inferiority complexes as the immigrants became increasingly aware that they were considered problems by many of their native American neighbors. On the negative side, too, should be credited a certain increase in nativism, later to break forth in the 1920's in the form of the revived Ku Klux Klan, which was strengthened by the fear of possible unassimilation. On the other hand, the criticisms directed at the immigrants by the more zealous and less thoughtful of the Americanizers made for a strengthening of the 'racial' ties, and stimulated the leaders of the various ethnic groups to challenge many of the superiority assumptions of the crusaders and to defend their own cultures and the contributions of their own peoples to America. This new attitude, coupled with the fact that various and sundry of the 'new' immigrant elements had entered the political field and had begun to feel their voting strength, soon forced a retreat on the part of many native Americans from the extremist positions assumed at the height of the patriotic war fever.

On the positive side may be mentioned the growth of an attitude of tolerance on the part of a greater proportion of the American people than heretofore. Zealots and super-patriots might have overdone matters here and there, but the message of understanding and appreciation of the foreign-born contained in the literature issued by the various governmental bureaus must have aroused within many native Americans a feeling of responsibility for their new neighbors, and engendered within them a sincere desire to do their part to stamp out intolerance and bigotry. The Americanization movement which brought together the native and foreign-born, in many cases for the first time, was thus a lineal ancestor of those movements in the 1920's, 1930's, and the present-day national brotherhood drive, which, through association and mutual understanding of the various religious and ethnic groups, strove or are striving to abolish bigotry and intolerance in America.

On the positive side of the ledger, too, credit should be assigned to the Americanization movement for the impetus which it gave to the budding adult education movement. In this respect, the passage of state Americanization legislation providing night schools and facilities for the education of the adult immigrant paved the way for later legislation on behalf of other types of adults as well as immigrants. In many cases, the original Americanization acts provided these features. Legislation on behalf of adult education and evening schools might not have been passed so easily had it not been for the crusading zeal of the Americanizers in sponsoring such legislation on behalf of the foreign-born. With precedent taken, the stage was set for better things to come.

The " Movement to Americanize the Immigrant " was the product of an America that was still suffering its industrial growing pains and had not as yet digested the huge mass of humanity that had flocked to its shores from an impoverished Europe. As such, it forms an interesting phase of American history during the first two decades of the 20th century. Idealistic in tone, nationalistic in goal, patriotic in expression, it takes its place, alongside those other great crusades of the past, abolitionism, woman's suffrage, civil service reform, and universal education. Like these other movements, it reveals itself as a manifestation of the buoyant optimism and enthusiasm of a people ever confident of their ability to proselytize successfully and of their ability to win converts to their cause.

# APPENDICES

# APPENDIX A

ARTICLES EXPRESSING DOUBT AS TO THE POSSIBILITY OF THE
ASSIMILATION OF THE 'NEW' IMMIGRANT

Chetwood, John, "The Problem of Immigration", *Arena*, XXVII (Mar. 1902), pp. 254-260.

Commons, John R., "Amalgamation and Assimilation", *Chautauqua*, XXXIX (May 1904), pp. 217-260.

Devine, Edward T., "Immigration as a Relief Problem", *Charities*, XII (Feb. 6, 1904), pp. 129-133.

Fairchild, Henry P., "Foreign-Americans", Nation, XCIII (Dec. 28, 1911), pp. 626-627.

——, "The Restriction of Immigration", *American Journal of Sociology*, XVII (Mar. 1912), pp. 637-646.

Halifax, Guy Raymond, "The Immigration Scourge", *Overland Monthly*, XLIII (Jan. 1904), pp. 65-69.

Hall, Prescott F., "The Future of American Ideals", *North American Review*, CXCV (Jan. 1912), pp. 94-102.

——, "New Problems of Immigration", *Forum*, XXX (Jan. 1901), pp. 555-567.

——, "Selection of Immigration", American Academy of Political and Social Science, *Annals*, XXIV (1904), pp. 169-184.

"Immigration", *Public Opinion*, XIV (Dec. 10, 1892), p. 221.

Knight, John Watrus, "The Working Man and Immigration", *Charity Review*, IV (May 1895), pp. 363-375.

Lodge, Henry Cabot, "Efforts to Restrict Undesirable Immigration", *Century Magazine*, LXVII (Jan. 1904), pp. 466-469.

Norton, Eliot, "The Diffusion of Immigration", American Academy of Political and Social Science, *Annals*, XXIV (1904), pp. 161-165.

Penrose, Boies, "Chinese Exclusion and the Problem of Immigration", *Independent*, LIV (Jan. 2, 1902), pp. 12-15.

Roebling, John A., "Economic Aspects of Immigration", *American Magazine of Civics*, IX (Oct. 1896), pp. 235-245.

Sanborn, Alvan F., "The New Immigration to America", *Independent*, LIV (Nov. 13, 1902), pp. 2696-2698.

Sargent, Frank P., "Problem of Immigration", American Academy of Political and Social Science, *Annals*, XXIV (1904), pp. 153-158.

Sherman, Philip Edward, "Immigration from Abroad into Massachusetts", *New England Magazine*, new series, XXIX (Feb. 1904), pp. 671-681.

Walker, Francis A., "Immigration", *Yale Review*, I (Aug. 1892), pp. 125-145.

——, "Immigration and Degradation", *Forum*, XI (Aug. 1891), pp. 634-644.

——, "Restriction of Immigration", *Atlantic Monthly*, LXXVII (June 1896), pp. 822-829.

Ward, Robert DeCourcey, "The Immigration Problem", *Charities*, XII, (Feb. 6, 1903), pp. 138-151.

——, "Immigration and the South", *Atlantic Monthly*, XCVI (Nov. 1905), pp. 611-617.

——, "The Restriction of Immigration", *North American Review*, CLXXIX (Aug. 1904), pp. 226-237.

Whelpley, James Davenport, "International Control of Immigration", *World's Work*, VIII (Sept. 1904), pp. 5254-5259.

Williams, B. W., "Our Attitude toward Foreigners", *American Magazine of Civics*, VIII (Jan. 1896), pp. 64-68.

# APPENDIX B

ARTICLES STRESSING A FAVORABLE ATTITUDE TOWARD THE ASSIMILATION
OF THE NEW IMMIGRANT AND ADVOCATING THE EDUCATION
OF THE IMMIGRANT

Abbott, Grace, "Adjustment—Not Restriction", *Survey*, XXV (Jan. 7, 1911), pp. 527-529.

Addams, Jane, "Autobiographical Notes Upon Twenty Years at Hull House", *American Magazine*, LXX (Sept. 1910), pp. 638-646.

Byington, Margaret F., "The Mill Town Courts and Their Lodgers", *Charities and the Commons*, XXI (Feb. 6, 1909), pp. 913-922.

Cance, Alexander E., "Immigrant Rural Communities", American Academy of Political and Social Sciences, *Annals*, XL (Mar. 1912), pp. 69-80.

Castiglione, G. E. DiPalma, "Classes in English for Immigrants", *Survey*, XXV (Oct. 15, 1910), p. 105.

Godkin, Edward L., "The Harm of Immigration", *Nation*, LVI (Jan. 19, 1893), pp. 42-43.

Goldenweiser, E. A., "Immigrants in Cities", *Survey*, XXV (Jan. 7, 1911), pp. 596-602.

Grant, Percy Stickney, "American Ideals and Race Mixture", *North American Review*, CXCV (Apr. 1912), pp. 513-525.

Jenks, Jeremiah W., "The Urgent Immigration Problem", *World's Work*, XXII (May 1911), pp. 14368-14374.

Kellogg, Paul U., "The Minimum Wage and Immigrant Labor", National Conference on Charities and Correction, *Proceedings*, 1911, pp. 165-177.

Lauck, W. Jett, "The Cotton-Mill Operatives of New England", *Atlantic Monthly*, CIX (May 1912), pp. 706-713.

——, "Industrial Communities", *Survey*, XXV (Jan. 7, 1911), pp. 579-586.

——, "The Real Significance of Recent Immigration", *North American Review*, CXCV (Feb. 1912), pp. 201-211.

Marshall, Louis, "The Way Out", *Survey*, XXIII (Jan. 1, 1910), pp. 472-475.

Norton, Eliot, "The Diffusion of Immigration", American Academy of Political and Social Science, *Annals*, XXIV (1904), pp. 161-165.

Orenstein, Marie Sabsovich, "The Servo-Croats of Manhattan", *Survey*, XXIX (Dec. 7, 1912), pp. 277-286.

Poole, Ernest, "A Mixing Bowl for Nations", *Everybody's Magazine*, XXIII (Oct. 1910), pp. 554-564.

Repp, Paul Joseph, "Why America is Better", *Independent*, LXVIII (Feb. 24, 1910), pp. 409-410.

"The Selection of Immigrants", *Survey*, XXV (Feb. 4, 1911), pp. 715-716.

"The So-Called American Wage Earner and the Strike at Lawrence", *American Review of Reviews*, XLV (June 1912), pp. 746-747.

Speranzo, Gino C., "Handicaps in America", *Survey*, XXIII (Jan. 1, 1910), pp. 465-472.

Willcox, W. F., "Popular Delusions about Immigration", *Independent*, LXXII (Feb. 8, 1912), pp. 304-307.

Willey, Day Allen, "Americans in the Making", *Putnam's Monthly and the Reader*, V (Jan. 1909), pp. 456-463.

Williams, Hattie Plum, "The Road to Citizenship", *Political Science Quarterly*, XXVII (Sept. 1912), pp. 399-427.

Wilson, J. G., "The Crossing of the Races", *Popular Science Monthly*, LXXIX (Nov. 1911), pp. 486-495.

# BIBLIOGRAPHY

[The symbol ( * ) indicates a pamphlet or leaflet]

Abbott, Clarence M., "Education of the Immigrant Adult", U. S. Bureau of Education, *Bulletin*, 1913, No. 51, pp. 33-36.

——, "On the Education of the Immigrant", *American Leader*, III, No. 11 (June 12, 1913), pp. 698-701.

Abbott, Grace, "Adjustment—Not Restriction", *Survey*, XXV (Jan. 7, 1911), pp. 527-529.

——, "Democracy of Internationalism; Which We are Working Out in Our Immigrant Neighborhoods in America", *Survey*, XXXVI (Aug. 5, 1916), pp. 478-480.

——, "The Education of Foreigners in American Citizenship", National Municipal League, *Proceedings*, 1910, pp. 375-384.

——, *The Educational Needs of Immigrants in Illinois*, Springfield, Ill., 1920.

——, *The Immigrant and Coal-Mining Communities of Illinois*, Springfield, Ill., 1920.

——, *The Immigrant and the Community*, New York, 1917.

Abelson, Paul, "The Education of the Immigrant", American Social Science Association, *Journal of Social Science*, XLIV (Sept. 1906), pp. 163-172

Adams, Samuel Hopkins, "Invaded America", *Everybody's Magazine*, XXXVIII (Mar. 1918), pp. 55-64.

Addams, Jane, "Autobiographical Notes upon Twenty Years at Hull House", *American Magazine*, LXX (Sept. 1910), pp. 638-646.

——, "Dangers to American Traits and Characteristics from Immigration", *Educational Review*, XXIX (Mar. 1905), pp. 245-263.

——, "Nationalism, a Dogma?", *Survey*, XLIII (Feb. 7, 1920), pp. 524-526.

——, "The Public School and the Immigrant Child", National Educational Association, *Journal of Proceedings and Addresses*, 1908, pp. 99-102.

Alexander, Hartley Burr, "Americanization", *Nation*, CIX (Sept. 13, 1919), pp. 367-369.

"Alien-Baiting", *Jewish Immigration Bulletin*, IX, No. 2 (Feb. 1919), p. 8.

"Alienating the Aliens", *Literary Digest*, LXVI (Sept. 25, 1920), pp. 62, 64 and 66.

Alleman, A., "Immigration and the Future American Race", *Popular Science Monthly*, LXXV (Dec. 1909), pp. 586-596.

Allen, L. A., "Making Americans by Motion Pictures", *American City*, XI (Sept. 1914), p. 205.

Alsberg, E., "Education of the Immigrant", National Educational Association, *Proceedings*, 1916, pp. 786-792.

American Baptist Home Missionary Society, *Annual Reports*, 1900-1925.

*American City*, Research Division, *Americanization*, November 1920.*

American Federation of Labor, *Proceedings of Annual Conventions*, 1900-1930.

American Fellowship Incorporated, *Buffalo's Part in Americanization*, 1920.*
" The American House of Cincinnati ", *Americanization Bulletin*, I, No. 5
    (Jan. 1, 1919), p. 10.
American International College, *Annual Reports*, 1908-1925.
——, *Immigration*, 1909-1914.
American Legion, *American Legion Weekly*, 1919-1925.
——, *Proceedings of the National Conventions*, 1919-1930.
——, *Reports to the National Conventions*, 1919-1930.
——, National Americanism Commission, *Bulletins*, 1919-1920.
——, *A Reprint of Bulletins Issued*, June 1920.
*American Leader, The*, 1912-1915.
American Library Association, *Work with the Foreign Born* [bibliography]
    n. d. [*circa*. 1919].*
——, Committee on Work with Foreign-Born, *Reading Service to the
    Foreign Born*, 1929.*
American Red Cross, *Work of Foreign Language Information Service of
    the American Red Cross*, June 20, 1920.*
"American Spirit That Overcomes Race Prejudice ", *Current Opinion*, LVII
    (Dec. 1914), pp. 417-418.
"Americanization ", *Nation*, CVIII (May 24, 1919), pp. 823-824.
"Americanization ", *New Republic*, V (July 29, 1916), pp. 322-323.
"Americanization ", *Public*, XXII (Jan. 18, 1919), pp. 54-55.
"Americanization ", *Report of the Commissioner of Education for the Year
    Ended June 30, 1919*, I, 42-46.
"Americanization " *Scientific American*, CXVIII (June 22, 1918), p. 562.
"Americanization ", *Survey*, XLV (Feb. 26, 1921), pp. 750-752.
"Americanization and the Lack of a National Epic Consciousness ", *Current
    Opinion*, LXI (Sept. 1916), pp. 183-184.
"Americanization and the Shortage of Teachers ", *World's Work*, XL
    (May 1920), pp. 15-16.
"Americanization by the Public Library ", *Survey*, XLI (Jan. 18, 1919),
    pp. 537-538.
"Americanization Courses at the Summer Session of the University of
    California ", *School and Society*, IX (Mar. 29, 1919), pp. 377-378.
"Americanization Day ", *American Leader*, VIII, No. 4 (Aug. 26, 1915),
    pp. 240-246.
"Americanization Day ", *Immigrants in America Review*, I, No. 2 (June
    1915), p. 23.
"Americanization Day, a Marked Success ", *Jewish Immigration Bulletin*,
    IX, No. 4 (Apr. 1919), pp. 7, 9-11.
"Americanization Day, a New Idea for July 4 ", *Survey*, XXXIV (May
    25, 1915), p. 189.
"Americanization Day Appeal ", *Immigrants in America Review*, I, No. 2
    (June 1915), p. 23.
"Americanization Day in 150 Communities ", *Survey*, XXXIV (July 31,
    1915), p. 390.

"Americanization Developments", *Foreign-Born*, I, No. 6 (May 1920), p. 12.

"Americanization—How It Can Best Be Accomplished", *Jewish Immigration Bulletin*, X, No. 3 (Mar. 1920), p. 8.

"Americanization in New York State", *School and Society*, X (Oct. 11, 1919), pp. 423-424.

"The Americanization Movement", *Immigration Journal*, I, No. 2 (Apr. 1916), p. 19.

"The Americanization Movement", *School and Society*, IX (Jan. 11, 1919), pp. 52-54.

"Americanization Notes", *Survey*, XLV (March 26, 1921), p. 924; XLVI (July 16, 1921), p. 519.

"The Americanization of the Jewish Immigrant, a Symposium", *Jewish Immigration Bulletin*, V, No. 5 (May 1915), pp. 7-12.

Americanization School Association of the District of Columbia, *Americanization Bulletin*, 1932.

"Americanization Starting Point", *Ladies' Home Journal*, XXXVI (Sept. 1919), p. 32.

"Americanization—What It Means", *American Architect*, CXIV (Aug. 28, 1918), p. 263.

"Americanization Work in Seattle Public Library", *Public Libraries*, XXV (Oct. 1920), pp. 448-449.

"Americanization Work of Women's Clubs", *Immigrants in America Review*, I, No. 4 (Jan. 1916), p. 64.

"Americanizing America", *North American Review*, CCVI (Oct. 1917), pp. 517-520.

"Americanizing Employees; Features of an Effective Campaign in Connecticut", *Iron Age*, CIII (Apr. 10, 1919), p. 966.

"Americanizing the 'Rookie'", *Literary Digest*, LXIV (Mar. 20, 1920), pp. 41-43.

Anderson, Alice T., "Christian Americanization", *Missions*, IX (Sept. 1918), pp. 678-679 (Oct. 1918), pp. 796-770.

Andreae, Percy, "The Foreign-Language Newspaper in the United States", *American Leader*, VIII, No. 1 (July 8, 1915), pp. 25-35.

——, "The Foreign-Language Press", *American Leader*, IV, No. 9, (Nov. 13, 1913), pp. 552-553.

Andrew, A. Piatt, "The Crux of the Immigrant Question", *North American Review*, CXCIX (June 1914), pp. 866-878.

Antin, Mary, "American Miracle", *Atlantic Monthly*, CIX (Jan. 1912), pp. 52-67.

——, "First Aid to the Alien", *Outlook*, CI (June 29, 1912), pp. 481-485.

——, "Kingdom in the Slums", *Atlantic Monthly*, CIX (Mar. 1912), pp. 368-370.

——, "The Making of a Citizen", *Atlantic Monthly*, CIX (Feb. 1912), pp. 211-226.

——, *They Who Knock at Our Gates*, Boston, 1914.

Arizona, State of, *Reports of the Superintendent of Public Instruction*, 1915-1925.

——, *School Laws of Arizona*, 1919.

——, State Council of Defense, *Arizona Service Bulletin*, Feb. 1, 1919.

Aronovici, Carol, *Americanization*, St Paul, c. 1919.

——, "Americanization: Its Meaning and Function", *American Journal of Sociology*, XXV (May 1920), pp. 695-730.

——, "Fallacies of the Americanization Movement", *Social Welfare*, St. Paul, Minn., I (Nov. 1917), pp. 1-2.

Ashe, G. F., "Americanization Program", *Playground*, XI (July 1917), pp. 190-191.

Aspden, T. F., "Americanization of Our Alien Population", *Bankers' Magazine*, XCVIII (June 1919), pp. 676-679.

"Assimilating the Adult Immigrant", *Outlook*, LXXXVIII (Feb. 1, 1908), p. 245.

Avery, Eunice H., "Americanization Is Not at All Bad", *Outlook*, CXXIV (Feb. 25, 1920), pp. 340-342.

Avery, Lewis B., "A New Heaven", *School and Society*, X (Oct. 11, 1919), pp. 416-422.

Bacon, Albion Fellows, "American Housing and the Immigrant", *Immigrants in America Review*, II, No. 2 (July 1916), pp. 42-44.

Baghdigian, Bagdasar Krekor, *Americanism in Americanization*, Kansas City, Mo., 1921.

——, *Essentials of Americanization*, St. Louis, 1919.

Bagley, G. H., "Americanization as War Service", *Woman Citizen*, I, (June 30, 1917), pp. 84-87.

Bakay, A., "Evangelization and Americanization", *Outlook of Missions*, XII (June 1920), p. 252.

Balch, Emily Greene, "*Our Slavic Fellow Citizens*, New York, 1910.

——, "Question of Assimilation", *Charities and the Commons*, XIX (Dec. 7, 1907), pp. 1162-1164.

——, "A Shepherd of Immigrants", *Charity*, XIII (Dec. 3, 1904), pp. 193-194.

Ball, W. R., "Federal and Public-School Cooperation in Citizenship Training", National Educational Association, *Addresses and Proceedings*, LVII, 1919, pp. 475-477.

Bame, Irene S., *Beginners' Lessons for Adult Immigrants*, 1921.*

——, *English Lessons for Home Makers*, 1922.*

Barge, C. M., "Training of Religious Leaders and Workers among Immigrants in America", *Religious Education*, IX (Feb. 1914), pp. 62-63.

Barnes, Earl, "Spoken English as a Factor in Americanization", National Educational Association, *Addresses and Proceedinggs*, LVI, 1918, pp. 171-173.

——, "Language as a Factor in Americanization", *Public*, XXI (July 27, 1918), pp. 954-957.

Barnes, M. E., *Neighboring New Americans*, New York, 1920.

Barnes, Mary C., "New Day in Christian Americanization", *Missionary Review*, XLII (Jan. 1919), pp. 57-59.

——, "Urgent Needs in 'Americanization Work'", *Missions*, XII (Apr. 1921), p. 234.

Bartholomew, Allen R., "The Immigrant at the Door and in the City", *Outlook of Missions*, XII (Apr. 1920), p. 151.

"The Basis of Americanization", *Unpartisan Review*, New York, 1921.

Batten, S. Z., "Christian Leaders for Immigrant Peoples", *Religious Education*, VII (Dec. 1912), pp. 538-543.

Baughman, Ruby, *Easy Lessons in Everyday English for Citrus Fruit Workers*, 1920.*

——, "Elementary Education for Adults", American Academy of Political and Social Science, *Annals*, XCIII (Jan. 1921), pp. 161-168.

Baustein, Dorothy, "Work of the Educational Alliance", *Charities and Correction*, X (Apr. 4, 1903), pp. 337-343.

Becht, J. George, "Americanization as a War-Time Duty of the Schools", National Educational Association, *Addresses and Proceedings*, LVI, 1918, pp. 363-364.

Beck, A., "Promotion of Citizenship", *Catholic World*, CIX (Sept. 1919), pp. 735-743.

Benjamin, Eugene S., "The Baron de Hirsch Fund", *Jewish Immigration Bulletin*, V, No. 5 (May 1915), pp. 9-11.

Berconvici, Konrad, *On New Shores*, New York, 1925.

Berkson, Isaac B., *Theories of Americanization, a Critical Study, with Special Reference to the Jewish Group*, New York, 1920.

Berman, Henry, "Stirring the Melting Pot", *Jewish Immigration Bulletin*, IV, No. 9 (Sept. 1914), pp. 2-4.

Bernheimer, Charles S., "Americanizing the Immigrant", *American Hebrew and Jewish Messenger*, XCVII (June 18, 1915), pp. 160-161.

Berry, Charles Scott, "Some Problems of Americanization as Seen by an Army Psychologist", *School and Society*, XIII (Jan. 22, 1921), pp. 97-104.

Beukema, J. C., "Americanization Work in Manistee", *American City*, XVIII (Apr. 1918), p. 357.

Beveridge, Albert J., "The School and the Nation", National Educational Association, *Addresses and Proceedings*, LV, 1917, pp. 678-690.

Bierstadt, Edward Hale, *Aspects of Americanization*, New York, 1922.

——, "Pseudo-Americanization", *New Republic*, XXVI (May 25, 1921), pp. 371-373; XXVII (June 1, 1921), pp. 19-23.

Blackwell, Nancy Gary, "Making Americans in a Public School", *Churchman*, CXVII, No. 3 (Jan 19, 1918), pp. 87 and 109.

Blanpied, Charles W., "Americanization of the Gradowskis", *World Outlook*, V (May 1919), pp. 9-10.

——, "Report of the Special Survey of the Pacific Coast", Conference of Charities and Correction, *Proceedings*, 1913, pp. 42-72.

Bloch, Joshua, "Americanization and the Foreign-Born", *Jewish Immigration Bulletin*, X, No. 2 (Feb. 1920), pp. 6, 7 and 9.

"Blunders about Immigration", *Independent*, LV (Aug. 27, 1905), pp. 2064-2066.

Bogardus, Emory S., *Essentials of Americanization*, New York, 1919.

Bok, E. W., *Americanization of Edward Bok*, New York, 1924.

Bond, William A., *Practical Americanization—a Business Man's View*, Chicago, Sept. 11, 1919.*

Boston Committee for Americanism, *A Little Book for Immigrants in Boston*, Boston, 1921.*

Boston Public Library, *Americanization*, 1919 [bibliography].*

Boswell, H. V., "Promoting Americanization", American Academy of Political and Social Science, *Annals*, LXIV (Mar. 1916), pp. 204-209.

Bourne, Randolph S., "Trans-National America", *Atlantic Monthly*, CXVIII (July 1916)), pp. 86-97.

Bradford, Mary Davison, "Training for Social Adjustment—the Citizens of the Future", National Educational Association, *Addresses and Proceedings*, 1918, pp. 160-163.

Braun, W. A., "University in Americanization", *Columbia University Quarterly*, XXI (July 1919), pp. 244-247.

Breckinridge, Sophonisba P., "Family in the Community but Not Yet of the Community", National Conference of Charities and Correction, *Proceedings*, 1914, pp. 69-75.

——, "Education for the Americanization of the Foreign Family", *Journal of Home Economics*, XI (May 1919), pp. 187-192.

——, *New Homes for Old*, New York, 1921.

Bremer, Edith Terry, "Foreign Community and Immigration Work of the National Young Women's Christian Association", *Immigrants in America Review*, I, No. 4 (Jan. 1916), pp. 73-82.

——, *The International Institutes in Foreign Community Work, Their Program and Philosophy*, New York, 1923.*

Bressler, David M., "The Industrial Removal Office", National Conference of Charities and Correction, *Proceedings*, 1909, pp. 227-230.

Brewer, Daniel Chauncey, "A Patriotic Movement for the Assimilation of Immigrants", *Editorial Review*, III (Aug. 1910), pp. 786-800.

Bridges, Horace J., *On Becoming an American, Some Meditations of a Newly Naturalized Immigrant*, Boston, 1919.

Brink, B. D., "Play in Immigrant Communities", *Rural Manhood*, X (Apr. 1919), pp. 161-162.

Brissenden, Paul Frederick, *The I. W. W., a Study of American Syndicalism*, New York, 1920.

Brodie, Robert B., "The Content and Method of Instruction", U. S. Bureau of Education, *Bulletin*, 1913, No. 51, pp. 47-48.

Brooks, Christian Alvin, *Christian Americanization, a Task for the Churches*, New York, 1919.

——, "City and Foreign-Speaking Missions", *Missions*, X (Sept. 1919), pp. 600-603.

——, "Missions to People of Foreign Speech Affected by the War", *Missions*, IX (Nov. 1918), pp. 820-823.

——, "Shall America Be American", *Missions*, XII (Sept. 1921), pp. 469-470.

Brown, Lawrence Guy, *Immigration*, New York, 1933.

Brunner, Edmund D., *Immigrant Farmers and Their Children*, New York, 1929.

Buchanan, J., "How to Assimilate the Foreign Element in Our Population", *Forum*, XXXII (Feb. 1902), pp. 686-694.

Buffalo Public Library, *Our Immigrants of Foreign Tongues in Their Old Homes and in America*, 1920, [bibliography].*

Burgess, Thomas, "The Church and the Foreign Born, the Work of the National Organization", *Churchman*, CXXII, No. 15 (Oct. 9, 1920), pp. 13-14.

——, *Foreign Born Americans and Their Children*, 1921.

——, *Foreigners or Friends, a Handbook: the Churchman's Approach*, 1920.

——, "Our Work Among the Foreign Born Americans", *Spirit of Missions*, LXXXV, No. 3 (Mar. 1920), p. 173; No. 5 (May 1920), p. 325; No. 6 (June 1920), p. 396.

Burns, Allen T., "American Americanization", Courts: Municipal Court, *Public Service Series*, 1919-1920, No. 4, Philadelphia, 1920.

——, ed., *Americanization Studies*, 10 volumes, New York, 1920-1924.

Burr, Clinton Stoddard, *America's Race Heritage*, New York, 1922.

Butler, F. C., "Community Americanization", U. S. Bureau of Education, *Bulletin*, 1919, No. 76.

——, "State Americanization", U. S. Bureau of Education, *Bulletin*, 1919, No. 77.

Byington, Margaret F., "The Mill Town Courts and their Lodgers", *Charities and the Commons*, XXI (Feb. 6, 1909), pp. 913-922.

Byrnes, James C., "Selection of Evening-School Teachers", U. S. Bureau of Education, *Bulletin*, 1913, No. 51, pp. 42-43.

Cahan, Abraham, "The Russian Jew in America", *Atlantic Monthly*, LXXXII (July 1898), pp. 128-139.

California, State of, *School Laws of California*, 1919.

California, State of, Commission of Immigration and Housing, *Americanization, California's Answer*, Sacramento, July 1, 1920.*

——, *Americanization, the California Program*, 1919.*

——, *Americanization, Suggested Lines for Speakers and Workers*, 1919.*

——, *Annual Reports*, 1915-1930.

——, *Bulletin of Information for Immigrants*, 1920.*

——, *The California Immigration and Housing Bulletin*, 1920.*

——, *A Community Survey Made in Los Angeles City*, 1918.*

——, *Discussion of Methods of Teaching English*, 1917.*

——, *Heroes of Freedom*, 1919.*

——, *A Manual for Home Teachers*, 1919.*

——, *Our Soldiers and the English Language*, 1918.*

——, *Report on Experiment Made in Los Angeles in the Summer of 1917 for the Americanization of Foreign-born Women*, 1917.*

——, *Report on Fresno's Immigration Problem*, 1918.*

——, *A Primer for Foreign Speaking Women*, parts 1 and 2, 1918.*

——, *The Spirit of the Nation as Expressed in Song and the Words of Famous Americans*, 1918.*

——, *A Suggested Program for Americanization*, 1919.*

California, State of, Council of Defense, Woman's Division, *Bridging the Atlantic: a Discussion of the Problems and Methods of Americanization*, Los Angeles, 1919.*

California, State of, Superintendent of Education, *Biennial Reports*, 1901-1930.

Cance, Alexander E., "Immigrant Rural Communities", American Academy of Political and Social Science, *Annals*, XL (Mar. 1912), pp. 69-80.

——, "Immigrant Rural Communities", *Survey*, XXV (Jan. 7, 1911), pp. 587-595.

Cannon, Joseph G., "Native American", *Outlook*, CXII (Apr. 5, 1916), pp. 787-788.

Carney, C. S., "National Conference on Americanization in Industries", *Applied Psychology*, III (Sept. 1919), pp. 269-276.

Carr, John Foster, "The Library and the Immigrant", *American Leader*, VIII, No. 1 (July 8, 1915), pp. 37-45.

"Centers in Americanization", *Americanization Bulletin*, I, No. 8 (Apr. 1, 1919), p. 16.

Chamber of Commerce of the United States, *Proceedings*, 1913-1925.

——, *Report of Committee on Immigration of the Chamber of Commerce of the United States of America*, 5th Annual Meeting, Washington, 1917.*

Chamber of Commerce of the United States, Committee on Immigration, "Americanizing Industrial Workers, Vitally Important Task of To-day ... Strong Presentation of Case in Report of the Immigration Committee of the U. S. Chamber of Commerce", *Manufacturers' Record*, Apr. 5, 1917.

——, *Bulletins*, 1916-1918.*

"Chester Holds a Pageant", *Americanization Bulletin*, I, No. 9 (May 1, 1919), p. 8.

Chetwood, John, *Immigration Fallacies*, Boston, 1896.

Chicago Association of Commerce, *A Year of Americanization Work, July 1918–July 1919; Has It Paid? Read the Answer*, Chicago, 1919.*

——, Committee on Americanization, *Organizing English and Citizenship Classes in Industrial Plants*, 1921.*

Chicago Community Trust, *Americanization in Chicago*, Chicago, 1920.*

"Christian Americanization", *Missions*, X (Jan. 1919), pp. 45-48.

Cincinnati, City of, *Course of Study in History and Government for Petitioners for Naturalization in the Citizenship Schools*, Cincinnati, Jan. 1916, [mimeographed].*

Civic Education Association of Buffalo, *Participating Americans: the Story of One Year's Work for the Americanization of Buffalo*, Buffalo, 1918.*

——, *New Citizens' Handbook: a Manual of Information for Buffalo's Immigrants Who Wish to Become Citizens*, Buffalo, 1917.*

Claghorn, Kate Halladay, "First Year's Work of a New State Bureau", *Survey*, XXVIII (May 11, 1912), pp. 269-271.

——, *The Immigrant's Day in Court*, New York, 1923.

Clark, Bertha V., "American Attitude the Essential in Americanization", *Missions*, XII (Mar. 1921), pp. 162-164.

Clark, E. Everett, "The Akron Plan", *Survey*, XLVI (July 16, 1921), pp. 518-519.

——, "The Worcester Plan", *Survey*, XLV (Mar. 26, 1921), p. 924.

"Classes in English for Immigrants", *Survey*, XXV (Oct. 15, 1910), p. 105.

Claxton, P. P., "Churches and Americanization", *Religious Education*, XIV (Feb. 1919), pp. 24-25.

——, "Education for the Establishment of a Democracy in the World", National Educational Association, *Addresses and Proceedings*, LVII, 1919, pp. 81-88.

——, "What is Americanization?", *Jewish Immigration Bulletin*, VIII, No. 7 (Nov. 1918), p. 14.

Cleveland, Americanization Committee of, *Americanization in Cleveland*, Nov. 25, 1919.*

——, *A Handbook on Industrial Americanization*, c. 1917.*

——, *The Czechs of Cleveland*, 1919.*

——, *The Italians of Cleveland*, 1919.*

——, *The Jugo-Slavs of Cleveland*, 1920.*

——, *The Lithuanians of Cleveland*, 1920.*

——, *The Magyars of Cleveland*, 1919.*

——, *The Poles of Cleveland*, 1919.*

——, *Report of the Work of the Cleveland Americanization Committee*, n. d. *circa.* 1919.*

——, *Report of the Work of the Cleveland Americanization Committee of the Mayor's Advisory War Board, July 1917–July 1918.**

——, *The Slovaks of Cleveland*, 1918.*

Cleveland, Board of Education of, Division of Educational Extension, *Lessons in American Citizenship for Men and Women Preparing for Naturalization*, c. 1918.*

Cleveland Chamber of Commerce, Committee on Education, *Report on Organized Americanization Work in Cleveland*, 1918.*

Cleveland Citizens' Bureau, *The Citizens' Bureau*, n. d., [*circa*, 1919].*

——, *Lessons in American Citizenship*, c. 1919.*

Cody, F., "Americanization Courses in the Public Schools", *English Journal*, VII (Dec. 1918), pp. 615-622.

Cohen, H. L., "Americanization by Class-Room Practice", *Teachers' College Record*, XX (May 1919), pp. 238-249.

Cohen, Henry, "The Immigrant Publication Society", *Jewish Charities*, Aug. 1915, n. p.

Cole, Raymond E., "Around John Rocco's Store: Experiment in Rural Americanization", *Rural Manhood*, X (Apr. 1919), pp. 151-152.

——, "The City's Responsibility to the Immigrant", *Immigrants in America Review*, I (June 1915), pp. 36-44.

Colgrove, P. P., "Night Schools of the Iron Range of Minnesota", *Immigrants in America Review*, I, No. 4 (Jan. 1916), pp. 65-69.

Colletti, Umberto, "Assimilating the Adult Immigrant", *Outlook*, LXXXVIII (Feb. 1, 1908), pp. 244-245.

——, "The Italian Immigrant", Conference of Charities and Correction, *Proceedings*, 1912, pp. 249-254.

——, "Schools for Immigrant Laborers", *Outlook*, XCII (Aug. 7, 1909), pp. 823-824.

Colorado, State of, *Educational Laws, Passed by the Twenty-Second General Assembly*, 1919.

Colorado, University of, *The Need for Americanization Teachers*, 1919.*

"Colorado's 'America First' Societies", *Americanization Bulletin*, I, No. 6 (Feb. 1, 1919), p. 9.

"Commencement Addresses by Some Recent Graduates in 'Americanization'", *Literary Digest*, LXVI (July 17, 1920), pp. 54, 56, 57 and 58.

Committee for Immigrants in America, *Americanizing a City—Getting the Adult Immigrant to School*, 1915.*

——, *The City's Responsibility to the Immigrant*, 1915.*

——, *Immigrants in America Review*, 1915-1916.

——, *Memorandum to the Advisory Commission of the Council of National Defense Concerning the Committee for Immigrants in America, National Americanization Committee, and Affiliated Organizations*, Oct. 12, 1917.*

——, *Memoranda to the Advisory Commission of the Council of National Defense Concerning a War Policy for Aliens*, Oct. 31, 1917.*

——, *A National Bureau of Employment*, 1915.*

——, *A Professional Course for Social Service among Immigrants*, 1915.*

Commons, John R., "Amalgamation and Assimilation", *Chautauqua*, XXXIX (May 1904), pp. 217-225.

——, *Races and Immigrants in America*, New York, 1907.

——, "Social and Industrial Problems", *Chautauqua*, XXXIX (Mar. 1904), pp. 13-22.

"Compulsory Education", Report of the Committee on State School Systems, National Educational Association, *Journal of Addresses and Proceedings*, 1891, pp. 294-305.

Condon, Randall, J., "Education of the Immigrant", National Educational Association, *Journal of Addresses and Proceedings*, LVII, 1919, pp. 558-560.

"Conference for Industrial Peace", *Metal Worker*, XCI (Feb. 28, 1919), pp. 283-284.

"Conference in Cambridge", *Americanization Bulletin*, I, No. 8 (Apr. 1, 1919), p. 7.

Congregational Home Missionary Society, *Annual Reports*, 1900-1925.

Connecticut, State Board of Education, *Americanization Bulletins*, 1920-1921.*

——, *Annual Reports*, 1900-1930.

——, *Circular Letters on Americanization*, 1919.*

——, *Classes for Foreign-Born Adults, Organization and Maintenance*, Hartford, Sept. 1920.*

——, *Information for New Americans*, Hartford, Feb. 14, 1921.*
——, *Information Regarding Naturalization with Outline of History and Government of the United States*, Hartford, 1920.*
——, *A Suggested Course of Study and Syllabus for Non-English Speaking Adults*, 1918.*
Connecticut, State Council of Defense, *An Aid to Americanization in Industry*, Hartford, 1920.*
——, *State Campaign of Americanization*, New Haven, 1918.*
——, *State Campaign of Americanization, Purpose and Aims*, New Haven, 1918.*
Cooper, Charles C., "Necessity for Changes in Americanization Methods", *Jewish Immigration Bulletin*, IX, No. 2 (Feb. 1919), pp. 9-10.
Corkran, Harriet C., "Little Adventures in Americanization", *Christian Advocate*, XCV, No. 40 (Sept. 30, 1920), pp. 1301-1302.
Costa, Alfonzo Arbib, "Americanization and Reaction", *Living Age*, CCCV (Apr. 10, 1920), pp. 69-71.
Council of Jewish Women, *The Immigrant*, 1921-1930.
——, *Proceedings of the Triennial Conventions*, 1896-1930.
——, *Programs of Work*, 1900-1930.
——, *Study in Literary Americanization Program*, Oct. 1918.*
Craig, Laura G., *America, God's Melting Pot*, New York, 1913.
Creel, George, "The Hopes of the Hyphenated", *Century Magazine*, XCI, new series, LXIX (Jan. 1916), pp. 350-362.
Crist, Raymond F., "Education of Foreigners for American Citizenship", National Educational Association, *Journal of Addresses and Proceedings*, 1916, pp. 1045-1048.
——, "The Federal Plan of Americanization Work with the Foreign-Born", National Educational Association, *Journal of Addresses and Proceedings*, LVII, 1919, pp. 471-475.
Daniels, John, *Americanization via the Neighborhood*, New York, 1920.
——, "Americanizing Eighty Thousand Poles", *Survey*, XXIV (June 4, 1919), pp. 373-385.
——, National Immigration Conference", *Survey*, XXVII (Dec. 16, 1911). pp. 1358-1359.
Davies, George R., "Americanization Program for the Schools", North Dakota University, *Quarterly Journal*, IX (July 1919), pp. 337-350.
Davis, M. M., *Immigrant Health and the Community*, New York, 1921.
Davis, Philip, ed., *Immigration and Americanization*, Boston, 1920.
Delaware, Service Citizens of, *Americanization in Delaware, 1921-1922*, Sept. 1922.*
——, *Bulletins*, 1919-1922.
——, *Report Made to the Annual Meeting of the Service Citizens of Delaware, May 7, 1920.*
——, *Six Months of Americanization in Delaware*, Wilmington, Sept. 1919.*
——, *Voices of the New America*, Apr. 15, 1920.*
Delaware, State of, *Annual Reports of the State Superintendent of Education*, 1910-1930.

——, *Delaware School Code*, 1919.

Delaware, State of, Council of Defense, *Americanization in Delaware, a State Policy Initiated by the Delaware State Council of Defense*, n. d., [*circa*. 1920].\*

Denny, Mary Putnam, "The Genius of America", *Missions*, XII (Sept. 1921), p. 470.

Desmond, Humphrey J., *The A. P. A. Movement*, Washington, 1912.

Detroit, Board of Commerce, *How to Become an American Citizen*, n. d. [*circa*. 1920].

——, *Information for Immigrants in Detroit, Michigan, Preparing to be American Citizens*, 1916.\*

Devine, Edward T., "Immigration as a Relief Problem", *Charities*, XII (Feb. 6, 1904), pp. 129-133.

——, *et al.*, "Social Reconstruction", *Survey*, XLII (June 7, 1919), pp. 403-404.

Dewey, John, "Nationalizing Education", National Educational Association, *Journal of Addresses and Proceedinggs*, LIV, 1916, pp. 183-189.

Dine, H. B., "School Center and the Immigrant", *Playground*, X (Feb. 1917), pp. 456-461.

Dingwell, James D., "The Civic Center and Better Citizenship", *Immigrants in American Review*, I, No. 3 (Sept. 1915), pp. 84-87.

District of Columbia, *Annual Reports of the Commissioners of the District of Columbia*, 1914-1930.

Dooley, William H., "Evening Elementary Schools", *Education*, XXXVI (Feb. 1916), pp. 357-361.

Doughty, Isabel, "Taking Uncle Sam's Foster Children into the Family", *Woman Citizen*, III (Jan. 4, 1919), pp. 650-651.

Downer, Harry E., *Chats with Possible Americans: Some Friendly Help in Civics Given Worthwhile Folks*, Davenport, Ia., 1918.\*

Dixon, Royal, *Americanization*, New York, 1916.

——, *Americanizing Our Foreign Born*, New York, 1918.

——, "Americanizing Our Foreign-Born; the Patriotic Work of the League of Foreign-Born Citizens", *Forum*, LX (Oct. 1918), pp. 444-452.

Drechsler, Julius, *Democracy and Assimilation*, 1920.

——, *Learning How to Feel at Home in America*, Oct. 4, 1923.\*

Duluth, Minn., Board of Education, Americanization Committee, *Night School Lessons*, Aug. 1920.\*

——, *How to Become an American; Information for Future Americans*, Duluth, 1919.\*

Dunbar, Olivia H., "Teaching the Immigrant Woman", *Harpers' Bazaar*, XLVII (June 1913), pp. 277-278.

Duncan, Hannibal G., *Immigration and Assimilation*, New York, 1933.

Dunning, Jane G., "Educational Work of the Daughters of the American Revolution", *Immigrants in America Review*, I (Sept. 1915), pp. 51-53.

Dykema, F. L., *Americanization Dictionary*, 1920.\*

Eastman, Fred, *Unfinished Business of the Presbyterian Church in America*, Philadelphia, 1920.\*

Eberle, Warren C., "Coordination of Welfare Agencies", U. S. Bureau of Education, *Bulletin*, 1913, No. 51, pp. 30-31.

"Educating the Immigrant for Citizenship", *American Review of Reviews,* LIII (Jan. 1916), pp. 79-80.

"Education of Adult Immigrants: Symposium", National Educational Association, *Journal of Addresses and Proceedings*, 1915, pp. 439-445.

"Education of the Immigrant", *Elementary School Teacher*, XIV (Feb. 1914), pp. 261-263.

"Education of the Immigrant", U. S. Bureau of Education, *Bulletin*, 1913, No. 51, pp. 1-52.

Educational Alliance, *Annual Reports*, 1893-1920.

——, *Souvenir Book of the Fair in Aid of the Educational Alliance and Hebrew Technical Institute*, New York, c. 1895.*

——, *25th Anniversary Program*, Mar. 21, 1915.*

Educational Committee for Non-English-Speaking Women, *Report*, 1925.

Edwards, Richard H., *Immigration*, Madison, Wis., 1909.

Eliot, Charles W., "What is an American?" *Jewish Immigration Bulletin*, VI, No. 11 (Nov. 1916), pp. 6-7.

Ellerbe, P. L., "Education for Citizenship", *Outlook*, CXX (Sept. 11, 1918), pp. 64-65.

Evans, Thomas, *A Plan for Co-operative Americanization*, 1924.*

Evemeyer, Mrs. Edward F., "Americanization", *Outlook of Missions*, XI (July 1919), pp. 323-325.

Ettinger, William L., "Americanization", *School and Society*, IX (Feb. 1919), pp. 129-133.

Fairchild, Henry Pratt, "Foreign Americans", *Nation*, XCIII (Dec. 28, 1911), pp. 626-627.

——, *Immigration, a World Movement and Its American Significance*, New York, 1913.

——, *The Melting Pot Mistake*, New York, 1926.

——, "The Restriction of Immigration", *American Journal of Sociology,* XVII (Mar. 1912), pp. 637-646.

Fairman, Charles G., "College Trained Immigrants, a Study of Americans in the Making", *New England Magazine*, new series, XLIII (July 1910), pp. 577-584.

Farrington, Frederick E., "Campaign for Americanization", *School and Society*, III (June 10, 1916), pp. 862-864.

——, "Public Facilities for Educating the Alien", U. S. Bureau of Education, *Bulletin*, 1916, No. 18.

Feeks, D., "Putting Mother in Her Right Place", *World Outlook*, IV, 1918, pp. 9-10.

Fernandez, Alice Barrows, "The Problem of Adult Education in Passaic, New Jersey", U. S. Bureau of Education, *Bulletin*, 1920, No. 4.

Finch, Charles E., "The Rochester Plan of Immigrant Education", *Twelfth Annual Report of the New York Education Department*, 1916.

Finegan, Thomas E., "The Education of the Illiterate Immigrant", The American Academy of Political and Social Science, *Annals*, XCIII (Jan. 1921), pp. 168-173.

Fitch, John A., "Lackawanna—Swamp, Mill, and Town", *Survey*, XXVII (Oct. 7, 1911), pp. 929-945.

Fleishman, Doris E., "Evolution in Americanization", *Foreign-Born*, I, No. 2 (June 1915), p. 18.

Fleishman, Henry, "The Educational Alliance", *Immigrants in America Review*, I, No. 2 (June 1915), pp. 68-71.

Fletcher, Henry P., "Our Divided Country", *Atlantic Monthly*, CXVII (Feb. 1916), pp. 223-233.

"For a Constructive Law on Immigration", *Survey*, XXXIX (Feb. 23, 1918), p. 575.

Ford English School, *Official 100 Facts Taught by the Teachers of the Ford English School*, Mar. 1, 1916.*

"Foreign Editors Endorse Night Schools", *American Leader*, IX (Jan. 13, 1916), pp. 10-11.

Foreign Language Information Service, *Bulletins*, 1920-1923.

——, *Five Years Work with the Foreign-Born*, New York, Oct. 12, 1922.*

——, *The Interpreter*, 1923-1925.

——, *A Job of Understanding*, Dec. 1924.*

——, *The Work of the Foreign Language Information Service, a Summary and Survey*, 1922.*

——, Czecho-Slovak Bureau, *Ako Sa Mozna State Obcanom Spojenych Statov*, 1923.*

——, *Jak Lze Se Stat Obcanem Spojenych Statu*, 1923.*

——, Finnish Bureau, *Miten Kansalaistuminen Yhdysvalloissa Tapahtuu*, 1923.*

——, Polish Bureau, *Jak Mozna Zostac Obywatelem Stanow Zjednieczonych*, 1922.*

Frank, Glenn, "The Fad of Americanization", *Century Magazine*, C, new series, LXXVIII (June 1920), pp. 219-222.

——, "A New Angle on Americanization", *Century Magazine*, CI, new series, LXXIX (Feb. 1921), pp. 538-539.

Franklin, Lawrence, "The Italian in America: What He Has Been, What He Shall Be", *Catholic World*, LXXI (Apr. 1900), pp. 67-80.

Frederick, J. George, "The American Leader, Why It Has Come to Stay, and What It Means to Accomplish", *American Leader*, I, No. 1 (Feb. 29, 1912), pp. 19-20.

Fry, C. L., *The New and Old Immigrant on the Land*, New York, 1922.

Fulcher, G. M., "Americanization of the Immigrant in Chicago: a Survey", *Social Science Review*, VIII (Jan. 1919), p. 8.

Garis, Roy L., *Immigration Restriction*, New York, 1927.

Gaus, John M., "New Frontiers of Assimilation", *Public*, XXI (Dec. 14, 1918), pp. 1501-1503.

——, "Municipal Program for Educating Immigrants in Citizenship", *National Municipal Review*, VII (May 1918), pp. 237-244.

Gavit, John P., *Americans by Choice*, New York, 1922.

Gadalecia, Joseph, "Americanizing the 'Shut-Ins'", *Survey*, XLII (May 24, 1919), pp. 317-318.

General Federation of Women's Clubs, Division on Americanization, *Americanization Programs*, 1920.*

Geringer, Vladimir A., "The Mission of the Foreign-Language Newspaper in the United States", *American Leader*, VIII, No. 2 (July 22, 1915), pp. 101-104.

"Getting the Immigrant to School", *Survey*, XXXIV (May 29, 1915), pp. 190-191.

Gibbs, Winifred, "Teaching Immigrant Mothers Proper Food", U. S. Bureau of Education, *Bulletin*, 1913, No. 51, pp. 10-11.

Gibson, Emily M., *English-Class Plays for New Americans*, 1921.*

Ginsburg, Jacob, "The Mission of the Foreign-Language Newspaper in the United States", *American Leader*, VII, No. 12 (June 24, 1915), pp. 739-740.

Goddard, Charles A., "How a Bank Helps Americanize the Foreign-Born", *Bankers' Magazine*, XCVII (Dec. 1918), pp. 757-760.

Godkin, E. L., "The Harm of Immigration", *Nation*, LVI (Jan. 19, 1893), pp. 42-43.

Goeldi, N., "Why I Became an American Citizen", *Survey*, XXXVI (Aug. 19, 1916), pp. 524-525.

Goldberger, Henry H., "Teaching English to the Foreign-Born", U. S. Bureau of Education, *Bulletin*, 1919, No. 80.

Goldenweiser, E. A., "Immigrants in Cities", *Survey*, XXV (Jan. 7, 1911), pp. 596-602.

Gompers, Samuel, "Americanizing Foreign Workers", *American Federationist*, XXIII (Aug. 1916), pp. 689-690.

——, "Educate-Americanize", *American Federationist*, XXV (May 1918), pp. 390-391.

Goodwin, Clarence Norton, "National Americanization", *Immigrants in American Review*, II (Apr. 1916), pp. 27-31.

Gordon, F., "The Mission of the Foreign-Language Newspapers in the United States", *American Leader*, VIII, No. 3 (Aug. 12, 1915), pp. 169-172.

Grabo, Carl H., "Americanizing the Immigrant", *Dial*, LXVI (May 31, 1919), pp. 539-540.

Grace, Alonzo G., *Immigration and Community Americanization*, Minneapolis, c. 1921.*

Grand Rapids, Michigan, American Citizenship Society of, *Citizenship Training through the Ballot*, c. 1921.*

Grand Rapids, Michigan, Americanization Society of, *Americanization Dictionary*, 1920.*

——, *Papers*, 1919-1921.*

Grant, Percy Stickney, "American Ideals and Race Mixture", *North American Review*, CXCV (Apr. 1912), pp. 513-525.

Gratiaa, Josephine, *Making Americans, How the Library Helps*, St. Louis Public Library, 1919.*

Gray, Robert Floyd, "The Teaching of English to the Foreign-Born", *School and Society*, XIII (Jan. 15, 1921), pp. 67-71.

——, "The Training of Americanization Teachers", *Educational Review*, LXI (Mar. 1921), pp. 224-229.

Greene, Amy B., *Handbook Bibliography on Foreign Language Groups*, 1925.*

Griscom, Jr., Elwood, *Americanization: a School Reader and Speaker*, 1920.

Gronert, Theodore G., *Problems of Women Citizenship and Women's Club Progress on Civic Problems*, 1921.*

Guernsey, Irwin S., "The United States", *The New International Yearbook*, New York, 1920, p. 707.

Guggenheimer, Frederick L., "The Americanization of the Jewish Immigrant", *Jewish Immigration Bulletin*, IX, No. 4 (Apr. 1919), pp. 12-13.

Gwiazdowski, A. P., "Increasing Efficiency of Foreign Employees", *American Machinist*, XLIX (Oct. 10, 1918), p. 650.

Haaren, John H., "Education of the Immigrant Child", U. S. Bureau of Education, *Bulletin*, 1913, No. 51, pp. 19-21.

Halifax, Guy Raymond, "The Immigration Scourge", *Overland Monthly*, XLIII (Jan. 1904), pp. 65-69.

Hall, Prescott, "The Future of American Ideals", *North American Review*, CXCV (Jan. 1912), pp. 94-102.

——, *Immigration and its Effects upon the United States*, New York, 1906.

——, "Immigration and the Educational Test", *North American Review*, CLXV (Oct. 1897), pp. 393-402.

——, "New Problems of Immigration", *Forum*, XXX (Jan. 1901), pp. 555-567.

——, "Selection of Immigration", American Academy of Political and Social Science, *Annals*, XXIV, 1904, pp. 169-184.

Hall, Robert C., "Camp Schools and the State", *Charities and the Commons*, XVII, pp. 892-893.

Halsey, Edward A., "Our Brothers, the Immigrants", *World Today*, XIX (Dec. 1910), pp. 1375-1381.

Hamilton, W. I., "America First Campaign in Massachusetts", *Education*, XXXVII (June 1917), pp. 622-629.

Hamlin, L. A., "Putting Americanism into Americanization: an Experiment in a Socialized Night School for Foreigners", *Community Center*, IV (Apr. 7, 1917), pp. 9-10.

Hammerling, Lewis N., "The Influence of the Foreign-Language Press in America", *American Leader*, I, No. 9 (June 27, 1912), pp. 33-36.

Hammond, Henry D., "Americanization, a Problem in Human Engineering", *Engineering News*, LXXX (June 13, 1918), pp. 1116-1119.

Hansen, Annie L., "Two Years as a Domestic Educator in Buffalo", *Journal of Home Economics*, V (Dec. 1913), pp. 433-437.

——, "The Work of the Domestic Educator", U. S. Bureau of Education, *Bulletin*, 1913, No. 51, pp. 7-10.

Harkness, Georgia E., *The Church and the Immigrant*, New York, 1921.

Harman, D., "Americans for America", *Ladies' Home Journal*, XXXV (Aug. 1918), p. 3.

Harriman, Raymond D., *Suggestions for Americanization Teachers*, Salt Lake City, 1920.*

Hart, Helen, "State Programs of Immigrant Education", *Survey*, XLVI (July 16, 1921), pp. 516-518.

Hart, Joseph K., "Americanizing Americanization", *Survey*, XLVI (July 16, 1921), p. 521.

Hartford, Conn., Mayor's Americanization Committee, *The Hartford Handbook for New Citizens—and Old*, 1919.*

Harvey, George, "Hyphens Must Go", *North American Review*, CCIII (Mar. 1916), pp. 343-344.

Haskin, Frederick J., *The Immigrant, an Asset and a Liability*, New York, 1913.

Hebrew Sheltering and Immigrant Aid Society, *Annual Reports*, 1909-1920.

Hedger, Caroline, "The Difficulties of Americanization", *Immigrants in America Review*, II (July 1916), pp. 26-31.

——, "The Kindergarten as a Factor in Americanization", National Educational Association, *Journal of Addresses and Proceedings*, LVI, 1918, pp. 167-171.

Hemphill, A. J., "Banker's Part in Americanization", *Guaranty News*, VIII (Mar. 1919), pp. 1-6.

Henrici, Max, "Americanization and the Foreign-Language Press", *American Leader*, IX, No. 8 (Apr. 27, 1916), pp. 479-480.

——, "The Lesson of the Melting Pot", *American Leader*, IX (Mar. 9, 1916), pp. 277-279.

Henry, Katherine, "The 'American' in Americanization", *Outlook*, CXXIV (Jan. 7, 1920), pp. 36-39.

Herlihy, Charles M., "Adult Education for Foreign-Born and Native Illiterates", U S. Bureau of Education, *Biennial Survey of Education, 1922-1924*, pp. 235-246.

Herring, H. C., "Uniting to Help the Immigrants", *Missionary Review*, XXXVIII (July 1915), pp. 515-519.

Hill, Howard C., "The Americanization Movement", *The American Journal of Sociology*, XXIV (May 1919), pp. 609-642.

Hodges, L., "Church and the Immigrants: a Record of Failure and the Remedy", *Missionary Review*, XXXV (Mar. 1912), pp. 167-172.

Home Missions Council, *Reports of Annual Meetings*, 1910-1925.

"The Honorable Hyphen", *Independent*, LXXXVI (June 12, 1916), pp. 429-430.

Hood, William R., "Review of Educational Legislation, 1917 and 1918", U. S. Bureau of Education, *Bulletin*, 1919, No. 88, pp. 491-530.

Hoose, J. H., "Educational Problem of Americanizing Immigrants", *Education*, XV (Jan. 1905), pp. 269-278.

Hough, E., "What One Hyphenate Thinks", *Outlook*, CXIX (Aug. 21, 1918), pp. 627-628.

Horvath, Joseph, "The Vocation of the Hungarian Press in the United States", *American Leader*, VIII, No. 7 (Oct. 14, 1915), pp. 421-424.

Hourwich, Isaac A., *Immigration and Labor, the Economic Aspects of European Immigration to the United States*, New York, 1912.

"How Montclair 'Mothers' Foreign Mothers", *Literary Digest*, LXVII (Oct. 23, 1920), p. 35.

"How to Make Americans", *Survey*, XLII (June 28, 1919), pp. 484-486.

Howard, C. B., "Making Americans in Four Months", *Colliers, the National Weekly*, LXV (Jan. 17, 1920), p. 14.

Howe, Frederick C, "Our Future Immigrant Policy", *Scribners' Magazine*, LXI (May 1917), pp. 542-546.

Hoyt, Homer, "The Literacy Test and Immigration", *Journal of Political Economy*, XXIV (May 1916), pp. 445-473.

Hoyt, Margaret H., "Making Americans in Minnesota", *Educational Review*, LVIII (June 1919), pp. 14-20.

Hrbkova, Sarka B., "'Bunk' in Americanization, a Laudable Propaganda Infected by Ignorance", *Forum*, LXIII (Apr.–May 1920), pp. 428-439.

Huebner, G. G., "Americanization of Immigrants", American Academy of Political Science, *Annals*, XXVII (May 1906), p. 653.

Humphrey, Grace, "Americanization in a Small Town", *Outlook*, CXXIV (Feb. 4, 1920), pp. 211-214.

——, "The Business Man and Americanization", *Everybody's Magazine*, XLI (July 1919), p. 71.

Illinois, State of, *School Laws of Illinois*, 1919.

——, Department of Registration and Education, *Bulletins*, 1920.

——, *The Educational Needs of Immigrants in Illinois*, Springfield, 1920.*

——, *The Immigrant and Coal Mining Communities of Illinois*, Springfield, 1920.*

——, Illinois, State of, Immigrants' Commission, *Bulletins*, 1920.

——, Superintendent of Public Instruction, *Biennial Reports*, 1912-1930.

"Illiteracy in the United States", *American Review of Reviews*, LXIII (Feb. 1921), pp. 220-221.

"The Immigrant and the Rest of Us", *Outlook*, CXII (Jan. 12, 1916), pp. 60-61.

"An Immigrant's Program of Americanization", *Survey*, XL (Aug. 24, 1918), pp. 596-597.

"Immigration and Americanization", *Outlook*, CXV (Jan. 31, 1917), p. 182.

"Immigration and Straight America", *World's Work*, XXXII (Oct. 1916), p. 607.

*Immigration Journal*, 1916-1917.

Immigrants' Protective League, *Annual Reports*, 1909-1920.

Indiana, State of, *Laws of Indiana Relating to the Public School System, 1917, Supplement*, 1919.

——, Board of Education, *Americanization Day in the Indiana Public Schools on October 24, 1919*, 1919.

International Workers of the World, *Industrial Worker*, Seattle, Wash., 1912-1913.

——, *Solidarity*, Chicago, 1918-1921.

Inter-Racial Council, *Bolshevist Movement in America*, 1920.*

——, *Brief in Opposition to the Exclusion of Foreign Language Newspapers from Second Class Mailing Privileges*, 1921.*

——, *The Inter-Racial Council, Aims and Purposes*, 1919.*

——, *Proceedings, National Conference on Immigration under Auspices of the Inter-Racial Council*, New York, Apr. 7, 1920.*

——, *Some Suggestions for Scenarios on Americanization*, New York, 1920.*

Iowa, State of, *School Laws of Iowa*, 1913, 1915, 1919.

——, State Board of Education, *Biennial Reports*, 1914-1930.

Iowa, University of, Extension Division, "Study of Americanization", *Bulletin*, new series, XXXII, No. 51, 1919.

Irwin, E. J., "An Americanization Program", U. S. Bureau of Education, *Bulletin*, 1923, No. 30.

Issacs, Michael J., "Supplementary Activities", U. S. Bureau of Education, *Bulletin*, 1913, No. 51, pp. 51-52.

Italian Baptist Missionary Association, *Report of the Committee on Americanization*, 1918.*

"The Italians in Americanization", *Missions*, X (Apr. 1919), pp. 236-237.

Jackson, H. E., *What Americanization Means to Me*, 1920.

Janak, Jan, "The Mission of the Foreign-Language Newspaper in the United States", *American Leader*, VIII, No. 3 (Aug. 12, 1915), pp. 173-175.

Janzow, Laura M., *The Library without the Walls*, 1927.

Jardine, Edith L., "Selection of Evening-School Teachers", U. S. Bureau of Education, *Bulletin*, 1913, No. 51, pp. 43-46.

Jenks, Mrs. A. E., "Christian Americanization", *Missions*, XI (Feb. 1920), pp. 104-105.

Jenks, Albert Ernest, "The Goal of Americanization Work", *Survey*, XLI (Jan. 11, 1919), p. 505.

——, "Assimilation in the Philippines as Interpreted in Terms of Assimilation in America", *American Journal of Sociology*, XIX (May 1914), pp. 773-791.

Jenks, Jeremiah W., "The Urgent Immigration Problem", *World's Work*, XXII (May 1911), pp. 14368-14374.

—— and Lauck, W. Jett, *The Immigration Problem*, New York, 4th ed., 1917.

*Jewish Immigrant Bulletin*, 1913-1921.

Johnson, Alex J., "The Mission of the Foreign-Language Newspaper in the United States", *American Leader*, VII, No. 9 (May 13, 1915), pp. 538-540.

Jump, Herbert A., "A Festival of Nations", *Survey*, XXIV (June 4, 1910), pp. 392-396.

Junior Order United American Mechanics, New Jersey Council, *Report of the Special Committee on Americanization, 1921-1924.**

Kallen, H. M., *Culture and Democracy in the United States*, 1924.

Kane, J. F., "Big Brother for the Naturalization Applicant", *Outlook*, CXVIII (Jan. 9, 1918), pp. 74-75.

Kansas, State of, *Laws Relating to Education*, Session of 1919.

Keeler, Floyd, "Suspicious Americanization", *America*, XXIII, No. 17 (Aug. 14, 1920), pp. 391-393.

——, "Work among the Foreign Born", *America*, XXV, No. 19 (Aug. 27, 1921), pp 440-442.

Kellogg, Paul U., "The Minimum Wage and Immigrant Labor", National Conference of Charities and Correction, *Proceedings*, 1911, pp. 165-177.

Kellogg, Vernon, "Race and Americanization", *Yale Review*, new series, X (July 1921), pp. 729-740.

Kellor, Frances A., "Americanization by Industry", *Immigrants in America Review*, II, No. 1 (Apr. 1916), pp. 15-26.

——, "Americanization: a Conservation Policy for Industry", American Academy of Political and Social Science, *Annals*, LXV (May 1916), pp. 240-244.

——, *Americanization of Women; a Discussion of an Emergency Created by Granting the Vote to Women in New York State*, New York [*circa.* 1918].*

——, "Education of the Immigrant", *Educational Review*, XLVIII (June 1914), pp. 21-36.

——, *The Federal Administration and the Alien, a Supplement to Immigration and the Future*, New York, c. 1921.

——, "How to Increase Night School Attendance among the Foreign-Born", *School and Society*, III (Feb. 15, 1916), pp. 570-572.

——, "The Immigrant and Preparedness", *Immigrants in America Review*, I, No. 4 (Jan. 1916), pp. 20-30.

——, "The Immigrant Woman", *Atlantic Monthly*, C (Sept. 1907), pp. 401-407.

——, "Immigrants in America, a Domestic Policy", *Immigrants in America Review*, I, No. 1 (Mar. 1915), pp. 1-27.

——, *Immigrants in America, Program for a Domestic Policy*, New York, 1915.*

——, *Immigration and the Future*, New York, 1920.

——, "Justice for the Immigrant", American Academy of Political and Social Science, *Annals*, LII (Mar. 1914), pp. 159-168.

——, "Lo, the Poor Immigrant!", *Atlantic Monthly*, CXVII (Jan. 1916), pp. 59-65.

——, "Loyalty Highways", *Chronicle*, October 1918.

——, "National Americanization Day—July 4th", *Immigrants in America Review*, I, No. 3 (Sept. 1915), pp. 18-29.

——, "Needed, a Domestic Immigration Policy", *North American Review*, CXCIII (Apr. 1911), pp. 561-573.

——, *Neighborhood Americanization; a Discussion of the Alien in a New Country and of the Native American in his Home Country* [New York, 1918?].*

——, "The Protection of Immigrant Women", *Atlantic Monthly*, CI (Feb. 1918), pp. 246-255.

——, "Standards of Living", *Immigrants in America Review*, I, No. 1 (Mar. 1915), pp. 45-55.

——, "The Tie that Binds Immigration, Work, and Citizenship", *Survey*, XXXI (Mar. 21, 1914), pp. 766-767.

——, "Unemployment and Immigration", American Academy of Political and Social Science, *Annals*, LXI (Sept. 1915), pp. 40-44.

——, "What is Americanization", *Yale Review*, new series, VIII (Jan. 1919), pp. 282-299.

——, "Who is Responsible for the Immigrant", *Outlook*, CVI (Apr. 25, 1914), pp. 912-917.

Kentucky, Commonwealth of, *Common School Laws*, 1918, vol. II, No. 2.

Kernan, Thomas J., "The Catholic's Sound Americanism", *Catholic Mind*, XVII, No. 21 (Dec. 8, 1919), pp. 433-444.

Kidd, Cecil A., "Education of the Immigrant Child", U. S. Bureau of Education, *Bulletin*, 1913, No. 51, pp. 22-23.

Kilpatrick, Van Evrie, "Americanization through School Gardens", National Educational Association, *Journal of Addresses and Proceedings*, 1918, pp. 174-175.

Kimball, Rosamond, "Education of the Immigrant Adult", U. S. Bureau of Education, *Bulletin*, 1913, No. 51, pp. 37-39.

Kinne, Helen, "The Training of the Domestic Educator", U. S. Bureau of Education, *Bulletin*, 1913, No. 51, pp. 11-12.

Kittredge, Mabel H., "The Training of the Domestic Educator", U. S. Bureau of Education, *Bulletin*, 1913, No. 51, pp. 12-13.

Knight, John Watrous, "The Working Man and Immigration", *Charity Review*, IV (May 1895), pp. 363-375.

Knights of Columbus, Educational Bureau, *Bulletins*, 1919-1920.

Kley, Michael, "Adult Education and the Immigrant", *Jewish Immigration Bulletin*, VI, No. 10 (Oct. 1916), pp. 6-7.

——, *How to Take Out Your First Papers*, Metropolitan Life Insurance Co., 1921.*

Knox, Margaret, "Coordination of Welfare Agencies", U. S. Bureau of Education, *Bulletin*, 1913, No. 51, pp. 29-30.

Kohns, Lee, "Americanizing the Immigrant", *American Hebrew and Jewish Messenger*, XCVII (May 14, 1915), pp. 27-28.

——, "The Educational Alliance", *Jewish Immigration Bulletin*, V, No. 5 (May 1915), pp. 11-12.

Kulamer, John, "Americanization: the Other Side of the Case", *Atlantic Monthly*, CXXV, 1920, pp. 416-423.

Labaree, Mrs. B. W., "What New Britain is Doing to Help the Immigrant", *Missionary Review*, XXXV (Nov. 1912), pp. 835-839.

LaGuardia, Richard D., *A New English System for New Americans*, Trenton, N. J., c. 1919.

Lambos, Peter S., "The Mission of the Foreign-Language Newspaper in the United States", *American Leader*, VII, No. 9 (May 13, 1915), pp. 535-537.

Lane, Franklin K., "How to Make Americans", *Forum*, LXI (Apr. 1919), pp. 399-406.

——, "I Will Show You America", *Jewish Immigration Bulletin*, IX, No. 2 (Feb. 1919), pp. 3-4.

——, "Interpreting America", *Churchman*, CXX, No. 13 (Sept. 27, 1919), pp. 14-15.

——, "The Living Flame of Americanization", *Current History*, XIV (July 1921), pp. 608-610.

——, "What I Mean by Americanization", *Ladies' Home Journal*, XXXVI (May 1919), p. 33.

——, "What Is It to Be an American?", *National Geographic Magazine*, XXXIII (Apr. 1918), pp. 348-354.

Lape, Esther E., "Americanization", *Columbia University Quarterly*, XX, 1918, pp. 59-80.

——, "The 'English First' Movement in Detroit", *Immigrants in America Review*, I, No. 3 (Sept. 1915), pp. 46-50.

——, "Putting America into Your City", *Ladies' Home Journal*, XXXVI (Sept. 1919), pp. 35-36.

——, "Putting America into Your Town, *Ladies' Home Journal*, XXXVI (Oct. 1919), p. 37.

——, "Putting America into Your Village", *Ladies' Home Journal*, XXXVI (Nov. 1919), p. 57.

Lapp, John A., "Bogus Propaganda, Dollar Mark Shows in Attempts to Control Americanization", National Catholic War Council, *Bulletin*, I, No. 11 (June–July 1920), pp. 9-10.

Lauck, W. Jett, "The Cotton Mill Operatives of New England", *Atlantic Monthly*, CIX (May 1912), pp. 706-713.

——, "Industrial Communities", *Survey*, XXV (Jan. 7, 1911), pp. 579-586.

——, "The Real Significance of Recent Immigration", *North American Review*, CXCV (Feb. 1912), pp. 201-211.

League for the Protection of Immigrants, *Annual Reports*, 1909-1920.

League of Foreign-Born Citizens, *League of Foreign-Born Citizens, Its Aims and Activities*, n. d. [*circa*.] 1916].*

"The League of Foreign-Born Citizens", *American Hebrew*, CVIII (Nov. 26, 1920), p. 27.

Ledbetter, Eleanor E., *The Czechs of Cleveland*, 1918.*

——, *The Jugo-Slavs of Cleveland*, 1918.*

——, *Polish Immigrant and His Reading*, 1924.*

——, *The Slovaks of Cleveland*, 1918.*

——, *Winning Friends and Citizens for America*, 1918.*

Leipziger, Henry M., "Education of Adults", American Social Science Association, *Journal of Social Science*, XLII (Sept. 1904), pp. 133-143.

Leiserson, W. M., *Adjusting Immigrants and Industry*, New York, 1924.

Lenz, Frank B., "Assimilation of the Immigrant", *Overland Monthly*, new series, LXVI (Sept. 1915), pp. 240-243.

——, "Education of the Immigrant", *Educational Review*, LI (May 1916), pp. 469-477.

——, ed., *Immigration—Some Phases of the Problem* [San Francisco, 1915?].*

——, "Young Men's Christian Association and the Immigrant", *Overland Monthly*, new series, LXVII (Feb. 1916), pp. 162-165.

Levey Printing Company, *The Manual of Americanism*, Indianapolis [1918?].*

Levy, Clifton H., "Americanization Then and Now", *American Hebrew*, CVII (Sept. 10, 1920), pp. 492-493.

——, "An Early Step in Americanization", *American Hebrew*, CIII (July 5, 1918), pp. 198-199.

Lewinski-Corwin, E. H., "Education of the Immigrant Adult", U. S. Bureau of Education, *Bulletin*, 1913, No. 51, pp. 36-37.

Lieberman, Elias, "Assimilation of the Immigrant", *American Hebrew*, CIII (July 5, 1918), pp. 198-199.

——, "The Human Side of Americanization Work", *American Hebrew*, CIX (Sept. 23, 1921), pp. 430, 442 and 447.

——, "The Iron Hand or Sympathy? a Problem of Americanization", *Outlook*, CXXIV, pp. 434-436.

"The Limit of the Melting Pot", *World's Work*, XXIX (Mar. 1915), pp. 491-492.

Lingle, Clara S., *A Course on Americanization; Studies of the Peoples and the Movements That Are Building Up the American Nation*, Chapel Hill, N. Car., 1919.*

Lodge, Henry Cabot, "Efforts to Restrict Undesirable Immigration", *Century Magazine*, LXVII (Jan. 1904), pp. 466-469.

Loeb, Max, "Compulsory English for Foreign-Born", *Survey*, XL (July 13, 1918), pp. 426-427.

Loewinthan, Albert, "Supplementary Activities," U. S. Bureau of Education, *Bulletin*, 1913, No. 51, pp. 49-50.

Los Angeles Library School, *Americanization*, 1919 [bibliography].*

Loughran, E. W., and Madden, M. R., *Outline Study of Immigration and Americanization*, c. 1921.*

Louisiana, State of, *School Laws of Louisiana*, 1916.

Lubin, Simon J. and Krysto, Christina, "The Strength of America; the Menace of Americanization", *Survey,* XLIII (1920), pp. 258-259, 252-256, 461-463, 610-612, 690-695 and 719.

McAndrew, William, *The Motion Picture in Americanization*, c. 1919.*

McAuliffe, W. J., "Problem of Americanization", Catholic Educational Association, *Bulletin*, XVI (Nov. 1919), pp. 184-191.

MacDonald, A. A., "Americanization; What it Means to the Employer", Pennsylvania Department of Labor and Industry, *Monthly Bulletin* (Jan. 1917), No. 4, pp. 18-24.

McDowell, Mary E., "Americanization", *United Mine Workers' Journal*, XXIX (June 20, 1918), pp. 6 and 11.

——, "The Struggle in the Family Life", *Charities*, XIII (Dec. 3, 1904), pp. 196-197.

Mackay, C. D., "Suggestions for a Simple Industrial Ceremonial", *Playground*, XIII (May 1919), pp. 70-74.

Maclean, Annie M., "Life in the Pennsylvania Coal Fields", *American Journal of Sociology*, XIV (Nov. 1908), pp. 329-351.

McClure, Archibald, *Leadership in the New America, Racial and Religious*, New York, 1916.

Magoshes, S., "Putting America into Americanization", *Jewish Immigration Bulletin*, IX, No. 6 (June, July and Aug. 1919), pp. 14-15.

Mahoney, John J., "Americanization in the United States", U. S. Bureau of Education, *Bulletin*, 1923, No. 31.

——, The Importance of State Aid to the Future Citizenship of the Commonwealth", *Education*, XXXIX (June 1919), pp. 628-634.

——, "Training Teachers for Americanization", U. S. Bureau of Education, *Bulletin*, 1920, No. 12.

—— and Herlihy, Charles M., *First Steps in Americanization, a Handbook for Teachers*, New York, c. 1918.

Maine, State of, *Laws of Maine Relating to Public Schools*, 1919.

——, State Superintendent of Schools, *Annual Reports*, 1910-1930.

"Make the Fourth of July, 1915, 'Americanization Day'", *American City*, XII (June 1915), pp. 492-493.

"Making Aliens Into Citizens", *Independent*, LXXV (Feb. 28, 1916), p. 294.

"Making Aliens out of Immigrants", *Outlook*, CXXV (June 30, 1920), p. 419.

"Making the Foreign-Born One of Us", *Survey*, XL (May 25, 1918), pp. 213-215.

Maltby, Adelaide B., "Education of the Immigrant Adult", U. S. Bureau of Education, *Bulletin*, 1913, No. 51, p. 37.

Mangano, Antonio, "Americanizing the Italian Mother", *Missions*, X (Jan. 1919), p. 42.

Manufacturers' and Dealers' Association of America, Chicago, Educational Publicity Department, *Be An American* [1918?].*

Marshall, Louis, "The Way Out", *Survey*, XXIII (Jan. 1, 1910), pp. 472-475.

Maryland, State of, *Maryland Public School Laws*, 1918.

Mason, G., "Americanization Factory; an Account of What the Public Schools Are Doing to Make Americans of Foreigners", *Outlook*, CXIV (Feb. 23, 1916), pp. 47-53.

——, "Americans First; How the People of Detroit Are Making Americans of the Foreigners in Their City", *Outlook*, CXIV (Sept. 27, 1916), pp. 193-201.

Massachusetts, Commonwealth of, *Report of the Commission on Immigration on the Problem of Immigration in Massachusetts*, Boston, 1914.

——, *Revised Laws Relating to Public Instruction, Enacted by the Legislature of November 21, 1901, to Take Effect January 1, 1902*, 1902.

——, *Subsequent Amendments and Additions from 1902-1914, Inclusive, and Other Laws of Interest to School Authorities*, 1914.

Massachusetts, Commonwealth of, Board of Education, *Annual Reports*, 1900-1930.

——, *Bulletins*, 1916-1925.*

——, *The Federal-State Program for Immigrant Education*, July, 1919.*

——, *Proceedings of State Conference on Immigrant Education in Massachusetts Industries*, Boston, 1920.*

——, *Thirty Lessons in Naturalization and Citizenship*, 1921.*

Massachusetts, Commonwealth of, Board of Education, Extension Division, *Americanization, Courses Given in Cooperation with the State Normal School at Hyannis, Massachusetts, during the Summer Session, August 2 to September 1, 1920*, Jan. 1920.*

——, *Americanization, One Language—One People*, July 1919.*

——, *Americanization Letters*, 1920.*

——, *Annual Reports*, 1915-1930.

——, *Civics for Naturalization*, July 1917.*

——, *English for American Citizenship; Suggested Plans through Which Industry Can Assist in Promoting Good Citizenship*, 1918.*

——, *Lessons in English for American Citizenship*, Sept. 1919.*

——, *Lessons in English for American Citizenship, Series for Women with Home Interests*, 1920.*

——, *The Problem of Immigrant Education in Massachusetts*, July 1919.*

——, *A Teacher's Handbook to Accompany Standard Lessons in English for American Citizenship*, May 1919.*

Massachusetts, Commonwealth of, Bureau of Immigration, *Annual Reports*, 1919-1930.

——, *Who Is Your Neighbor?*, 1918.*

Massachusetts, Commonwealth of, Committee on Public Safety and Woman's Committee of Council of Defense, *Co-ordination of Americanization Work in Massachusetts*, Sept. 9, 1918.*

Massachusetts, Commonwealth of, Department of Education, *Adult Immigrant Education in Massachusetts*, 1920-1921.*

Massachusetts, Commonwealth of, Department of Education, Division of Immigration and Americanization, *Americanization for Women's Organizations*, n. d. [*circa.* 1919.]

——, *Annual Reports*, 1920-1922.

Massachusetts, Commonwealth of, Department of Education, University Extension Division, *English for American Citizenship*, 1921.*

——, *The Massachusetts Problem of Immigrant Education in 1921-22*, Nov. 1922.*

——, *A Survey of Adult Alien Education in Massachusetts*, 1927.*

Matthews, Brander, "The American of the Future", *Century Magazine*, LXXIV (July 1907), pp. 747-780.

Maxwell, William H., "Education of the Immigrant Child", U. S. Bureau of Education, *Bulletin*, 1913, No. 51, pp. 18-19.

Mayer, Eli, *Americanization*, Albany, N. Y., 1920.

Mayper, Joseph, "Americanization in National Defense", *American City*, XVI (May 1917), pp. 497-501.

——, "Americanizing Immigrant Homes", *Immigrants in America Review*, II, No. 2 (July 1916), pp. 54-60.

——, "Immigrants in Labor Camps and Isolated Communities", U. S. Bureau of Education, *Bulletin*, 1913, No. 51, pp. 13-15.

Mead, George H., "The Adjustment of Our Industry to Surplus and Unskilled Labor", National Conference of Charities and Correction, *Proceedings*, 1909, pp. 222-225.

Methodist Episcopal Church, Board of Home Missions, *Reports*, 1910-1925.

Michaud, G. and Giddings, F. H., "Coming Race of America", *Century Magazine*, LXV (Mar. 1903), pp. 683-692.

Michigan, State of, *General School Laws*, rev. 1917.

——, Superintendent of Public Instruction, *Annual Reports*, 1912-1930.

Miller, G., "Americanization of Immigrants", *Outlook*, CXXI (Apr. 16, 1919), pp. 630-631.

"Milwaukee's 30 Races Present Unusual Problems", *Americanization Bulletin*, I, No. 9 (May 1, 1919), p. 14.

Minckley, Loren S., *Americanization Through Education*, Girard, Kan., 1917.*

Minneapolis, American Committee of, *Patriotism: Its Dangers and Duties* [circa. 1919].*

——, *Prospectus, Flying Squadron of Volunteer Speakers* [circa. 1919].*

Minnesota, State of, *Laws of Minnesota Relating to the Public School System*, 1919.

——, Department of Education, *Biennial Reports*, 1912-1930.

Minnesota State Americanization Conference, *Proceedings*, Minneapolis, 1920.*

Minnesota, University of, General Extension Division, *Short Course in Citizenship*, Minneapolis, 1919.*

Mintz, Frances S., *The New American Citizen, a Reader for Foreigners*, New York, 1923.

Missouri, State of, *Revised School Laws of the State of Missouri*, 1917.

Mitchell, John, "Protect the Workmen", *Outlook*, XCIII (Sept. 11, 1909), pp. 65-69.

Mitchell, Mrs. W. S., "Americanization", *Child Welfare Magazine*, XIII (March 1919), pp. 183-184.

Monaghan, J. C., "Immigration Problem", *Catholic World*, LXXIX (July 1914), pp. 512-523.

Montana, State of, *School Laws of the State of Montana*, June 1919.

Montgomery, George W., "Christian Americanization", *Presbyterian*, XC, No. 45 (Nov. 4, 1920), pp. 10, 30-31.

Moore, Annie Carroll, "Coordination of Welfare Agencies," U. S Bureau of Education, *Bulletin*, 1913, No. 51, pp. 32-33.

Moore, John H., "The Sons of the American Revolution and Better Citizenship", *Immigrants in America Review*, I (Sept. 1915), pp. 40-41.

Moore, Sarah Wool, "Labor Camp Schools", National Conference of Charities and Correction, *Proceedings*, 1909, pp. 236-238.

——, "New Recollections—Notes on Camp School No. 1, Aspinwall, Pa.", *Charities and the Commons*, XVIII, pp. 894-902.

——, "Teaching of Foreigners", *Survey*, XXIV (June 4, 1910), pp. 386-392.

Morley, Felix, "Making Americans", *Nation*, CVIII (May 31, 1919), p. 878.

Moskowitz, Henry, "The Real Jewish Immigrant", *Jewish Immigration Bulletin*, V, No. 5 (May 1915), pp. 7-9.

"The Movie and Trench Piano as Instruments of Americanization", *Outlook*, CXXIV (Jan. 21, 1920), pp. 102-104.

Muensterberg, Emil, "Impressions of American Charity", *Charities and the Commons*, XVII, pp. 740-743.

Mullen, Rosemary ·F., "Wherein Americanization Will Fail", *Educational Review*, LIX (Apr. 1920), pp. 341-344.

Murphy, John Bernard, "What America Needs and How to Americanize the Immigrant", *Immigrants in America Review*, I, No. 3 (Sept. 1915), pp. 88-92.

Myers, Carry Cleveland, *Some Psychology Applied to Americanization*, c. 1921.*

Nagel, Charles, "Americanization", *American Leader*, IX (May 25, 1916), pp. 588-592 (June 8, 1916), pp. 650-655 (June 22, 1916), pp. 716-720.

National Americanization Committee, *Actual Account of What We Have Done to Reduce Our Labor Turnover*, 1917.*

——, *Americanization Day—Fourth of July*, 1916.*

——, *Americanization of Foreign-Born within Controlled Districts*, 1918.*

——, *Americanization of Women, a Discussion of an Emergency Created by Granting the Vote to Women in New York State*, Jan. 17, 1918.*

——, *Americanization War Service, What You Can Do for Americanization*, Jan. 1918.*

——, *Americanization, What Women's Organizations Can Do*, 1918.*

——, *Americanizing a City, The Campaign for the Detroit Night Schools Conducted in Cooperation with the Detroit Board of Commerce and Board of Education, August–September, 1915*, New York, Dec. 15, 1915.*

——, *Bulletins on Industrial Engineering*, 1917-1918.*

——, *A Call to National Service*, 1916.*

——, *How to Reach Aliens with War Information*, Feb. 1918.*

——, *Immigrants In America Review*, 1915-1916.

——, *Invaded America*, 1918.*

——, *Neighborhood Americanization*, Feb. 8, 1918.*

——, *A New Era in the Industrial World*, Oct. 1918.*

——, *News Releases*, 1915-1918 [mimeographed material].*

——, *A Partial Record of Alien Enemy Activities, 1915-1917.*

——, *Pay Envelope Series*, 1915.*

——, *Safeguarding Industries from Enemies Within*, 1918.*

——, *Reprints* [of articles by Frances Kellor, and Joseph Mayper In the *North American Review, National Efficiency Quarterly, Engineering News-Record*, and *American City*, 1917-1918].*

——, *War Americanization for States*, Oct. 1917.*

——, *War Policy for Aliens*, Oct. 1917.*

——, *What Industrial Leaders Say about Americanization*, 1918.*

——, National Committee on Patriotic Literature, *Songs of Our Country*, c. 1917.*

——, *Your Flag and Mine*, c. 1917.*

National Association of Manufacturers, *Proceedings of Annual Conventions*, 1914-1924.

National Catholic War Council, Committee on Special War Activities, *A Program for Citizenship*, July 1919.*

National Catholic Welfare Conference, *Bulletins*, 1919-1925.*

National Civic Federation, *Facts about Immigration, Being the Report of the Conferences on Immigration Held in New York City, September 24 to December 12, 1906, by the Immigration Department of the National Civic Federation*, Jan. 1907.*

National Conference on Americanization in Industries, *Proceedings*, June 22-24, 1919, Boston.*

"National Conference on Immigration", *School and Society*, III (Jan. 22, 1916), p. 144.

"The National Conference on Immigration and Americanization", *Immigrants in America Review*, II, No. 1 (Apr. 1916), pp. 38-46.

National League of Women Voters, Committee on American Citizenship, *Bulletins*, 1920-1921.*

National Security League, *Americanization, What is It? What to do*, 1919.*

——, *Americanization Service, What You Can Do for America Through Americanization of the Foreign Born*, New York, 1918.*

——, *A Concept of National Service* [address of S. Stanwood Menken before the Congress of National Service, February 21, 1918].*

——, *Future Work*, Feb. 1919.*

——, *Handbook of War Facts and Peace Problems*, 1919.*

——, *How to Obtain Citizenship Papers*, Apr. 1920.*

——, *A Square Deal for the Public, a Working Program for Crushing the Radical Menace*, Dec. 1, 1919, New York.*

——, *Teachers' Patriotic Leaflets*, New York, 1919.*

——, *Work of the National Security League from 1914 to 1920*, New York, May 1920.*

National Society of the Colonial Dames of America, *The National Society of the Colonial Dames of America, its Beginnings, its Purposes, and a Record of its Work, 1891-1913*, 1913.

——, *Minutes of the Biennial Councils*, 1900-1930.

——, *Reports of the Historians of the Society*, 1920-1930.

National Society of the Daughters of the American Revolution, *Manual of the United States for the Information of Immigrants*, 1921 [revised 1923, 1926].

——, *Proceedings of the Continental Congresses*, 1900-1925.

National Society of the Sons of the American Revolution, *The Constitution of the United States*, 1915.*

——, *Official Bulletins*, 1906-1925.

——, *The United States, Information for Immigrants* [English, Polish, Greek, and Yiddish editions].*

Naylor, J. E., "Transformation—the Real Americanization", *Missions*, XIII (Feb. 1922), p. 112.

Nebraska, State of, *New School Laws Passed by the Thirty-Seventh Session of the Nebraska Legislature*, 1919.

Nevada, State of, *School Laws of Nevada*, 1919.

"New Americanism", *American Review of Reviews*, LIX (June 1919), p. 656.

"A New Approach to Americanization Work", *Outlook*, CXXII (July 23, 1919), pp. 459-460.

"A New Departure in Association Work", *Charities and the Commons*, XX (May 16, 1908), pp. 224-225.

New Hampshire, State of, *School Laws of 1919*.

——, State Board of Education, *Americanization Pamphlets*, 1918.*

——, *Reports, 1920-1930*.

——, Superintendent of Public Instruction, *Reports*, 1910, 1920.

"The New Independence Day", *Survey*, XL (July 13, 1918), pp. 419-421.

New Jersey, State of, *New Jersey School Laws*, 1918; Supplement, 1919.

——, *Report of the Commission of Immigration of the State of New Jersey*, Trenton, 1914.

——, State Board of Education and Commissioner of Education, *Annual Reports*, 1912-1930.

New Mexico, State of, State Board of Education, *Bulletin*, V, No. 3 (Sept. 1919).

New York, City of, Department of Education, *Guide for Applicants for Citizenship*, 1915.*

"New York City Day Schools", *Americanization Bulletin*, I, No. 3 (Nov. 1, 1918), p. 5.

*New York Times*, 1900-1925.

New York, State of, *Laws of 1918*.

——, *Report of the Commission of Immigration of the State of New York*, 1909.

——, *Report of the Joint Legislative Committee Investigating Seditious Activities, Filed April 24, 1920 in the Senate of the State of New York,* 4 vol., Albany, 1920.

New York, State of, Bureau of Industries and Immigration, *Annual Reports,* 1912-25.

New York, State of, Department of Education, *Americanization Through Women's Organizations,* 1919.*

——, *Immigrant Education,* 1919.*

——, *Lessons for Illiterate Foreign Women,* 1919.*

——, *Methods of Teaching English to the Non-English-Speaking Foreign-Born,* 1919.*

New York, State of, Reconstruction Commission, *Americanization,* 1919.*

New York, State of, University of the State of, *Community Organization and Program for Americanization Work,* 1919.*

——, *Immigrant Education,* 1919.*

——, *Organization of Schools in English for the Foreign-Born,* 1919.*

——, *Twenty Lessons in English for Non-English-Speaking Women,* 1919.*

New York—New Jersey Committee of the North American Civic League for Immigrants, *Bulletins,* 1910-1911.

——, *Reports,* 1909-1913.

Nicholes, S. Grace, "First Aid to New Voters", *Survey,* XXXIX (Dec. 8, 1917), pp. 275-279.

North American Civic League for Immigrants, *Abraham Lincoln,* n. d. [*circa.* 1910].*

——, *Annual Reports,* 1908-1920.

——, *First Paper, Pierwsze Papiery,* n. d. [*circa.* 1910].*

——, *George Washington,* n. d. [*circa.* 1910].*

——, *How to Become a Citizen of the United States,* n. d. [*circa.* 1910].*

——, *Messages for Newcomers to the United States,* Boston, 1915.*

——, *The Need of Learning English and the Advantages of an Education,* n. d. [*circa.* 1910].*

——, *The New Home Land and Opportunity Offered in Various Sections,* n. d. [*circa.* 1910].*

——, *A Patriotic Organization, Aims and Purposes,* 1915.*

——, *A Patriotic Movement for the Assimilation of Immigrants,* 1910.*

——, *A Primer for the Alien Desirous of Becoming a Citizen,* n. d. [*circa.* 1910].*

——, *Special Message of the President of the United States,* 1915.*

——, *A Square Deal for the Immigrant,* n. d. [*circa.* 1910].*

——, *Summary for the Information of Associated Committees and Contributors,* 1925.*

——, *War Bulletins,* 1917-1918.*

——, Committee on Legislation, *Bi-Monthly Bulletins,* 1913-1914.*

North Carolina, State of, University of, *Americanization Studies of the Peoples and the Movements That Are Building Up the American Nation,* 1920.*

North Dakota, State of, *General School Laws with 1917 Enactments*, 1917.
——, State Superintendent of Public Instruction, *Biennial Reports*, 1912-1930.
Northern Baptist Convention, *Annuals*, 1900-1925.
——, *Proceedings of Annual Meetings*, 1900-1925.
Norton, Eliot, "The Diffusion of Immigration", American Academy of Political and Social Science, *Annals*, XXIV, 1904, pp. 161-165.
O'Connor, A. W., "Americanization Work as a Field for College Women", *Intercollegiate Community Service Quarterly*, IV (Jan. 1919), pp. 3-5.
Ohio, State of, Americanization Committee, *Americanization in Ohio, a Constructive Program*, 1920.*
——, *A Handbook of American Citizenship*, 1920.*
Ohio, State of, Department of Education, Americanization Division, *Adult Education in Ohio*, 1923.*
——, *Fundamental Facts for New Citizens*, 1922.*
——, *Manual for Teachers*, 1922.*
——, General State Conference of All Agencies Interested in Americanization in Ohio, *Proceedings*, Columbus, 1920.*
Ohio, State of, Superintendent of Public Instruction, *Annual Reports*, 1912-1930.
Oklahoma, State, *School Laws of Oklahoma*, 1919.
Okuntsoff, Ivan, "The Mission of the Foreign-Language Newspaper in the United States", *American Leader*, VII (June 24, 1915), pp. 735-738.
"The Old Stock and the New", *Outlook*, CVII (June 13, 1914), pp. 334-335.
Omaha, Neb., Public Library, *Books for New Americans*, n.d. [circa. 1916].*
O'Neil, Robert T. and Estes, G. K., *Naturalization Made Easy*, San Francisco, 1917.*
Oregon, State of, *Oregon School Laws*, 1919.
——, University, Extension Division, *Americanization: a Suggested Outline for Teachers of Aliens*, 1919.*
Orenstein, Marie S., "The Servo-Croates of Manhattan", *Survey*, XXIX (Dec. 7, 1912), pp. 277-286.
O'Toole, Rose, *Practical English, First Series*, 1920.
"Our Foreign Born Citizens", *National Geographic Magazine*, XXXI (Feb. 1917), pp. 95-130.
"Overdoing Free Education", *Public*, XXII (June 14, 1919), p. 623.
"A Pageant of America in the Making", *Survey*, XXXVIII (Sept. 15, 1917), p. 529.
Palandech, John R., "Hyphenated Americans", *American Leader*, VIII (Dec. 9, 1915), pp. 675-679.
Palmer, Mitchell, "Americanization—Not Restriction", *Jewish Immigration Bulletin*, IX, No. 7 (May 1919), pp. 12-15.
Panunzio, Constantine, *Immigration Crossroads*, New York, 1927.

Park, R. E., *The Immigrant Press and its Control*, New York, 1922.
——, *Old World Traits Transplanted*, New York, 1921.
" Patriot Service of the Civic League for Immigrants ", *Outlook*, XCII
    (July 10, 1909), pp. 580-581.
Paull, Charles H., *Americanization, a Discussion of Present Conditions with
    Recommendations for the Teaching of Non-Americans*, Solvay Process
    Co., Syracuse, N. Y., 1918.*
——, "Aims and Standards in Industrial Americanization", *Industrial
    Management*, LVII (Feb. 1919), pp. 148-151.
——, "Development of Americanization Project, Experiment and Ex-
    perience of the Solvay Process Company", *Industrial Management*,
    LVII (Mar. 1919), pp. 213-217.
Pennsylvania, Commonwealth of, *School Laws of Pennsylvania*, 1917, 1919.
——, Commissioner of Labor and Industry, *Annual Reports*, 1913-1922.
——, Department of Labor and Industry, Bureau of Statistics and Infor-
    mation, Division of Immigration, *Reports*, 1913-1922.
Pennsylvania, Council of National Defense, Americanization Bureau,
    *Americanization in Pennsylvania; Plan of the Americanization Bureau,
    Pennsylvania Council of National Defense*, Philadelphia, 1918.*
Pennsylvania, League of Women Voters, *Correspondence Course on Citizen-
    ship*, Philadelphia, n. d. [*circa*. 1918].*
Penrose, Boies, "Chinese Exclusion and the Problem of the Immigrant",
    *Independent*, LIV (Jan. 2, 1902), pp. 12-15.
Peyser, Nathan, "Co-operating with the Immigrant", *Jewish Immigration
    Bulletin*, IX, No. 5 (May 1919), pp. 12-15.
Philadelphia Chamber of Commerce, Americanization Committee, *Ameri-
    canization in Philadelphia*, c. 1923.*
Phillips, Edna, *Easy Books for New Americans, with Reading List for
    Americanization Workers*, 1926.*
Phillips, Nathaniel, "The League of Foreign-Born Citizens", *American
    Leader*, VIII, No. 2 (July 22, 1915), pp. 109-113.
——, "The League of Foreign-Born Citizens", *Immigrants in America
    Review*, I, No. 3 (Sept. 1915), pp. 58-61.
Pickett, Charles E., *Helps Toward American Citizenship*, New Haven,
    Conn., 1919.
Pierce, David Henry, "What America Means and How to Americanize
    the Immigrant", *Immigrants in America Review*, I (Sept. 1915), pp.
    93-97.
Pittsburgh, Chamber of Commerce of, Americanization Bureau, *Annual
    Report for 1921-1922*.*
Plass, Anna A., *Civics for Americans in the Making*, 1920.
Poe, Elizabeth Ellicott, "America's Greatest Problem", *D. A. R. Magazine*,
    LIV, No 1 (Jan. 1920).
Pollak, Mrs. Bernard E., "Americanization That Works Both Ways",
    *American Hebrew*, CVI (Apr. 16, 1920), pp. 726-727.
Poole, Ernest, "A Mixing Bowl for Nations", *Everybody's Magazine*,
    XXIII (Oct. 1910), pp. 554-564.

Pratt, Julius W., *Expansionists of 1898*, Baltimore, 1936

"Preaching the 'Gospel of Americanization'", *Lutheran*, XXII, No. 21 (Feb. 21, 1918), p. 8.

Presbyterian Church, U. S. A., Board of Home Missions, *Annual Reports*, 1910-1925.

Prince, J. D., "Educating the Adult Immigrant", *Charities and the Commons*, XVII (Feb. 16, 1907), pp. 890-891.

"The Professor's Visit", *Outlook*, CXXV (May 26, 1920), pp. 150-151.

"Progress of Americanization: Symposium", *National Efficiency Quarterly*, I (Nov. 1918), pp. 179-213.

"Proposal for an Americanization Day", *Outlook*, CX (June 30, 1915), p. 485.

Protestant Episcopal Church in the U. S. A., *Journals of the General Conventions*, 1910-1925.

——, Board of Missions, Domestic and Foreign Missionary Society, *Annual Reports of the Board of Missions*, 1910-1925.

Providence, R. I., Public Library, *Americanization*, Mar. 1919 [bibliography].*

Providence, R. I., Union for Christian Work, *Report of the Immigrant Education Bureau*, 1913.*

"Public Education", *School and Society*, IX (June 14, 1919), pp. 720-721.

"Public Education", *Survey*, XLII (June 7, 1919), pp. 403-404.

Ravage, M. E., "Absorbing the Alien", *Century Magazine*, XCV (Nov. 1917), pp. 26-36.

——, "American in the Making", *Harper's Magazine*, CXXXIV (June 1917), pp. 111-125.

——, *An American in the Making, the Life Story of an Immigrant*, New York, 1917

——, "Democratic Americanization, a Criticism and a Policy", *New Republic*, XIX (May 31, June 14 and June 16, 1919).

——, "Immigrant's Burden", *New Republic*, XIX (June 14, 1919), pp. 209-211.

——, "The Loyalty of the Foreign Born", *Century Magazine*, XCIV (June 1917), pp. 201-209.

——, "My Plunge into the Slums", *Harper's Magazine*, CXXXIV (Apr. 1917), pp 658-665.

——, "Standardizing the Immigrant", *New Republic*, XIX (May 31, 1919), pp. 145-147.

——, "Task for Americans", *New Republic*, XIX (July 16, 1919), pp. 349-351.

Rea, Samuel, "Making Americans on the Railroads", *Social Service Review*, VIII (Sept. 1918), pp. 5-7.

Reformed Church in America, Board of Domestic Missions, *Annual Reports to the General Synod*, 1910-1925.

Reid, Marguerite, *Aids in Library Work with Foreigners*, 1912.*

Remnitz, Virginia Yeaman, "The Story of Senate Bill 5464; the Smith-Bankhead Americanization Bill", *North American Review*, CCX (Aug. 1919), pp. 203-211.

Repp, Paul Joseph, "Why America is Better", *Independent*, LXVIII (Feb. 24, 1910), pp. 409-410.

Repplier, Agnes, "Americanize", *Atlantic Monthly*, CXVII (Mar. 1916), pp. 289-297.

——, "The Modest Immigrant", *Atlantic Monthly*, CXVI (Sept. 1915), pp. 303-312.

Rhode Island and Providence Plantations, State of, *An Act to Promote Americanization*, 1919.

——, *Acts and Resolves Passed by the General Assembly of the State of Rhode Island ... at the January Session A. D. 1914*, Chapter 1078.

——, *Laws of Rhode Island Relating to Education*, 1919.

——, State Board of Education, *Annual Reports*, 1910-1930.

Rhodes, Anne, "Americanization through Women's Organizations", *Immigrants in America Review*, II, No. 1 (Apr. 1916), pp. 71-73.

Ridge, Jr., Fred H., "3,500 College Students Humanizing Industry", *World's Work*, XXVII (Mar. 1914), pp 505-511.

Ripley, William Z., "Races in the United States", *Atlantic Monthly*, CII (Dec. 1908), pp. 745-759.

——, "Race Progress and Immigration", American Academy of Political and Social Science, *Annals*, XXXIV (July–Dec. 1909), pp. 130-138.

Ritchie, Mrs. Jean, "An Individual Experiment in Americanization", *Missions*, XII (Sept. 1921), pp. 452-453.

Robbins, Barney R., *Immigration and Americanization*, New York, 1924.

Robbins, Jane E., "The Foreign Born American", *Outlook*, LXXXIII (Aug. 18, 1906), pp. 891-893.

——, "Immigrants in Labor Camps and in Isolated Communities", U. S. Bureau of Education, *Bulletin*, 1913, No. 51, pp. 15-18.

——, "Schools in Temporary Construction Camps", *Immigrants in America Review*, I (June 1915), pp. 28-30.

Roberts, Arthur J., "Selection of Evening-School Teachers", U. S. Bureau of Education, *Bulletin*, 1913, No. 51, pp. 46-47.

Roberts, Peter, *Anthracite Coal Communities, a Study of the Demography, the Social, Educational, and Moral Life of the Anthracite Region*, New York, 1904.

——, *Civics for Coming Americans*, New York, 1917.

——, "English for Coming Americans", *Teachers' Manual*, p. 9, n. d. [*circa.* 1918].

——, *The New Immigration*, New York, 1912.

——, "The New Pittsburgers", *Charities and the Commons*, XXI (Jan. 2, 1909), pp. 533-552.

——, "Night Schools", National Conference of Charities and Correction, *Proceedings*, 1909, pp. 232-236.

——, *The Problem of Americanization*, New York, 1920.

——, "The Y. M. C. A. among the Immigrants", *Survey*, XXIX (Feb. 15, 1913), pp. 697-700.

——, "The Y. M. C. A. Teaching Foreign-Speaking Men", *Immigrants in America Review*, I (June 1915), pp. 18-23.

——, "Work with Foreign-Speaking Men", *American Leader*, V, No. 4 (Feb. 26, 1914), pp. 275-282.

Rochester, New York, City of, *Provisional Course of Study in Immigrant Education and Citizenship*, Nov. 1915.*

Rochester, New York, Chamber of Commerce, *Report of Americanization Committee of Rochester Chamber of Commerce, 1916.*

Rockow, L., "Americanization and the Pillar of Democracy", *Education*, XXXVII (Nov. 1916), pp. 174-183.

Roebling, John A., "Economic Aspects of Immigration", *American Magazine of Civics*, IX (Oct. 1896), pp. 235-245.

Rogers, Sherman, "Tell the Truth Papers", *Outlook*, CXXV (May 26, 1920), p. 156.

Roosevelt, Theodore, *Americanism*, 1915.*

——, "Americanism and Americanization: Selections From His Writings", Pittsburgh, Carnegie Library, *Bulletin*, XXIV, Feb. 1919, pp. 81-86.

——, "Americanization Day", *Metropolitan Magazine*, XLII (July 1915).

Rose, Ernestine, *Bridging the Gap*, 1917.

Roseman, W. P., "Experiences with Americanization, with Suggestive Plan for Development", National Educational Association, *Journal of Addresses and Proceedings*, LVII, 1919, pp. 477-482.

Rosenstein, David, "Contributions of Education to Ethnic Fusion in America", *School and Society*, XIII (June 18, 1921), pp. 673-682.

——, "Crucial Issues in War-Time Education-Americanization", *School and Society*, VII (June 1, 1919), pp. 631-637.

——, "Social Settlements after the War", *School and Society*, IX (June 21, 1919), pp. 725-735.

Ross, Edward Alsworth, "American and Immigrant Blood", *Century Magazine*, LXXXVII (Dec. 1913), pp. 225-232.

——, *The Old World in the New*, New York, 1914.

Rossiter, William S., "A Common-Sense View of the Immigration Problem", *North American Review*, CLXXXVIII (Sept. 1908), pp. 360-371.

Rumball, Edwin A., "Rochester's Civic Banquet", *Survey*, XXIV (July 16, 1910), pp. 604.

St. Louis Public Library, *Americanization, a List Compiled by Marie Thomas*, 1919 [bibliography].*

——, *Making Americans, How the Library Helps*, 1919.*

Sampers, Isidore H., "The Mission of the Foreign-Language Newspaper in the United States", *American Leader*, VII, No. 11 (June 10, 1915), pp. 672-677).

Sanborn, Alvin F., "The New Immigration to America", *Independent*, LIV (Nov. 13, 1902), pp. 2696-2698.

Sanders, Leon, "Americanization", *Jewish Immigration Bulletin*, II, No. 10 (Oct. 1913), p. 12.

Saner, R. E. L., *American Citizenship*, 1922.

Sanville, Florence L., "In Franklin's Footsteps", *Survey*, XXXIV (May 1, 1915), pp. 118-120.

——, "Unemployment Education and the Immigrant's Chances in Pennsylvania Today", *Survey*, XXXIV (May 1, 1915), pp. 118-120.

Sargent, Frank P., "Problems of Immigration", American Academy of Political and Social Science, *Annals*, XXIV, 1904, pp. 153-158.

Sarkar, B. K., "Americanization from the Viewpoint of Young Asia", *Journal of International Relations*, X (July 1919), pp. 26-48.

Saunders, D. A., "Immigrant Mission Work at the Synods", *Outlook of Missions*, XII (Jan. 1920), pp. 13-14.

Saveth, Edward N., "Race and Nationalism in American Historiography: the Late Nineteenth Century", *Political Science Quarterly*, LIV (Sept. 1939), pp. 421-441.

Schaeffer, Charles E., "Evangelize, Christianize, Americanize", *Outlook of Missions*, XII (May 1920), pp. 203-205.

Schermerhorn, H. I., *Citizenship Instruction*, Hackensack, N. J., 1923.*

Schneider, William T., "How to Help Our New Citizens", *Jewish Immigration Bulletin*, X, No. 4 (Apr. 1920), pp. 13-14.

"Schools for Immigrant Laborers", *Outlook*, XCII (Aug. 7, 1909), pp. 823-824.

Schuster, S. J., "What the Evening School Is Doing for the Alien", *Journal of Education*, LXXIX (Mar. 5, 1914), pp. 261-262.

Sears, Charles, "Suggestions for Americanization", *Missions*, X (June 1919), pp. 446-447.

Seeds, Corinne A., "The Cottage Unit", *Survey*, XLV (Mar. 26, 1921), p. 923.

"Self-Americanization for the Foreign-Born", *Literary Digest*, LXII (Sept. 13, 1919), pp. 28-29.

"Self-Made Americans", *Independent*, C (Dec. 27, 1919), p. 292.

Senger, H. L., "American House: Auto-Americanization by Immigrant Clubs in an Abandoned Saloon", *Survey*, XLI (Mar. 1, 1919), pp. 788-790.

Sharlip, William and Owens, Albert A., *Adult Immigrant Education*, New York, 1925.

Sherman, Philip E., "Immigration from Abroad into Massachusetts", *New England Magazine*, new series, XXIX (Feb. 1904), pp. 671-678.

Sherwood, M., "Our Immigrant Young and the Anglo-Saxon Ideal", *Forum*, LVI (Sept. 1916), pp. 317-322.

Shiels, Albert, *Americanization*, Los Angeles, 1919.

——, "Americanizing the Foreigner—In What Sense?", *Jewish Immigration Bulletin*, VI, No. 5 (May 1916), pp. 5-6.

——, "Illiteracy and Industrial Efficiency in Large Cities", *School and Society*, I (Mar. 6, 1915), pp. 325-336.

——, "The Necessity for Evening Schools", U. S. Bureau of Education, *Bulletin*, 1913, No. 51, pp. 39-42.

Shetwood, John, "The Problem of Immigration", *Arena*, XXVII (Mar. 1902), pp. 254-260.

Silver, A H., "The Immigrant Versus the Foreigner", *Jewish Immigration Bulletin*, VI, No. 9 (Aug.–Sept. 1916), pp. 6 and 16.

Simons, S. E., "Social Assimilation", *American Journal of Sociology*, VII (Nov. 1901), pp. 386-404.

Slabey, F., "Only American in Our Family", *Ladies' Home Journal*, XXXVI (Sept. 1919), pp. 7-8.

Slaughter, John W., "Community Councils", *Jewish Immigration Bulletin*, IX, No. 2 (Feb. 1919), pp. 3-7.

Sleszynski, T., and Sleszynski, A., "Leadership in Americanization", *Survey*, XLII (Aug. 23, 1919), pp. 746-747.

Sleszynski, Thaddeus, "The Second Generation of Immigrants and the Assimilative Process", American Academy of Political and Social Science, *Annals*, XCIII (Jan. 1921), pp. 156-161.

Smith, M. G., "Foreign Child and the Teacher", *Education*, XXXVIII (Mar. 1918), pp. 504-507.

——, "Raphael in the Background", *Education*, XXXIX (Jan. 1919), pp. 270-279.

Smith, W. C., "Rural Immigrants; New York's Program of Cooperation for Americanization", *Rural Manhood* X (Apr. 1919), pp. 157-158.

Snyder, Edwin R., "Americanization", National Educational Association, *Journal of Addresses and Proceedings*, 1920, pp. 487-490.

Society for Italian Immigrants, *Reports*, 1904-1920.

Society for the Promotion of Social Service, *The Immigrant and the Community*, New York, 1910.

Solomon, William J., "The Mission of the Foreign-Language Newspaper in the United States", *American Leader*, VII, No. 11 (June 10, 1915), pp. 675-677.

Soltes, Mordecai, *The Yiddish Press, an Americanization Agency*, New York, 1924.

Somers, Arthur S., "The Gospel of Americanism", Brooklyn Training School for Teachers, *Bulletin*, IV, June 1919.

South Dakota, State of, *School Laws of South Dakota*, 1919.

——, Department of Public Instruction, *Americanization of South Dakota*, 1919.*

——, Americanization Department, *Patriotic and Civic Instruction*, 1920.*

——, Americanization Department, *Patriotism*, 1920.*

South Dakota, State of, Superintendent of Public Instruction, *Biennial Reports*, 1914-1930.

Spectorski, Isaac, "The Newcomer and the Night School", *Charities and the Commons*, XVII (Oct.–Apr. 1906-07), pp. 891-892.

Speek, Peter Alexander, *A Stake in the Land*, New York, 1921.

Speranza, Gino C., "Handicaps in America", *Survey*, XXIII (Jan. 1, 1910).
pp. 465-472.

——, "How It Feels to Be a Problem", *Charity*, XII (May 7, 1904), pp.
457-463.

——, *Race or Nation; a Conflict of Divided Loyalties*, Indianapolis, Ind.,
1925.

——, "Solving the Immigrant Problem", *Outlook*, LXXVI (Apr. 16, 1904),
pp. 928-933.

Sporburg, Mrs. William D., Americanization of the Foreign-Born", Am.
Institute of Mining Engineers, *Bulletin*, CXLVII (supplement) (Mar.
1919), pp. ix-xiv.

"Spread of Americanization Day Plans", *Survey*, XXXIV (June 19, 1915),
p. 261.

Springer, Isador, "The Content and Method of Instruction", U. S. Bureau
of Education, *Bulletin*, 1913, No. 51, pp. 48-49.

Stabler, H. S., "She Makes Americans", *Ladies' Home Journal*, XXXV
(May 1918), p. 114.

Steiner, Edward A., *Against the Current*, New York, c. 1910.

——, "Americanizing New York" *American Review of Reviews*, LIX (May
1919), pp. 517-520.

——, *From Alien to Citizen*, New York, c. 1914.

——, *Nationalizing America*, New York, 1916.

——, *On the Trail of the Immigrants*, New York, c. 1906.

Sternberger, E. M., "Gary and the Foreigner's Opportunity", *Survey*,
XLII (June 28, 1919), pp. 480-482.

Stevenson, George M., *A History of Immigration*, Boston, 1926.

Stewart, Wentworth, *The Making of a Nation; a Discussion of Americanism and Americanization*, Boston, 1920.

Stitt, Edward W., "Recreation for the Immigrant", U. S. Bureau of Education, *Bulletin*, 1913, No. 51, pp. 25-27.

Stone, E. F., "What the Woman's Club Can Do This Year", *Ladies'
Home Journal*, XXXVI (Oct. 1919), p. 53.

Straubenmueller, G., "Schools for Immigrants", *American Journal of
Social Science*, XLIV, p. 29.

Straubenmueller, Gustav, "The Work of the New York Schools for the
Immigrant Class", American Social Science Association, *Journal of
Social Science*, XLIV (Sept. 1906), pp. 175-182.

Strook, Samuel, "The Night Schools and the Immigrant", *Jewish Immigration Bulletin*, VI, No. 9 (Aug.–Sept. 1916), pp. 6 and 16.

Sweet, Frederick A., "Putting Over a Civic Educational Program", National Catholic War Council, *Bulletin*, I, No. 12 (Aug. 1920), pp.
10-11 and 30.

Switzer, C. F., "Larger Plans for Americanizing the Foreigner", *Elementary School Journal*, XIX (Jan. 1919), pp. 367-374.

Syracuse, New York, Americanization League, *Americanization in Syracuse
and Onondago County*, 1920.*

——, *The Home Class Review*, June 1925.*

——, *The Syracuse Plan of Americanization*, June 1919.*

Talbot, Winthrop, "American Illiterate", *World's Work*, XXXII (July 1916), pp. 303-305.

——, *Americanization*, 1920.

——, "Americanization in Industry", *Industrial Management*, LVI (Dec. 1918), pp. 510-511.

——, "Illiteracy and Democracy", *North American Review*, CCII (Dec. 1915), pp. 873-878.

——, "The One Language Industrial Plant, Practical Aim of Americanization", *Industrial Management*, LVIII (Oct. 1919), pp. 313-320.

Taylor, Arthur V., "Supplementary Activities", U. S. Bureau of Education, *Bulletin*, 1913, No. 51, pp. 50-51.

Taylor, Graham, "Distribution and Assimilation of Immigrants", Conference Charities and Correction, *Proceedings*, 1913, pp. 26-36.

"Teaching Americanism in the Factory", *Literary Digest*, LX (Feb. 1, 1919), pp. 28-29.

"Teaching English to Adult Women", *Survey*, XLI (Mar. 15, 1919), p. 873; XLII (April 26, 1919), p. 156.

"Teaching Immigrants and Illiterates", *Elementary School Journal*, XVIII (June 1918), pp. 729-732.

Texas, State of, Department of Education, *A Handbook of Information as to Education in Texas, 1918-1922*, 1923.*

"They Call New England Highbrow—But", *Independent*, C (Dec. 13, 1919), p. 196.

Thomas, C., "Making the Melting Pot Melt", *Columbia University Quarterly*, XX (July 1918), pp. 214-224.

Thompson, F. V., *Schooling the Immigrant*, New York, 1920.

——, "Americanization in the Schools", *Current Affairs* (Boston), X (June 30, 1919), p. 16.

Thurman, Arch M., *Americanization in Utah*, Salt Lake City, 1920.

Tieje, Ralph E., "Suggestions for Americanization", *School and Society*, XIII (May 21, 1921), pp. 598-601.

Todd, A. J., "Job for Every Alien; Plans for Fitting Immigration to the Labor Market", *Survey*, XXXVII (Jan. 20, 1917), pp. 452-453.

Towne, Charles F., "The Organization of Lessons in English for Americanization Classes", *School and Society*, XII (Sept. 11, 1920), pp. 183-186.

Townsend, M. L., "Value of Music in Americanizing the Alien", *Public*, XXII (Apr. 5, 1919), pp. 349-350.

"The Training of Americanization Workers", *Survey*, XLI (Jan. 11, 1919), p. 505.

"A Traveling Seminar", *Outlook*, LXXXIX (May 30, 1908), pp. 235-236.

Treacy, Gerald C., "The American Melting Pot", *America*, XXIII, No. 13 (July 17, 1920), pp. 295-296.

——, "Americanizing Americans", *America*, XXV, No 12 (July 9, 1920), pp. 272-274

Trumbull, Frank, "Report of the Committee on Immigration of the Chamber of Commerce of the United States", *Immigrants in America Review*, II, No. 1 (Apr. 1916), pp. 32-34.

Tully, F. W., "The Chamber and the Alien: Representatives of Racial Groups and Americanization Workers Urge Committee to Undertake Citizenship Work in Boston", *Current Affairs* (Boston), X (June 30, 1919), pp. 12-13.

Tupper, George W., *Foreign-Born Neighbors*, Boston, 1914.

Unassimilated Foreigner, An, "The Failure of the Melting-Pot", *Nation*, CX (Jan. 24, 1920), pp. 100-102.

United States, Bureau of Education, "Americanization As a War Measure", *Bulletin*, 1918, No. 18 [Americanization Conference, 1918].

——, *Americanization Bulletin*, 1918-1919.

——, *Bulletins*, 1900-1930.

——, *Biennial Surveys of Education*, 1916-1930.

——, *Proceedings, Americanization Conference Held under the Auspices of the Americanization Division of the Bureau of Education, Washingto, May 12, 13, 14 and 15, 1919*, Washington, 1919.

——, *Reports of the Commissioner of Education*, 1900-1930.

United States, Bureau of Naturalization, *An Outline Course in Citizenship to be Used in the Public Schools for the Instruction of the Foreign and Native Born Candidates for Adult-Citizenship Responsibilities*, 1916.*

——, *Proceedings of the Naturalization Reception Held at Philadelphia, Pa., May 10, 1915*, 1915.*

——, *Reports of the Commissioner of Naturalization*, 1915-1930.

——, *Second Year of the Work of the Public Schools with the Bureau of Naturalization*, 1918.*

——, *Student's Textbook*, 1918.

——, *Suggestions for Securing and Holding Attendance of Foreign-Born Adults upon Public-School English and Citizenship Classes*, 1922.*

——, *Syllabus of the Naturalization Law, an Aid to Public-School Teachers in the Instruction of Aliens in the Requirements of the Naturalization Law*, 1916.*

——, *Teacher's Manual*, 1918.*

——, *The Work of the Public Schools with the Bureau of Naturalization in the Preparation for Citizenship Responsibilities of the Candidates for Naturalization*, 1917.*

United States, Committee on Public Information, *Complete Report of the Chairman of the Committee on Public Information, 1917, 1918, 1919, 1920*.

——, *Official Bulletins*, 1917-1919.

United States, Council of National Defense, *Americanization*, Bulletin 108 (Aug. 10, 1918); Bulletin 17 (Dec. 21, 1918).*

——, *Americanization*, General Letter 47 (Dec. 30, 1918) ; General Letter 53 (Jan. 11, 1919).*

——, *Americanization, Cooperation with the United States Bureau of Naturalization*, Bulletin 91 (Apr. 18, 1918).*

——, *Americanization, Instruction in English to Adult Foreigners* (Sept. 26, 1918).*

——, *Americanization—Local Organizations and an Americanization Magazine*, Bulletin 112 (Sept. 5, 1918).*

——, *Americanization of Aliens*, Bulletin 86 (Feb. 12, 1918).*

——, *Americanization, Organization of Local Committees* (Sept. 25, 1918).*

——, *Americanization, Questionnaire on War Information Service for Immigrants*, Bulletin 3 (Oct. 17, 1918).*

——, *Americanization, Request for Americanization News*, Bulletin 4 (Oct. 18, 1918).*

——, *Americanization, a Suggestion for Thanksgiving*, General Letter 20 (Nov. 2, 1918).*

——, *Americanization, Teaching English to Registrants*, Bulletin 8 (Nov. 2, 1918).*

——, *Americanization, Transmitting from the Bureau of Education to Industrial Plants*, Bulletin 2 (Oct. 17, 1918).*

——, *Americanization—War Information Service for Immigrants*, Bulletin 92 (Apr. 20, 1918).*

——, *Annual Reports*, 1917-1920.

——, *Bulletins*, 1917-1920.*

——, *Circular Letters*, 1917-1920.*

——, *Foreign-Born People and Public Libraries*, General Letter 40 (Dec. 21, 1918).*

——, *General Letters*, 1917-1920.*

——, *Readjustment and Reconstruction Information*, 2 vol., 1919-1920.

——, Reconstruction and Research Division, *Readjustment and Reconstruction Information, Bills and Resolutions Introduced in the 65th Congress*, May 15, 1919.

——, Woman's Committee, *An Interpretive Report, April 21, 1917 to February 27, 1919.*

United States, Department of the Interior, *America, Americanism, Americanization*, 1919.*

——, *Annual Reports of the Secretary of the Interior*, 1910-1922.

United States, Department of Labor, *Proceedings of the First Citizenship Convention Held at Washington, D. C., July 10-15, 1916, under Auspices of the Bureau of Naturalization*, 1917.*

United States, Immigration Commission, *Abstracts of Reports of the Immigration Commission with Conclusions and Recommendations and Views of the Minority*, 2 vols., Washington, 1911.

United States, Library of Congress, Division of Bibliography, *List of References on American Immigration Including Americanization*, Washington, 1918; *Supplement*, 1920.*

United States, House of Representatives, Committee on Education, *Hearing before the Committee on Education, House of Representatives, 65th Congress, 2nd Session, on HR 6490*, Washington, 1918.\*

——, *Hearing before the Committee on Education, House of Representatives, 65th Congress, 3rd Session, on HR 15402*, 2 parts, Washington, 1919.\*

United States, Senate, Education and Labor Committee, *Hearing before the Committee on Education and Labor, United States Senate, 66th Congress, 1st Session, on S. 17*, Washington, 1919.\*

United States, War Department, *Education for Citizenship*, 1918.\*

Utah, State of, *School Laws, Reprinted from the Session Laws of Utah*, 1919.

——, Superintendent of Public Instruction, *Biennial Reports*, 1914-1930.

Van Rensselaer, L. C., " Protection of the Immigrant Woman ", *Forum*, LVI (Oct. 1916), pp. 469-475.

Van Sickle, J. H. and Whyte, John, " Public Education in the Cities of the United States ", U. S. Bureau of Education, *Bulletin*, 1919, No. 88, pp. 115-120.

Vaughn, J., " The Evening Schools of Chisholm, Minnesota ", *Immigrants in America Review*, II, No. 1 (Apr. 1916), p. 83.

Veterans of Foreign Wars of the United States, Americanization Department, *Americanism, Addresses by Woodrow Wilson...at the Convention Hall, Philadelphia, May 10, 1915; Franklin K. Lane, New York, January 11, 1919; Theodore Roosevelt...New York, October 12, 1915*, 1926.\*

Vlasto, S. J., " The Mission of the Foreign-Language Newspaper in the United States ", *American Leader*, VII, No. 10 (May 27, 1915), pp. 612-614.

Wade, Joseph H, " Education of the Immigrant Child ", U. S. Bureau of Education, *Bulletin*, 1913, No. 51, pp. 23-24.

Waid, E. C., "Americanization—the Duty of Haste ", *Missionary Review*, XLI (Nov. 1918), pp. 818-820.

Waid, Eva Clark, *Presbyterian Woman and Americanization*, n. d. [circa. 1918].\*

Walker, Anne, "An Americanization Tea ", *Woman's Home Companion*, XLVII (Jan. 1920), pp. 29 and 34.

Walker, Francis A., " Immigration ", *Yale Review*, I (Aug. 1892), pp. 125-145.

——, " Immigration and Degradation ", *Forum*, XI (Aug. 1891), pp. 634-644.

——, " Restriction of Immigration ", *Atlantic Monthly*, LXXVII (June 1896), pp. 822-829.

Walsh, Frank P., "Americanization and Liberty Eliminated ", *United Mine Workers' Journal*, XXV (Feb. 3, 1916), p. 7.

Ward, Robert deCourcey, "Americanization and Immigration ", *American Review of Reviews*, LIX (May 1919), pp. 512-516.

——, " Immigration and the South ", *Atlantic Monthly*, XCVI (Nov. 1905), pp. 611-617.

——, "The Immigration Problem", *Charities*, XII (Feb. 6, 1904), pp. 138-151.

——, "The Restriction of Immigration", *North American Review* (Aug. 1904), CLXXIX, pp. 226-237.

Warne, Frank Julian, *The Immigrant Invasion*, New York, 1913.

——, *The Tide of Immigration*, New York, 1916.

Washington, State of, *School Laws of Washington*, 1919.

——, Superintendent of Public Instruction, *Biennial Reports*, 1913-1930.

Weber, S. E., "The Kindergarten as an Americanizer", *Educational Review*, LIX (Mar. 1920), pp. 206-212.

Webster, Hanson H., *Americanization and Citizenship, Lessons in Community and National Ideals for New Americans*, New York, c. 1919.*

Wehl, Walter E., "New Americans", *Harpers' Monthly Magazine* (Sept. 1914), pp. 615-622.

Weiss, Feri F., *The Sieve or Revelations of the Man Mill, Being the Truth about American Immigration*, Boston, 1921.

Welliver, J. C., "Campaign to Absorb the Alien in America", *Printers' Ink*, CIII (June 6, 1918), pp. 3-6.

West Virginia, State of, *The School Laws of West Virginia*, 1919.

——, State Superintendent of Free Schools, *Biennial Reports*, 1914-1930.

Wheaton, H. H., "Making Real Americans out of Many Races", *American Review of Reviews*, LVIII (Aug. 1918), pp. 161-166.

——, "United States Bureau of Education and the Immigrant", American Academy of Political and Social Science, *Annals*, LXVII (Sept. 1916), pp. 273-283.

Whelpley, James D., "International Control of Immigration", *World's Work*, VIII (Sept. 1904), pp. 5254-5259.

——, "Naturalized American", *Fortnightly Review*, LVIII (Oct. 1917), pp. 594-603.

——, "The Overtaxed Melting Pot", *Living Age*, LXIII (Apr. 11, 1914), pp. 67-72.

Whipple, Caroline A., *Selected Bibliography of Texts and References in Immigrant Education*, Albany, 1921 [issued by the University of the State of New York].*

Whitehouse, Vira Boarman, "The Immigrant Woman and the Vote", *Immigrants in America Review*, I, No. 3 (Sept. 1915), pp. 63-69.

Whiteside, Alexander, "Our New Americans and War Activities", *Survey*, XL (June 15, 1918), pp. 309-312.

Whitman, Governor, "The Address of Governor Whitman before the Americanization Committee of Schenectady", *Immigrants in America Review*, II, No 1 (Apr. 1916), pp. 51-54.

Wiernik, Peter, "The Mission of the Foreign Language Newspaper in the United States", *American Leader*, VII, No. 10 (May 27, 1915), pp. 609-612.

Wiley, Louis, "Americanizing the Immigrant", *American Hebrew*, XCIX (Sept. 26, 1916), pp. 712-713.

Willcox, W. F., "Popular Delusions about Immigration", *Independent*, LXXII (Feb. 8, 1912), pp. 304-307.

Willcox, Walter F., "Distribution of Immigrants in the United States", *Quarterly Journal of Economics*, XX (Aug. 1906), pp. 523-546.

Willey, Day Allen, "Americans in the Making", *Putnams' Monthly and the Reader*, V (Jan. 1909), pp. 456-463.

William, D. A., "Americans in the Making; New England's Method of Assimilation", *Putnams'*, V (Jan. 1909), pp. 456-463.

Williams, Hattie Plum, "The Road to Citizeznship, a Study of Naturalization in a Nebraska County", *Political Science Quarterly*, XXVII (Sept. 1912), pp. 399-427.

Williams, B. W., "Our Attitude toward Foreigners", *American Magazine of Civics*, VIII (Jan. 1896), pp. 64-68.

Wilson, Huntington, "Our Living Fences", *North American Review* CXCIX (Mar. 1914), pp. 383-393.

Wilson, J. G., "The Crossing of the Races", *Popular Science Monthly*, LXXIX (Nov. 1911), pp. 486-495.

Wilson, Woodrow, "Address of President Wilson Delivered at Convention Hall, Philadelphia, May 10, 1915", *Immigrants in America Review*, I (Sept. 1915), pp. 30-32.

Winkler, H., "Laggards at Night School; Factory Classes Essential for Americanization", *Survey*, XXXIX (Jan. 26, 1918), pp. 462-463.

Winter, K. B., "Made-in-America Democracy", *World Outlook*, IV (Nov. 1918), pp. 24-25.

Wisconsin, State of, *Laws of Wisconsin Relating to Common Schools*, 1919.

——, *Report of Special Legislative Committee on Reconstruction*, 1919.

——, State Department of Public Instruction, *Biennial Reports*, 1914-1930.

Wisconsin, University of, Extension Division, *Americanization; a Preliminary Bulletin Outlining Americanization Plans of the University of Wisconsin*, Madison, 1919.*

——, *Americanization Course in English and Citizenship for Teachers of Immigrants at Milwaukee, Wisconsin, February 25 to May 8, 1919*, Madison, 1919.*

Wise, Leo, "The American Israelite", *American Leader*, VIII, No. 2 (July 22, 1915), pp. 105-108.

Wise, Stephen S., "What Americanization is Not", *Jewish Immigration Bulletin*, X, No. 3 (Mar. 1920), p. 14.

Woellner, Frederic P., "The Teaching of History as a Factor in Americanization", *School and Society*, XIII (May 21, 1921), pp. 588-591.

Wolfson, Arthur M, "The Stranger within Our Gates", *Independent*, XCIV (Apr. 8, 1918), pp. 25 and 46.

Woman's American Baptist Home Mission Society, *Annual Reports*, 1900-1925.

Woman's Home Missionary Society of the Methodist Episcopal Church, *Reports*, 1910-1925.

Women's Relief Corps, *Circular Letters*, 1918-1920.*

Woodward, Elizabeth A., "English Classes for Foreign-Born Mothers", *Foreign-Born*, II (May 1921), pp. 222-223.

——, "Language and Home Links", *Survey*, XLV (June 15, 1918), pp. 696-697.

Wright, Carroll D., "Influence of Trade Unions on Immigrants", U. S. Bureau of Labor, *Bulletin*, X (Jan. 1905), pp. 1-8.

Wyoming, State of, *School Laws of the State of Wyoming*, 1919.

——, State Department of Education, *Biennial Reports*, 1914-1930.

Young Men's Christian Association, International Committee, *Americanization*, n. d. [*circa*, 1920].*

——, *The American Blend, Report of Americanization Work for 1919-1920.*

——, *Making Americans, Report of Americanization Work for 1919-1920.*

——, *Three Steps in Americanization*, n. d. [*circa.* 1919.] *

Young Men's Christian Association, Education Department, *Annual Reports,* 1913-1924.

Young Men's Christian Association of Brockton, Mass., Immigration and Industrial Committee, *New American*, 1913-1914.

Young Women's Christian Association, *Proceedings of the Biennial Conventions*, 1900-1928.

——, Committee of Research and Investigation, *Some Urgent Phases of Immigrant Life*, 1910.*

——, National Board, *Co Ameryka ma dla was*, 1920.*

——, International Service, *Foreign-Born*, 1919-1922.

"Your Government of the United States Making New Americans", *World's Work*, XXXII (May 1916), pp. 30-33.

Zezierska, A., "Soap and Water and the Immigrant", *New Republic*, XVIII (Feb. 22, 1919), pp. 117-119.

Znaniecki, Florian, "Social Attitudes of the Peasant and the Problem of his Americanization", *Immigrants in America Review*, II, No. 2 (July 1916), pp. 28-32.

# INDEX

APA, *see* American Protective Association

Abbott, Grace, 74, 135; studies of Chicago's ethnic groups, 52

Addams, Jane, 23

Adult education, country-wide survey of facilities for, 109; efforts to extend, 154; impetus given by Americanization, 273

Aguilar Free Library, 25

Aidline, Elbert, 225

Aliens, hostility toward, 106 ff., 217 ff., 254; propagandizing by, 106; handling in wartime, 167

Ambridge, Pa., labor camp school, 27-28.

'America First' campaign, 127, 175; posters, 132; demand for support of, 172; pledge, 204; societies in Colorado, 250

American ideals, 7-8, 17, 25

American International College, 30-31

American Legion, 264

American Protective Association, 7, 19-20

American Red Cross, 210

American way of life, 7, 17

Americanization, background, 7, 8, 13 ff.; need for, 23; early efforts, 23 ff.; use of term, 112; defined, 124 f.; 'Industrial', 131-132, 195; and preparedness program, 162; 'War Americanization,' 163, 187ff.; Conferences, 189-191, 211, 224, 228 ff., 239, 241, 247; 'bills', 190-191, 230-233; meaning of, 269-271; results of movement, 271-273

Americanization Day, 112, 115, 117*n*, 123; Kellor *re* meaning of, 122*n*

Anarchists, alien, 217

Anthracite Coal Fields, 16

Anti-red campaign, 216-218, 253, 268

Arizona, legislation *re* Americanization, 243

Aronovici, Carol, quoted, 254-255

Ashokan Dam, N. Y., labor camp school, 28

Aspinwall, Pa., labor camp school, 27

Assimilation of the immigrant, necessity for, 7-8, 22-23, 24, 33, 37

Associated Industries of Massachusetts, 241

Association of Foreign-Language Newspapers, 223, 225

Astor, Mrs. Vincent, 113*n*, 138, 143, 167*n*, 168*n*, 220*n*

Baltimore, 'New Voters' Day', 109-110

Bankhead, William B., 230

Baron de Hirsch Fund, 26

Barr, William H., 220, 223; quoted, 224*n*

Bennett, William S., 65*n*, 68*n*

Berkman, Alex, 216

Blumenthal, Walter Hart, 225

Bolshevism, propaganda against, 220, 222, 223; fear of, 244

Boston, 16, 24; selected as center by North American Civic League, 42

Boy Scouts, cooperation with U. S. Bureau of Naturalization, 236

Breed, Donald, 209

Brewer, D. Chauncey, 56, 92; *re* program of the Civic League for Immigrants, 39; quoted *re* education of the immigrant, 45*n*; quoted *re* growing popularity of Civic League, 50*n*; prevention of industrial disturbances, 93-95

Brooklyn, 62, 70

Bryan, William Jennings, 110

Buffalo, 16, 24, 61, 70, 161; Civic Educational Association, 161-162

*Buford*, transport, the so-called 'Soviet Ark', 216

Bureau of Promotion and Information of Foreigners, Rochester, N. Y., 60

Burgess, John W., 19

Burns, Allen T., 191, 228, 260

California, Commission of Immigration and Housing, 77 ff., 179-80; powers and policy, 77; recommendations, 81; labor camp inspection, 81; Americanization legislation, 250-251

California Exposition, 118

Carnegie Corporation of New York, Americanization studies, 191, 260

Chambers of Commerce, local, 92, 96, 123; active *re* Americanization, 150-151, 162, 192; list of local

cooperation with other agencies, 192; periodical, *Americanization*, 195*n*, 200-201, 233; conflict with U. S. Bureau of Naturalization, 212-213; appropriations for work of, 225; final efforts, 225 ff.; summary of achievements, 234

  Bureau of Naturalization, 102, 153 ff.; cooperation with public schools, 108, 182-83, 235, 236; survey of facilities for adult education, 109; reaction to Americanization Day, 123 ff.; literature, 153-154, 185; text book on citizenship, 185; efforts to extend immigrant education, 154 ff.; syllabus on naturalization, 156; sponsors citizenship convention, 157-158; notes progress of Americanization 180 ff., 210 ff.; supports campaign for 'Industrial Americanization,' 184; conflict with Bureau of Education, 212-213; work with Boy Scouts, 236

  Chamber of Commerce, Immigration Committee: organized, 131-132; members, 132*n*; part in campaign, 146 ff., 176-178, 183; program, 147-148; industrial survey, 148; suggested program for cities, 149; 'Industrial Americanization' conferences, 152; aided by National Americanization Committee, 195

  Committee on Public Information, 187, 196, 215; survey of agencies *re* Americanization, 196 ff.; activities *re* Americanization, 205 ff.; Division of Work among Foreign-Born, 206 ff., 209

  Congress, 18, 21; and Americanization, 173-174, 213

  Council of National Defense, 169, 187, 215; endorses program of Bureau of Education, 188; plan of Americanization, 188-189; action *re* Americanization, 201 ff.; Woman's Committee on Defense, 189, 203-205

  Department of Commerce and Labor, 34-35

  Department of Justice, 216-217, 237, 254

  Department of Labor, 217

  U. S. Food Administration, Vernacular Press Division, 166

  U. S. Immigration Commission, 53, 85; effect of work of, 64; *Report*, 65; attitude toward restriction, 67; members, 65*n*

Universal military training, 219

Utah, compulsory Americanization law, 245-246

Valhalla, N. Y., labor camp school, 28, 58

Vanderbilt, Mrs. Cornelius, 113*n*, 120, 143 167*n*

Vestel, Albert H., 231

Walsh, Frank P., quoted *re* Americanization, 142

'War Americanization', 163, 187 ff.

Wappinger's Falls, N. Y., labor camp school, 28

Washington, George, "Farewell Address," 31

Washington, D. C., 63; Americanization center, 198

Washington, State of, efforts *re* Americanization, 249

Washington University of St. Louis, 32

West Virginia, efforts *re* Americanization, 249

Wheaton, H. H., 85*n*, 100, 175*n*, 190

White, Andrew D., 19

Wilson, William B., 158*n*, 214

Wilson, Woodrow, 71, 107, 110, 111*n*, 207-208; letter to Trumbull, 119*n*

Wisconsin, 33; efforts *re* Americanization, 248-249

Women's organizations, aid to the Americanization movement, 135

Women's Trade Union League, Chicago, 50

World War I, 7, 37, 268; effect on Americanization movement, 105 ff., 164 ff., 268

Wyoming, Americanization legislation, 246

Young Men's Christian Association, immigrant education classes, 28-29

Young Men's Hebrew Association, 25

Young Women's Christian Association, periodical, *Foreign-Born*, 235

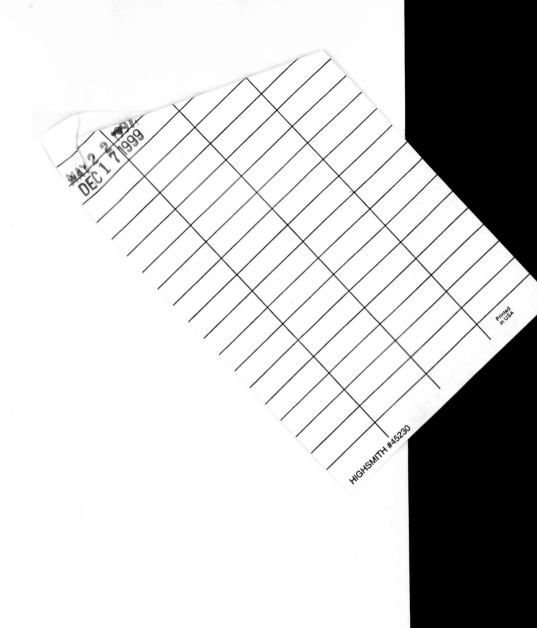